PRAISE FOR Inner River

"Inner River sails into the ageless world of Eastern Christianity, and along the way, spirituality is found in monasteries, in the lives of saints and living sages, in mystical experiences, and in the daily praxis of people seeking the meaning of life in the Orthodox faith. Markides, through his superb dialectic skills, blends reason with faith, and while his inspirational book has an end, the inner river keeps flowing, stirring the heart and mind of the reader, Western or Eastern, in a spiritual journey of self-discovery." —Dr. Christos P. Ioannides, director of the Center for Byzantine and Modern Greek Studies, Queens College, CUNY

"Dr. Markides welcomes readers into a reliving of another of his personal pilgrimages. His vulnerable exchanges with insightful elders prompt meaningful reflection, and these joyous experiences lead each reader to renewal and resolve of their own journey in spiritual development. The entire text is replete with enlightenment of the treasures found in *catharsis, fotisis,* and *theosis.*" —Fr. Nicholas C. Triantafilou, president of Hellenic College, Holy Cross Greek Orthodox School of Theology

"Professor Markides is a true philosopher and an inspired writer. *Inner River* is to date his most important work. Written in simple, clear, and practical words, it takes us to the core of our spiritual tradition, providing what is truly essential but most lacking in our contemporary educational system and secular society: meaning for the mind, motivation for the heart, and purpose for the will. If you want to know yourself and live to the fullest, this book is truly a must, a priceless jewel!" —Dr. Peter Roche de Coppens, Professor Emeritus, East Stroudsburg University of Pennsylvania, former UN consultant, writer

"With his engaging blend of travelogue, conversations with a wise and charismatic spiritual father, and musings on the big questions of life and death, Professor Markides takes us as companions on his journey of discovery. The insights that he communicates with such enthusiasm are timely ones: here at last is a writer who challenges the seeker after mystical understanding and Eastern spirituality to discover Christianity." —Dr. Elizabeth Theokritoff, independent scholar and co-editor of *The Cambridge Companion to Orthodox Christian Theology*

"Dr. Kyriacos Markides is a consummate scholar whose writings are so very accessible that his readers are ushered into a world of inquiry that might otherwise remain impenetrable. Whether specifically articulated or tacit, his message becomes increasingly clear that the laws of the spiritual world are far different from the laws of the material world. Armed with such a framework, his gentle invitation enables the reader to navigate the planet with an increasingly deeper understanding of both worlds. When one reads—or rather experiences—Markides, it is like acquiring a new friend and mentor who has come to live with you, in that he is only a reach away, an 'educator' who can stow away in a briefcase or knapsack, ready to offer further illumination on call. In *Inner River*, we journey with him in his further quest for a deeper understanding of the mystical path as informed by Eastern Orthodox spirituality. Through his writings we can come to embrace his beloved mentor, Father Maximos, as he 'educates' us as well. Following him from a conference and accompanying dialogues with learners, faculty, and friends at Holy Cross Theological School near Boston, to his further encounters with Father Maximos in his homeland of Cyprus, and beyond, Markides's informed, detailed, and engaging writing style makes one feel present in the conversation. Moreover, like a trusted friend, Markides invites us into his private thoughts as he makes meaning and ponders additional questions that arise. Like proceedings from a conference, one can return repeatedly to re-experience in greater depth the lessons learned. Accordingly, his writing holds the potential to transform one's very way of navigating life." —Marcie Boucouvalas, Ph.D., editor of *Journal of Transpersonal Psychology*

"A vast source of spiritual knowledge, understanding, and practice that is largely unknown to us." —Professor Jacob Needleman, author of *What Is God?*

"This is a book every man, woman, and child must become familiar with." —Antonio T. de Nicolas, professor of philosophy, SUNY

"Markides continues to explore the fascinating world of the mystical and deftly interprets its connections not just to Orthodox Christianity but to all spirituality." —Professor Harvey Cox, Harvard Divinity School

"This is a book of marvels. Markides has gifted us with his remarkable grasp of the implications of the philosophy and practice of those who would re-enchant the world." —Dr. Jean Houston, author of *A Mythic Life*

"A penetrating insight into profound spiritual truths. It is written with the critical eye of a scholar and the courage of a true spiritual adventurer." —Dr. Larry Dossey, author of *The Extraordinary Healing Power of Ordinary Things*

"A compelling glimpse into the heart of mystical Christianity. It sparkles with the wisdom of modern saints." —Dr. Joan Borysenko, author of *Minding the Body, Mending the Mind*

"Under the sacred spirit of Mount Athos, Kyriacos Markides transforms ordinary vision." —Lynn Andrews, author of *Love and Power*

"Strongly reminiscent of the old Platonic dialogues, where questions and answers are interspersed with anecdotes, stories, and experiences." —Richard Leviton, author of *The Galaxy on Earth*

"His viewpoint is extremely radical in nature and has great breadth in its implications . . . These are great questions, and this book poses them in a very calm and palatable way. . . . The tone is even-paced and the text is never heavy or hard to read. For one thing, the author is generous in his descriptions of his surroundings where all these discussions occur. . . . He shines his light and then lets his colleagues speak at length. . . . The presentation is often persuasive but always dispassionate. It is, above all, brave, for as the reviewer knows, to come out with evidence for truths inimical to the paradigm that flows through U.S. universities often gives rise to painful reaction from powerful colleagues." —J. O' M. Bockris, distinguished professor of chemistry, Texas A&M University, in *Journal of Scientific Exploration*

INNER RIVER

INNER RIVER

A Pilgrimage to the Heart of Christian Spirituality

KYRIACOS C. MARKIDES

IMAGE BOOKS ~ NEW YORK

Copyright © 2012 by Kyriacos C. Markides

Published in the United States by Image,
an imprint of the Crown Publishing Group,
a division of Random House, Inc., New York.
www.crownpublishing.com

IMAGE and the Image colophon are registered
trademarks of Random House, Inc.

Library of Congress Cataloging-in-Publication Data
Markides, Kyriacos C.
   Inner river : a pilgrimage to the heart of Christian spirituality / Kyriacos
Markides.—1st ed.
       p.   cm.
Includes bibliographical references.
   1. Mysticism—Orthodox Eastern Church.   2. Markides, Kyriacos C.
I. Title.
BX384.5.M37 2011
248.2'20882819—dc23

                                                              2011016829

ISBN 978-0-307-88587-6
eISBN 978-0-307-88588-3

PRINTED IN THE UNITED STATES OF AMERICA

Book design: Elizabeth Rendfleisch
Cover design: Alison Forner
Cover painting: *Starry Night over the Rhone* by Vincent van Gogh,
oil on canvas (photograph © Getty Images/Superstock)

1   3   5   7   9   10   8   6   4   2

First Edition

To
Emily J. Markides
Constantine Markides
Vasia Markides
and
Michael H. Lewis

A pilgrim to the Holy Mountain of Athos asked an old hermit,

"Father, how can I attain my salvation?" The venerated holy man replied,

"Every day at dusk go to the cemetery and for an hour hurl insults

to the dead. Do that for a month and pay attention to everything that

happens around you. Then come and report to me." After a month the

pilgrim returned. "Father, I have done what you told me but nothing

happened!" The hermit then said, "Go to the cemetery again for another

month and sing praises to the dead. Then come and tell me what

happened." After a month the pilgrim returned. "Father, I did what you

told me but nothing happened!" The holy father then said, "My son, if you

wish to attain your salvation, be like the dead, indifferent to insults and

indifferent to praise."

CONTENTS

As with my previous volumes, I have employed the Greek con-
jugation when directly addressing Greek males in the dialogues.
For example, Father Maximos is addressed as "Father Maxime,"
Lavros as "Lavro," and so on. Female names do not pose such
idiomatic problems. With the exception of historical names,
most names used in the dialogues are pseudonyms in order to
protect the subjects' privacy.

INNER RIVER

REMINISCENCES

I faced a major problem while working on my dissertation. I had accumulated a substantial amount of good material related to my topic, but I had no viable theoretical framework to give shape and meaning to my data. I was at a loss. Unless I resolved that problem, I could not finish my doctorate. One warm night in July, at midnight, feeling that I had reached a dead end and almost at the point of giving up, I took a walk on campus and sat on a bench to gaze at the starry sky. Then a pot-smoking hippie came and sat next to me, and we began talking about the vastness of the universe. Suddenly it was as if I was struck by lightning: I clearly saw the way out of my dilemma. My entire dissertation flashed in my mind, written and finished with the relevant theoretical framework. Overcome with emotion, I felt like running around campus screaming "Eureka!" I could hardly wait until morning to see my advisor. When we met, he readily approved my proposal. I was soon able to finish my dissertation, which eventually was published as a book, thereby initiating my academic career. This is one of the myriad coincidences that shaped my life. I often wonder how my life would have developed had that anonymous hippie not sat on that bench next to me to chat about the universe during that warm night in July.

Such coincidences take place continually in our lives, but we hardly pay attention. As they pass by we easily forget them, shrug them off, or simply take them for granted. I take it for granted that I've lived in Maine most of my life. But it didn't have to happen this way. Thirty years ago, after finishing my studies, I visited a friend and former professor in Evanston, Illinois, to bid him farewell. I planned to return home to Cyprus. While in Evanston, I accidentally met a leading professor of sociology at Northwestern University who in a month's time, and without me asking for it, was instrumental in landing me a job at the University of Maine. What if I had never visited my friend to say farewell and instead simply called him? At that time I was not searching for and was not interested in a job in America.

I never would have met Emily, my wife, had she not changed her mind as she was about to enter her car after a lecture I had given in Nicosia on the history of sociology. She fatefully thought of a question and returned to the lecture hall to ask for clarification. Similarly, had I not accepted a friend's invitation to join him on a visit to remote Mt. Athos, I would not have met Fr. Maximos, the charismatic monk and elder who became the subject of several of my books, including this one, leading me toward a radical shift of my spiritual life and professional career.

Coincidental events that constantly shape and reshape our lives, in both seemingly positive and seemingly negative ways, were among the subjects that I discussed with my artist friend and colleague Mike Lewis while having breakfast on a warm October morning in Bar Harbor, the well-known tourist town on Mt. Desert Island in Maine. Mike and I had common interests, and for many years we habitually met and engaged in casual conversations about academic life as well as wider concerns of politics, history, and religion. Recently, we had been toying with "counterfactual" history. We both had read the works of leading historians who speculated on how history might have developed if seemingly accidental events that had cataclysmic effects had not taken place.[1]

Just imagine, I said to Mike as we reminisced about our student years, if those tantalizing what-ifs had come to pass. What if Oswald's bullet had missed President Kennedy? What if Sirhan Sirhan was caught at the nick of time, just as he was about to shoot Robert Kennedy, a favorite to win the next presidential election? The history of America and of the world would have been different. What are we to make of all this? Change one such key event, and history, like our lives, would have followed a radically different direction.

We contemplated the myriads of apparently accidental events that have been shaping history and our biographies and concluded that intuitively we "knew" there must be a deeper level of reality that defies our rational understanding, and all things that happen in our lives and in history could not be accidental.

Having in mind the works of great sages, I shared with my friend some tentative thoughts. Every single event, I suggested, emerges out of an infinite ocean of probabilities and possibilities that exist inside God's Mind. Once a probable event becomes a concrete fact, as a result of human choices and decisions, the entire history of the world follows a different pathway. New settings emerge with radically new sets of infinite probabilities awaiting the possibility of becoming concrete realities. This is so because of the freedom that we humans are endowed with as self-conscious beings. One could say that we are cocreators with God. It appears as if history is the product of human choices and actions unfolding within the infinite wisdom of Divine Will. And what is true of history is also true of our individual biographies. "I wouldn't be sitting here with you in this Bar

Harbor café," I told Mike, "if any of the myriads of seemingly insignificant and coincidental encounters had not taken place in my own life."

"On the surface, one can easily conclude that both history and our lives are the results of random events," Mike pointed out.

"That's one way of seeing it. We can say that both history and our lives' trajectories are arbitrary, the products of apparently meaningless coincidences. Externally, at least, that's how it appears. History and biography are the results of strings of accidents. The Darwinians based their theory on that very presupposition, that evolution is the product of an infinite number of random and meaningless events. A monkey fooling around with paints and canvases will eventually create a *Mona Lisa*! Yet this is only an assumption, a preposterous one at that, which is taken as a fact engraved on granite. A noted Cabbalist philosopher, a reputed mystic, once told me, 'There is an esoteric history that manifests itself whenever external conditions are ready.' He implied that things of this world are not random, as the Darwinians believe, but rather the results of deep causes beyond the reach of physical science or rational thought. I believe all mystics from around the world would share this view."

I went on to tell my friend that if we assume all of our personal experiences are products of random events, and history, as well as biological evolution, is also the result of random events, then the only conclusion we can draw is that in the final analysis life itself is absurd and meaningless and that a human being, as the French existentialists claim, is a cruel joke. I personally repudiate such a conclusion not only because it is nihilistic but also because I strongly believe it is false.

An outside observer overhearing our conversation that sunny October morning could not have failed to realize that the themes we talked about were to a great extent reflections of our concerns about growing old and realizations of the imminence of our mortality. Both of us had just entered our sixties, with all the potentially unsettling emotions that such a pivotal turning point unveils. We were aware in a deep, visceral way that we were marching along the last leg of our life's journey. I reminded my friend, half seriously, that based on current national statistics we could look forward to a couple more decades of life at most and only if we were blessed with good health. Several of our longtime colleagues at the University of Maine, where we had been teaching for many years, had already made the transition to the beyond, some had retired to the Sunbelt, and others had begun struggling with geriatric health problems. It is no wonder, therefore, that, besides politics and health (comparing our cholesterol levels and sharing the latest research updates about enlarged prostates), spirituality, the nature of death, and the possibility of life after life would often arise in our conversations.

Questions of ultimate concern have also come increasingly to define our professional lives. Mike's artwork, which began with oil paintings portraying Freudian and social themes, evolved over the years to Jungian images, which in turn paved the way for his current interest in using the Maine landscape as a metaphor of timeless mystical, inner realities. Likewise, I began my career as a sociologist focusing on politics and nationalist movements. But thanks to a series of uncanny coincidences, I moved on to the study of healers, monks, hermits, and spiritual elders, the reputed specialists in unseen realities, from around the world.

"If what we are saying here is true," Mike said with deliberation, "why do you suppose the possibility of spiritual, suprapersonal dimensions is so commonly ignored in our understanding of the world?"

I had just discussed this issue with my students in social theory, and it was fresh in my mind. I believe, I told Mike, it is because of the worldview that has become crystallized in modern times, within which we conduct our everyday affairs. Alas, this worldview may be a key factor, if not the key factor, that could lead humanity to self-destruct. I mean that the ideology of materialism, the syndrome of modernity, has come to dominate the thinking of the cultural elite.

I told my friend modernity led us to believe that the only reality is the observable physical universe; that the only truth is the one discovered by our senses with the help of the scientific method; that there is no objective basis for values and moral rules other than what cultures and societies "construct"; and that human beings are ultimately and exclusively products of biological and sociocultural forces.[2] These taken-for-granted tenets of modernism allow no room for the workings of spiritual or nonmaterial forces in human affairs. We as human beings are considered nothing other than our genes and our cultural conditioning. Only matter exists, and only matter matters.

"However," Mike pointed out, "modernity helped us to understand our physical universe and also to develop a better understanding and tolerance of other societies and cultures."

"This is absolutely true. No one in his right mind would want to return to the state of affairs of medieval times. However, we have paid a heavy price for our modernity. Spirit simply vanished from our understanding of the human condition. We are seen not as creatures made in the image of God but as the products of blind natural forces of animal evolution. From God's icon we became the human animal."

I went on to tell Mike that modernity has convinced us that this universe we experience with our senses is the only one there is and that it is essentially bereft of Spirit. It has no sacred foundation, no Creator. And even if we grudgingly accept the possibility of a Creator (how else can one explain 100 billion galaxies that emerged about 14 billion years ago ex nihilo?), we assume that He has nothing to do with its daily operations. God is totally outside His Creation, leaving it to work on its own like a clock through mechanistic laws of His making. Following this logic, God created us but abandoned us to our own devices and to the laws of physics. To believe otherwise, that God not only created the universe but also is omnipresent in every particle of His Creation, appears singularly naïve to the modern scientific and philosophical imagination.

There is a well-known story relating to an exchange between Napoleon and the French scientist Pierre-Simon Laplace. When the emperor inquired about where God was situated in Laplace's system, the celebrated scientist replied, "Sir, I have no need for such a hypothesis." In fact, that declaration is considered a turning point in the history of science and its relationship to religion. Since Laplace's time the universe was believed not to need Spirit for its functioning. It was considered dead matter governed by "natural" laws. This is like saying that a human body can exist and function without life in it, without soul or Spirit. Yet great saints and sages tell us that if Spirit were to be removed, even for an instant, this world of concrete matter would instantly disintegrate, in the same way that when a soul abandons a human body what remains is a corpse. As my mentor Fr. Maximos would say, it is the Holy Spirit that keeps the world in operation in the same way that it is the Holy Spirit that animates our bodies and keeps them alive.

"So you see, Mike," I continued, "modernity with all its technological marvels and appeals paved the way to the desacralization of Creation and the consequent dehumanization of the individual. The world exists without the need for the 'God hypothesis.' So God was declared 'dead' by the end of the nine-teenth century. And this led unavoidably to the 'death of man' in the twentieth century, as postmodernists are fond of pro-nouncing like a mantra. They mean that there is no inherent meaning to human existence. This is the tragedy of modern cul-ture, its achievements notwithstanding. The French-Lithuanian writer Oskar Milosz (1877–1939) said, 'Unless a man's concept of the physical universe accords with reality, his spiritual life will be crippled at its roots, with devastating consequences for every other aspect of his life.'[3] This is what happened to us on a global, collective scale. With the emergence and dominance of scientific materialism, we have developed a grossly distorted view of reality. Why is that so? you may ask. The answer is that we have come to deny the spiritual origins of the physical world. So, perhaps our contemporary malaise and the massive prob-lems we are faced with, from global warming to the 'war on terrorism,' may spring, at least partly, from this fundamental distortion. Is it then accidental that the last hundred years have been characterized by unrestrained violence, the bloodiest pe-riod in the history of the world, with more than one hundred million dead from global wars and revolutions?"

"So which way do you think we're heading? Are you an op-timist or a pessimist?" Mike asked, breaking a brief period of silent reflection.

"In an ultimate sense I am always an optimist. In fact, I am hopeful that if during the nineteenth century we 'killed' God, and if in the twentieth century we killed 'man,' the twenty-first century may be the beginning of the resurrection of God, the resacralization of Creation, and the corresponding rehuman-ization of humanity. I see signs that we are heading toward a broader and clearer understanding of reality. Or let us say, if it does not go that way, our grandchildren may not have a world to inherit. As strange as this may sound, and notwithstanding what we discussed earlier, I daresay that this entire historical process is a form of spiritual development. Let's think about it: thanks to modernity, we have come a long way from the time when we accepted slavery as 'natural' and considered women inferior beings or 'defective males.' Even racists today will deny that they are racists. Not to mention that the notion of universal human rights was not part of our collective consciousness during previous centuries. So, in spite of everything, there has been progress."

"Let's discuss these issues further, but we should pay our bill first," Mike suggested. "There are people waiting in line for a table."

We walked around Bar Harbor enjoying the brilliant fall colors and the unusually warm weather. It was past eleven when we got back to the car. We then drove to nearby Acadia National Park and proceeded toward the entrance gate, the start of the spectacular twenty-seven-mile ocean drive. I had stopped the car at the booth and pulled out my wallet to pay the fee when Mike preempted me. "For ten dollars senior citizens can buy a card that gives them free access for life to all the national parks in America. Here, I've got one," he said and pulled out the plastic from his wallet.

I'd never thought of myself as a "senior citizen" until I entered Acadia that October morning. I was reminded of a colleague, three years older than myself, who first realized that he was a "senior" when he boarded a bus in Munich and a young German stood up and offered him his seat.

"How do you explain your own liberation from the dominance of a materialist worldview? What do you consider the key events in your life that made a difference?" Mike asked after we had completed a half-hour stroll along Sand Beach, where both of us had built sand castles for our children in our younger years.

"It was actually a gradual process that sprang from my unenthusiastic acceptance of the modern view dominant during my student years. Many people played a role in helping me overcome materialism. I can think of three, however, who were very important in my formulating a new worldview that I found to be more satisfying both psychologically and spiritually."

I went on to tell Mike that the first was the Russian sociologist Pitirim A. Sorokin, a refugee from the Bolshevik revolution and the founder of the Harvard sociology department during the early thirties. Then there was a group of controversial alternative therapists that I studied during the eighties. And finally, there was Fr. Maximos, the monk and elder from Mt. Athos. The latter became my spiritual mentor and had been the central character in my writings since the early nineties. All these people entered my life through a series of breathtaking coincidences. I then reminisced about the roles they played in my liberation from the dominant ideology of scientific materialism and reductionism.

During my graduate years, I stumbled onto Sorokin's work as the result of a class assignment. I was intrigued by his Russian background and his role in the revolution as a Menshevik. His story read like a novel penned by Tolstoy. But it was Sorokin's sociology that fascinated me the most.[4] I realized that it offered a radically different perspective on the nature of reality than what I had found in the writings of other classic founders of the discipline. His vision of the world was integral, holistic, and nonreductionistic.

Sorokin was convinced that human beings are made up not only of a conscious and an unconscious mind, as Freud had argued, but also of a "supraconscious" mind. In fact, for Sorokin the real source of creativity in all fields of endeavor is the supra-conscious part of the mind. Phenomena such as the mystical experiences of the great saints and psychic functions such as clairvoyance, telepathy, and precognition cannot be reduced to the unconscious or subconscious levels of the mind but are products of higher forms of mental energy. Of all the leading social scientists, Sorokin recognized the reality of higher forms of consciousness and did not dismiss as nonsense the "paranormal" experiences that people have been reporting in tribal and premodern as well as modern societies. For me that was an eye-opener. All along I'd felt asphyxiated by the materialistic reductionism that was the common denominator of just about all the great thinkers of the nineteenth and twentieth centuries to whom I was exposed as a student. I assumed I had no choice but to accept the materialist worldview as articulated by the leading exponents of modern thought, from sociology to psychology, from philosophy to physics. The only world out there was seen as the world of gross matter, of the five senses. Unusual experiences that people may have were explained as forms of regression or delusion. For example, the experiences of the great mystics were reduced by Freud to the "oceanic" state of mind characteristic of infants. Sorokin argued that such experiences must be seen as realities unto themselves, nonreducible to lower levels of awareness. The experiences of great saints and mystics, he claimed, are authentic results of higher levels of awareness and cognition, not infantile regression. Sorokin was a pioneer in his insistence that there are worlds beyond the physical universe and beyond the physical brain. Out of these worlds spring all of our deepest forms of creativity and insight.

Another important point in Sorokin's work was his claim that knowledge comes from three sources: the senses, the mind, and intuition. Our senses give us "sensate knowledge." Empirical science is the tool that allows us to gather knowledge about the visible, physical universe. That is its domain. For Sorokin, experimental science is the authoritative method invented by the human mind to acquire knowledge of the physical world. Neither religion nor philosophy is qualified to do that.

The second method of acquiring knowledge is through the mind. Mathematics, philosophical thought, and logical reasoning come under this form. The leading thinkers of the West have acknowledged the reality of these two sources of knowledge but not of intuition, the province of the great saints and mystics. This is Sorokin's most controversial argument and one of his major contributions.[5] He opposed the prevailing notion that subjective intuitions are less scientifically verifiable than empirically derived facts. He argued passionately for the emergence of an Integralist Truth, which honors all three forms of knowledge leading to a more holistic understanding of reality. Furthermore, Sorokin recognized only the great mystics and saints as authorities who can speak for the reality of higher forms of cognition, that is, cognition that penetrates the boundaries of the senses and the rational mind.

Finally, Sorokin claimed, based on an exhaustive examination of Western civilization, that the historical pendulum was heading toward a revival of religious faith and spiritual awakening. He made this prediction in the midst of the carnage of World War II and at a time when all indicators led to a consensus that religion was destined to disappear from the world with the advance of modernity, that secularization, the increasing displacement of religion to the margins of social life, was an irreversible process.

Sorokin was ignored during his lifetime because his thinking and work did not fit the mold of the nineteenth- and twentieth-century mechanistic understanding of life. However, his work was like a raft that rescued me from a turbulent ocean of historical materialism. It helped me overcome the agnosticism I acquired during my student years in the 1960s and offered me the green light to become receptive to mystical experiences as valid material for study while allowing me to continue to think of myself as a legitimate sociologist. After all, Sorokin was the founder of sociology at Harvard, one of the most prestigious universities in the world. He was one of the most prolific sociologists of the twentieth century, and, in spite of his controversial views, shortly before his death, in 1968, he was voted president of the American Sociological Association. I would not have been able to pursue my studies of mystics had I not discovered Sorokin's work. I would have thought of myself as treading on academically shaky ground.

"How did you move from Sorokin to the alternative therapists you mentioned?" Mike asked as we crossed the long bridge over the Penobscot River on our return home. By then it was night and the lights of the twin cities Bangor and Brewer were reflected in the water that separated them. The steeples of the Catholic and Protestant churches, high on the surrounding hills, offered a typical and picturesque New England nightscape.

My encounter with them was the empirical validation of what Sorokin taught. His ideas would have simply remained interesting theories had I not met those out-of-the-ordinary individuals who eventually, and providentially, paved the way for my discovery of Mt. Athos and Fr. Maximos.

Again, as a result of a series of coincidences, I met these therapists in Cyprus at the beginning of my first sabbatical leave from the university when I was planning to research and write a book on international terrorism. Their reputation on the island was highly controversial. Skeptics considered them charlatans who fooled the gullible and the naïve. The devoutly religious considered them possessed by diabolical forces. When I met them, I realized that they possessed unusual mental gifts. Sorokin had sensitized me to the possible reality of intuitive knowledge. So in spite of their reputation, I was ready to take them seriously as subjects of study instead of either ignore them or dismiss them as frauds.

I gave up the terrorism project as I came to find these people much more interesting than terrorists. Contrary to the sober advice of friends and relatives, I plunged into an exploration of the world of this unusual group. I became the outside observer doing anthropological field research.

These alternative therapists were fascinating to me because of their "paranormal" abilities, which I could not make any rational sense of.[6] For example, one of them could see things from a distance, as if his mind could travel through space like a radio or television signal. I remember how he described in great detail the inside of our house in Maine, something that he could not possibly have known.

Such abilities contradicted conventional scientific, materialist dogma. Of course, I could not prove scientifically that what I witnessed were objectively real phenomena. I did not conduct repeatable experiments. I did not, to use the scientific jargon, control the independent variables. But for me, what I witnessed were real, ontologically real experiences. I did, however, contact other anthropologists, such as Professor Michael Harner of the New School for Social Research, who had witnessed and recorded similar phenomena in other cultures. I sought their advice to make sure that I was not deceiving myself.

After reporting my research about these unusual people, I began receiving letters, e-mails, and telephone calls from people everywhere who claimed that my work provided them with an intellectual map of their inner worlds. That was extremely in-triguing to me. I was visited by people who led normal and or-dinary lives, held responsible positions in society, yet had rich inner experiences that they dared not reveal publicly. They were afraid of being stigmatized as mentally unbalanced, vilified as charlatans, or denounced as being possessed by demons. These were people who lived simultaneously in two worlds, the world of ordinary consciousness and that of their inner experiences. I concluded that there is a "para-culture" that mainstream sci-ence has ignored or failed to recognize because of its materialist blinders.

It is very clear to me that, without these experiences with Sorokin and the alternative therapists, I would not have taken Mt. Athos seriously. I would not have gone there, and, therefore, I would not have met Fr. Maximos.[7] That is why I am grateful for everything that has happened to me, which opened the way for a journey to the Holy Mountain. I am convinced that, had I not had those accidental encounters with alternative therapists during the eighties, I would still be studying international ter-rorism.

Mike understood what I meant. He had followed my adven-tures closely ever since Antonis, a friend from Cyprus, urged me to join him on a visit to Mt. Athos to meet, as he claimed, real holy men and saints. I reluctantly took up his invitation, and, in the spring of 1991, I joined him on a journey to the thirty-mile-long and ten-mile-wide peninsula in northern Greece, reserved since the ninth century as a refuge for Christian hermits and monks. At the time I was deeply prejudiced against "organized" religion. I believed that among monks one could find only fanat-icism, superstition, and narrow-mindedness. All of my higher learning had taken place in America, where monasticism is frowned upon because, among other things, of the lingering memories of the Holy Inquisition, a horrendous historical crime in which the Eastern part of Christianity played no part whatsoever.

It was Fr. Maximos who changed my attitude toward the Church. With him as my mentor, spiritual guide, and research informant, I discovered that there is a mystical lineage going all the way back to the early Christian Church that was preserved in some monasteries of Eastern Christianity. I realized that what many Western intellectuals searched for in the ashrams of India and the lamaseries of Tibet—that is, an experiential pathway to the Divine—has been all along within the very heart of Christianity. Furthermore, I discovered that phenomena I assumed were only part of the lore of shamanic cultures and of Eastern religions such as Hinduism, Taoism, and Buddhism have been an integral part of Christianity from its very inception. I learned that miraculous phenomena were integral in the lives of the great elders and hermits of Mt. Athos. With Fr. Maximos, I was introduced to the lives of extraordinary sages such as Elder Sophrony, St. Silouan the Athonite, and Elders Paisios and Porphyrios.[8] Eyewitness reports of the feats of these elders overshadowed by far everything that I had heard or known about from other cultures or witnessed through my association with the Cypriot alternative therapists. I was intrigued by the fact that great Christian elders and saints were reputed for extraordinary gifts such as clairvoyance, prophetic vision, healing abilities, levitation, teleportation, and the like, which are presumed to be part only of Eastern religions and tribal shamanism.

I felt more comfortable with the presence of such "powers" in the lives of Christian saints and elders. In every case that I had studied or encountered, the elders denied having such abilities. When I met Elder Paisios, in 1991, he refused to acknowledge that he had healing gifts. Yet people, fully convinced of his extraordinary powers, would travel hundreds or thousands of miles to seek his help. I soon learned that, within the Eastern Orthodox tradition, elders speak not of "powers" but of "gifts of the Spirit" offered to the human soul after she undergoes purification from egotistical passions. Those who have such abilities, therefore, must never consider them as their own and definitely not use them to further their fame or personal interests. When one possesses such abilities without prior personal purification, the consequences can be catastrophic for both the possessor and others. That is why the mix of psychic abilities and narcissism is not a blessing or a manifestation of the Holy Spirit but a curse, a "satanic" condition that must, according to the holy elders, be avoided at all costs. Persons who possess such "powers" without humility and deep *metanoia*, that is, a radical transformation of thinking, feeling, and acting, can easily regress to black magic, consciously or unconsciously. That was a great lesson that I learned after my exposure to the spiritual tradition of Mt. Athos.

"Regardless of the spiritual origin of extraordinary abilities and powers," Mike commented as we entered Orono, "their publicly acknowledged reality can have monumental repercussions for our understanding of the nature of the world and our own nature."

I agreed. Even negative spiritual realities can function positively in overcoming materialism. If nothing else, they provide evidence of realities beyond this world, and if the gatekeepers of our higher culture accept the fact that there are spiritual realities, positive as well as negative, we are bound to witness a real revolution in consciousness. At the moment, we are still under the spell of modernity, a "flatland" understanding of reality that reduces everything to the physical level.

It was nine in the evening when we reached Mike's house. "What we talked about today may come in handy for your upcoming roundtable discussion," Mike suggested as I dropped him off.

"Most probably," I replied. Then I drove off to my house, a mile and a half away on the same side of the Stillwater River.

A few weeks earlier I had been asked by the dean of our college to take part in a program titled Great Conversations. It was an initiative to bring the liberal arts to the general public by asking several faculty members from the university to have Saturday afternoon roundtable discussions on topics that would be of interest to the wider community. My topic was "The Forgotten Path of Christian Spirituality: My Research with Healers, Monks, Mystics, and Hermits of Eastern Christianity." I was asked to write a short abstract for my presentation to be included in the program. Ten other such "conversations," on a variety of topics, would be offered simultaneously by my colleagues.

The next morning I jotted down a few questions that I proposed to explore with my fellow roundtable participants: "Is there a Christian spirituality that is mystical, experiential, and focused on the fundamental and existential healing of the self? What are the basic characteristics of this spiritual tradition? What is its relevance for contemporary living? Why has the Christian West ignored this cultural and spiritual tradition?"

I planned to discuss these questions and many others in the context of my many years' relationship with Fr. Maximos. However, after these conversations, to my pleasant surprise, I received the news that Fr. Maximos would visit America for the first time. After repeated phone calls, e-mails, and faxes, he had finally, albeit reluctantly, accepted an invitation to be the keynote speaker at an early spring conference on religion and healing at the Holy Cross Greek Orthodox seminary in Boston. Both Emily, my wife, and I looked forward to reconnecting with him.

TWO

ATHOS IN AMERICA

Emily and I headed south on Route I-95 toward Boston. The air was refreshingly crisp as the sun rose above the forest-covered earth. The snow that had blanketed the land until mid-March had melted away. By the first week in April, thanks to a warming spell, the trees had begun to show the first signs of nature's awakening. Driving at that early hour in a region full of lakes, rivers, and forests was an invigorating delight. I never stop reminding my students of the enviable uniqueness of their relatively unspoiled environment and their responsibility to preserve it. With a stable population of 1.3 million, yet larger in size than all of the other New England states combined, Maine is a magnet for environmentalists, hunters, and bird-watchers and can boast a vast expanse of pristine nature in the American Northeast.

We were upbeat that morning as we prepared to meet Fr. Maximos. We were to join him and the organizers of the conference for dinner at a Greek restaurant in Cambridge. We hadn't seen him since the previous year, and we looked forward to hearing, among other things, his impressions of America. Since his knowledge of English was minimal, I had volunteered to be his simultaneous translator, something I had never done before.

My anxiety, however, was tempered by the knowledge that Emily, a polyglot and an experienced translator, would be there to give me not only moral support but also a hand.

In spite of a heavy schedule at home, what finally attracted Fr. Maximos to visit America was not just the conference itself but the opportunity to visit the newly established St. Anthony's monastery, southeast of Phoenix. An even greater attraction was his desire to reconnect with Elder Ephraim, one of his venerated elders, who had left Mt. Athos in 1996 with a mission to set up Greek Orthodox monasteries for men and women all over North America. In only ten years the septuagenarian elder, with financial backing from American philanthropists, created twenty monasteries, from Montreal to Arizona and from New York to Florida. It was an extraordinary feat, interpreted by his devout followers as nothing short of a miracle. It is interesting that the number of monasteries the elder created in America was equal to those on Mt. Athos itself. The central and largest monastery, built in the Arizona desert, was St. Anthony's, a sanctuary that Emily and I had visited some years back.[1]

Fr. Maximos had arranged his flight so that he could first visit Arizona, where he stayed for a week in the company of his beloved elder. Having spent many years on Mt. Athos before his return to his native Cyprus, Fr. Maximos wished to relive briefly his life as an Athonite monk. This visit also gave him a few days to recover from the substantial jet lag.

In Cambridge, the conference organizing committee was in a reserved room of the restaurant, awaiting Fr. Maximos's arrival from Logan Airport. No one had met him or knew what he looked like except Emily and myself. For this reason we were asked to welcome him at the front door.

"America is blessed to have you walk on its soil, Fr. Maxime," I pronounced with a humorous intonation and with spread-out arms as he stepped out of the taxi. "I am the one who is blessed to be here, Kyriaco," Fr. Maximos replied in equal measure. In fact, when I later mentioned to him in all seriousness that a lot of people benefited from his presence in America, he responded that it was he who benefited the most. "I have overcome," he confided to us later, "some of my prejudices and misconceptions about this country."

I was pleased to hear that. The overseas image of America was severely tarnished by the Iraq war and the unpopular policies of the Bush administration. Fr. Maximos told me that he saw an America that was very different from what he had imagined. Among other things, he was surprised to find Americans so friendly and hospitable and so religiously devout.

"Did you have a good flight?" Emily asked.

"The flight from London to Phoenix was without exaggeration the best twelve hours I've had in a long time," Fr. Maximos retorted.

"Really?" Emily asked in surprise, knowing from experience how taxing such a long trip could be.

"Nobody was talking to me!" Fr. Maximos quipped. "There was a young boy sitting next to me who was asleep most of the time. No one paid attention to me, and nobody asked me any questions. In fact, I enjoyed it so much that I could not let myself fall asleep lest I miss the joy of being alone so high up in the sky and in silence for so many hours."

We both knew how rare it was for Fr. Maximos to have time to himself. Ever since he'd arrived in Cyprus in the early nineties, with the mission to revitalize monasticism on the island, his popularity had skyrocketed, leaving him little time to live in silence like a monk. His eventual election as bishop compounded the problem. It was no wonder, therefore, that he had cherished the silence during the long flight from London to Arizona. "I couldn't believe how huge that plane was!" Fr. Maximos marveled, shaking his head as we went to meet his hosts. It had been his first transatlantic flight in a jumbo jet.

In the informal setting of this evening meal, I practiced simultaneous translation so as to feel better prepared for the next day. After the meal, we strolled to Harvard Square and walked the groomed paths of Harvard Yard, where Fr. Maximos got a glimpse of a nerve center of contemporary Western, rational civilization.

In spite of being a bearded, black-robed clergyman, he attracted no particular attention. It was one of the advantages of being in a cosmopolitan, urban area. In their attempt to fence themselves off from the cascade of city stimuli, urbanites, as the early twentieth-century German sociologist Georg Simmel argued, maintain an indifferent attitude toward their surroundings. Strange-looking folks are not curiosities as they would be in small towns and villages. "I love being in Athens," Fr. Maximos once told me, "because there I can walk the streets, go to bookshops, and have a bite at a restaurant without people paying any attention to me." In Cyprus, however, he cannot walk down the street without taxis stopping to offer him a ride or people running after him asking for his blessing or kissing his hand. As a result, and unlike his years on the Holy Mountain, where he was an unknown monk, he had accumulated unnecessary weight because of a lack of walking and other physical exercise. No wonder he was enjoying his sojourn in the New World.

~~~

Fr. Maximos was the first speaker at the conference. He began his presentation with a slight bow, a smile, and a cheerful

"Good morning," the only English words he uttered. He then turned toward me and signaled that he was ready for his address. Not surprisingly, he had no written text. As far as I knew, since he'd left Mt. Athos twelve years earlier, Fr. Maximos had never delivered a speech from a written text, even though he had given over one thousand tape-recorded talks that were circulating around the globe among Greek-speaking devotees. Somehow the Holy Spirit worked more freely through him if he remained spontaneous in his delivery. That way he had the opportunity to illustrate his lectures with personal anecdotes, humor, and attention-grabbing vignettes. This was another sign of Fr. Maximos's charisma.

Covering the microphone with my palm, I whispered to him to speak slowly so that I could translate precisely what he would say. I feared that my mind would not work fast enough to capture all the nuances and details of his sentences. I too was relying heavily on the Holy Spirit to not unduly distort what the elder was about to say. Fortunately, he focused on a theme that we had discussed many times before, so I felt that I had a definite advantage over a professional interpreter unfamiliar with Orthodox Christianity and healing.

After offering apologies for his lack of knowledge of English, Fr. Maximos began. "First and foremost," he said as he faced an audience of two hundred, a number of them preparing to become priests or ministers, "I would like to convey to you a message of greetings and blessings from the Orthodox Church of Cyprus, the Apostolic Church of Cyprus."

I suspected that very few knew what the "Apostolic Church of Cyprus" meant. I took the liberty, therefore, to signal to Fr. Maximos to wait a few seconds so that I could explain. I mentioned that it was called so because Christianity came to Cyprus, less than two hundred miles west of the Holy Land, with the arrival of Apostle Paul, who went to teach Christianity to the gentiles. Accompanied by his friend Barnabas, he converted the Cypriots to the new religion and laid the foundations of one of the earliest churches in Christendom.

Fr. Maximos went on to say that he was going to speak about the *Ecclesia*, or the Church, which includes the practices, homilies, and teachings of the holy elders of Christianity throughout the ages, not just the formal organization. He proceeded to state some well-known presuppositions of the Christian faith: that the Bible holds that God created human beings in His own image, that a human being is an icon of God and a reflection of how God is in His very nature, in His very essence. The true state of health, therefore, of human beings is their state prior to the primordial Fall. It follows that, to understand what the natural and healthy state of a human being is, we first have to contemplate the nature of God.

Fr. Maximos spoke slowly to give me time to process the translation. I felt like someone learning how to ride a bike or drive a car. But in spite of my anxiety, the translation seemed to be going smoothly. He went on to summarize the key themes of Eastern Orthodox spirituality: that God is love and that human beings made in the image of God are also love in their very depth. Therefore, to be truly healthy means to think, feel, and act in conformity with our innermost nature. The Fall shattered our original healthy state, and the divine gifts we were originally endowed with degenerated into destructive passions. Egotism, not love, became the primary motivation in human affairs.

Fr. Maximos then explained that Christ's historic presence, the Divine Archetype becoming manifest, was meant to help us heal our estrangement from God. It was a "therapeutic event." According to Fr. Maximos and the Orthodox tradition he represented, the Church must be seen as a spiritual hospital. Its real mission is to help human beings overcome their existential, spiritual illness. Fr. Maximos then elaborated on the meaning of *askesis*, or spiritual exercises such as fasting, systematic and ceaseless prayer, study of the scriptures and the lives of saints, charitable activities, all-night vigils, confession, and communion. This is the methodology employed by the *Ecclesia* for the restoration of humanity's wholeness and spiritual health. He described what could be considered the Threefold Way of Eastern Orthodoxy, a theme I had explored extensively with Fr. Maximos in earlier encounters and conversations.[2]

Orthodox elders speak of three distinct stages that every human being must traverse on his or her path toward reunion with God: *Catharsis*, or purification of the self from egotistical passions; *Fotisis*, or the illumination and enlightenment of the soul that follows *Catharsis*; and *Theosis*, or union with God, the final destination and healing of the human soul. In my years of exposure to this tradition, I understood these three stages as archetypal in that the elders consider them part of the structure of the human soul and its ultimate destiny. That means, regardless of one's religion or religious beliefs, salvation implies a movement through these stages. Simply put, you cannot reach or know God without first purifying your heart from lowly passions.

"The verification of the Gospel and the claims of the Church about its therapeutic promise," Fr. Maximos went on to say, "is the presence among us of the very people who have been healed, that is, the saints. We are talking not about some extraterrestrial beings but people like you and me who, after implementing the therapeutic methods of the *Ecclesia*, have witnessed it in themselves and have proved to the world that its pedagogy leads to the healing and the salvation of human beings. During the last two thousand years, the saints offer witness to the fact that the Grace of God heals human beings at their very core.

"When we speak of the salvation of a human being in this world, we are talking not about someone who prays and reads all day long by himself or herself but about a human being who may live an ordinary, normal life. The perfected human being in Christ manifests certain characteristics that demonstrate the presence of God. St. Paul, following Christ's message that one can understand a tree by its fruit, goes on to enumerate for us the fruits of the Holy Spirit: love, joy, peace, patience, kindness, goodness, faithfulness, gentleness, and self-control."

Fr. Maximos ended his talk by saying that if we demonstrate these qualities in our way of thinking, feeling, and acting, it is a sign that the Holy Spirit is manifest in our lives. This, he concluded, is the real healing of human beings according to the Gospel and the real goal of the therapeutic pedagogy of the *Ecclesia*.

~~~

In the afternoon, Fr. Maximos met with about twenty participants, mostly seminarians and students of religion, who had requested a private audience with him. They were second- and third-generation Greek Americans. It was decided that, since all of them had a working knowledge of Greek, there would be no need for an interpreter. Consequently, I was free to observe and take notes. Emily volunteered to sit next to Fr. Maximos and serve as an interpreter if the need arose.

Fr. Maximos stroked his beard, smiled broadly, looked around, and invited his small audience to raise whatever issues or questions were on their minds. After a few seconds, a young seminarian took the microphone and spoke in accented Greek. He was clearly born and raised in America.

"Last year we had a debate at the seminary in regard to the role of an elder. We wondered whether each one of us must have a spiritual guide and whether we should obey unconditionally the instructions of such an elder. This is a real problem for us when friends pose such questions and we have no satisfactory answers. Obedience is a controversial theme for modern people. I wonder whether you can clarify this issue for us."

"Do you understand the question that Michael raised?" Fr. Maximos asked. He apparently had already met that seminarian during lunch and knew him by name. Michael's question dramatized the clash between two seemingly incompatible values: a modern, pluralistic American culture, which nurtures individualism and self-reliance as the highest of values (partly an outgrowth of the Protestant work ethic), and the Athonite prescription of obedience to an elder as a means of attaining deification in Christ. Obedience in this case means the complete abandonment of your wishes, opinions, and desires.

Fr. Maximos leaned back. "We need," he began, "discernment in order to understand the difference between obedience in the context of monasticism and obedience in the context of an ordinary life in the world. In monasticism, there is an absolute relationship between the elder and his disciple. We consider it a mystery, a sacred bond based on the promise of the monk to absolutely obey God 'unto death' through the guidance of an elder. This is very important to understand," Fr. Maximos emphasized. "We do not obey the elder for the sake of the elder. This relationship is not an end in itself. The goal is to establish an eternal union with Christ through Grace.

"Obviously, this form of monastic obedience cannot be part of ordinary life in the world. Unlike the monks, who are totally free from social obligations, ordinary people are also subjected to a great variety of duties and obligations: to families, to husbands, to wives, to children, to employers, and so on.

"A spiritual father who ministers to ordinary people must have great discernment if he is to function as a doctor of their souls. He must know up to what point he should expect obedience. The disciple must also be aware of the limits of obedience."

"But isn't obedience antidemocratic? Isn't it contrary to the modern spirit of individual freedom?" a young woman objected.

"Again, when we talk about obedience, we really mean obedience to the commandments of God, not to the whims of a particular individual. The spiritual guide must not be the object of obedience and worship; it must be Christ Himself. The spiritual guide is simply a servant of Christ. The elder is like a medical doctor, in this case a doctor of the soul. When we obey the prescriptions of a medical doctor, we do so because we believe that he or she has the knowledge to restore our health. We are free to ignore the doctor's advice. Similarly, we are free to ignore the spiritual prescriptions of an elder."

"Isn't there a possibility of abuse and corruption in the elder-disciple relationship?" Michael asked. "These are problems and concerns we face when we talk to our friends about the role of the spiritual elder."

"Of course there is the possibility of corruption," Fr. Maximos confirmed. "That is why I emphasize the need for discernment, which can guard against such abuses. We need to realize that we must be obedient to the commandments of God, as they are revealed through the gospels, not to the whims of any particular person. The proper role of the *Ecclesia* and the spiritual guide is to help interpret for laypeople God's divine laws and not to exercise power over them. As I mentioned before, it is similar to obeying a doctor who tells you that you must get this or that medicine if you wish to get well. Nobody is forcing you to get well.

"So our personal freedom is not and must not be compromised by obedience to an elder. This is particularly important for people who live in the world. There are many things that concern our lives beyond the role and scope of the spiritual guide. Purchasing a house, for example, is not something about which we should seek advice from our spiritual guide. Spiritually speaking, it presupposes, of course, that what I plan to do will address my needs rather than satisfy my vanity and egotism. That is, when we make such personal choices and we wish to be in alignment with spiritual laws, we must act within the boundaries of need and not within the bottomless pit of unbridled desires."

"That is not what happens with monks and nuns," I interjected.

"That's right. If I am a monk or a nun, I will need to get the blessing of my elder even if I wish to buy a single pencil. This is different. So, again, we need discernment here. I hasten to add that more discernment is needed on the part of the spiritual guide than by the disciple."

"How so?" Michael asked.

"Well, as a rule, someone who is spiritually inexperienced could not be expected to demonstrate high levels of discernment."

"Fr. Maxime," a man in his forties asked in broken Greek, "what is the key for the attainment of discernment?"

"The Fathers say that discernment is a gift of the Holy Spirit and a child of humility. In order to attain discernment, one should free the mind from its own prejudices. The mind must be completely cleansed so that it can accept what God will instruct. We can see what this means by how the holy elders admonish prospective spiritual guides to handle confessions. They say that in order to be able to hear someone who comes to you for confession, you must avoid having any preconceptions in your mind."

"This is what modern counseling teaches," interjected Emily, who got her doctorate in that field.

"I'm glad to hear that modern science agrees with what the Fathers of the *Ecclesia* have taught about this matter," Fr. Maximos replied. "You must be in a prayerful state so that God may guide you on what to advise the person who comes to you for confession. In that prayerful state, what you may receive from God may be contrary to what you would have liked to tell that person. But if you are prejudiced, even when your prejudice may be motivated by good intentions, you will never be able to tell the other person what God actually wishes for him or her. That means discernment presupposes humility, which itself is the product of obedience. It is obedience that washes away your desires and pride and demolishes your preconceptions. Once your tendency for self-centeredness is abated with the help of your spiritual guide, you are free not only to accept the wishes of others but also to be of service to them. Most important, as a consequence of your obedience, the way is paved for you to hear and do God's Will.

"I know that what I am saying may be difficult to accept, but that is how things work within the context of monasticism based on the experiences of the holy elders."

In previous conversations, Fr. Maximos had emphasized the importance of confession as a "mystery" and as a method that helps people attain all those virtues such as *metanoia*, humility, and obedience to God's commandments, which can pave the way for the acquisition of the Holy Spirit.

There was a pause as Fr. Maximos signaled that he was ready for the next question. "During the morning session you said something very significant," said Eleni, a professional accountant who had decided to get an M.A. in theology. "You mentioned that in order to understand the essence of who we are as human beings we need to understand the nature of God. What did you mean by that? Who is God? What can you tell us about God over and beyond prayer?" It was a question that gave Fr. Maximos the opportunity to elaborate on a key issue in Orthodox spiritual practice.

"Right. We need to learn about our archetype. It means that in order to understand who we truly are, we need to get to know Christ Himself. As I said this morning, Christianity teaches that we were created in the image of God, an image that was shattered as a result of the Fall. Therefore, in order to know who we are in the very essence of our being, we will have to get to know the very nature of God's Image. That is, the Christ who is our archetype and model of what we may be."

"Do you mean that we could get to know God through prayer?"

"Not only through prayer. Yes, prayer is the most perfect way of knowing God, but it may not necessarily be a method for beginners. We must first get to know God through ordinary human knowledge."

"I'm not sure I understand."

"Someone must speak to us about God before we can begin to believe in God. As St. Paul asks, how can they believe if they do not hear? How will they be able to hear if nobody speaks to them? That is, the first step for people to come to love and know God usually presupposes that somebody speaks to them about

God. Another way is to read the work of someone who can introduce them to the reality of God. That is, the first step in getting to know God will depend on our natural inheritance as human beings."

"In other words?"

"In other words, our spiritual age and level of knowledge and understanding will determine the relevant ways of approaching God."

"Isn't it also possible, Fr. Maxime," I interjected, "that one can have a mystical knowledge of God without these preliminary stages? The life of St. Paul himself is a good example."

"Oh yes, of course. There are cases when God reveals Himself directly to a human being without the need of intermediaries, as in the case of Paul on the road to Damascus. In fact, the first record in the scriptures about God's manifestation is in Genesis, when God speaks to Abraham directly and tells him, 'I am your God and I will guide you.' Then God makes all those promises to Abraham. He tells Isaac, 'I am the God of Abraham.' To Jacob He declares, 'I am the God of Abraham, Isaac, and Jacob.' And then, according to the Hebrews, He becomes 'the God of our Fathers.' "

"The God of Israel," I volunteered, "is a talking God. He speaks through the prophets."

"That's right. But it is more than that. God makes Himself known through various means, such as the study and knowledge of His Creation."

"This is what people try to do in universities."

"Right. But most important, God reveals Himself to human beings through the heart. This is the most perfect way of knowing God, as far as human existence is concerned. The revelation of God in the human heart happens only when a person engages in sustained and systematic prayer."

There was a pause before the next question. "Yes, Teresa," Fr. Maximos said, giving the floor to a woman in her thirties who had raised her hand. I was always impressed with his capacity to remember people's names.

"Would you say that we know God through our experience rather than through our logic?"

"I believe we know God through both our experience *and* our logic. Human beings are also rational creatures."

"But I thought," Teresa added, "that with pure reason we cannot know God."

"Correct. Reason is just a stage. You must step through it in order to go to the next one. You can truly come to understand God through love and direct experience."

"Fr. Maxime," Emily interjected, "you said that we can know God through the Creation, through knowledge, and through the heart. Do you mean by the way we treat nature?"

"No, not on the basis of how we treat nature," Fr. Maximos clarified. "As we contemplate the magnificence of Creation and the wisdom embedded in Creation, we come to understand that everything was created by an omnipotent and all-wise God. And He created everything for the sake of human beings so that they may get to know Him. It is what the Fathers of the Church call the *logoi ton onton*, meaning the logics of beings. That is, the purpose of the cosmos is the gnosis or knowledge of the Creator and the divinization of Creation."

"Isn't there a danger, Fr. Maxime," Emily mused, "in saying that the Creation came into being for the sake of human beings?"

"What do you have in mind, Emily?" Fr. Maximos asked quizzically.

"Doesn't such an understanding place human beings as the dominant species over all other creatures of nature, giving them the right to use and abuse other species? Is it not this very human privilege that has led us to our ecological predicament today? What I have in mind is what Thomas Berry writes in his *Great Work*,[3] that it is precisely this anthropocentrism, the notion that human beings are the privileged crowning of Creation, that gave them exclusive dominion over nature and paved the way toward its destruction and the decimation of other species."

"No," Fr. Maximos responded, "I believe this is a false interpretation of what the Bible teaches. A good father or a good mother does not try to undermine the well-being of his or her family but looks after it, helps it grow and prosper. A loving parent becomes the custodian of the family. That is how our relationship with the created world ought to be. In other words, when the Bible teaches that God made man king of Creation, it should not be interpreted that man should become a destroyer of Creation. It says *ergazesthe kai fylatteen* [belabor and protect], which means you should work and protect the Creation so that you may come to know the Creator and attain *Theosis*."

"We should, but we don't," Emily insisted. "People misinterpreted certain words in Genesis, such as when it says *kai katakyriefsate ten Gen*, that is, that we are urged to act like conquerors of the earth rather than stewards of the earth."

"This is a gross misconception," Fr. Maximos replied. "The word *kyrievo* in the original Greek means 'I become master of,' just like God is master of the world, not to destroy it but to save it and protect it. This is how we should properly understand the meaning of the created cosmos. God did not provide us with a green light to destroy nature but to become its stewards and glorify the Creator in the form of a Divine Eucharist."

"Meanings were lost in translation," I muttered.

"That's what I was just thinking," Teresa added. "Much distortion sneaked into the Bible through flawed translations."

"It is always a problem with translation," Fr. Maximos agreed. "That is why many Christians who rely exclusively on the words of the Bible for guidance generated such great diversity of beliefs, interpretations, and, alas, distortions."

"And that is why a rigid and literal adherence to words can lead to all sorts of misconceptions and fundamentalisms," I added.

"For sure." Fr. Maximos nodded. "That is why we consider the Bible as only one of several spiritual sources in our under-standing of God." He then pointed out that in the Orthodox way, the entire holy tradition and experience of the *Ecclesia* must be taken into consideration. It includes the mystical experiences of the saints along with the homilies and testaments they left behind.

Fr. Maximos then raised a hypothetical question. What would happen in the event that all the Bibles in the world were destroyed in a massive catastrophe? The answer, he said, is that the saints would rewrite the Bible because, as St. Silouan the Athonite once said, the Bible is eternally written in the hearts of the saints, from where it can be retrieved whenever external conditions permit it.[4] It is for this reason, Fr. Maximos contin-ued, that the true interpreters of sacred scripture are not the Bible scholars or the theologians but the saints, who base their knowledge on direct personal experience and mystical illumi-nation. That is why the guidance of an elder is so important in a serious spiritual struggle for "the acquisition of the Holy Spirit." It is for this reason also that Fr. Maximos mentioned to me sev-eral times how impatient he is with academic theologians, with their obscurantist wordiness and theories that have nothing to do with a direct experience of divine realities. A true theologian, for Fr. Maximos, is someone who has tasted the reality of God directly.

"The *Ecclesia*," Fr. Maximos claimed, "is over and beyond scripture. It includes the Holy Bible, but the *Ecclesia* is the Holy Tradition itself. This is what some people do not understand."

"This is a most crucial difference between how the Fathers of the *Ecclesia* view scripture and how Protestantism, particularly its fundamentalist version, understand it," I interjected. With Fr. Maximos's encouragement, I briefly explained that fundamentalist Protestantism considers the Bible the inerrant word of God, innately infallible and beyond questioning. In the Eastern Orthodox mystical tradition, on the other hand, the Bible is considered to be divinely inspired but written down and recorded by fallible human beings. Traditional and fundamentalist Protestants believe in *sola scriptura*, which means that the Bible solely and exclusively speaks the Truth.[5] Furthermore, the holy scripture can be understood by the faithful directly and without intermediaries such as priests, monks, and saints. A person is like a maverick who can search for God using his reason with the aid of infallible Holy Scripture.

With modern scholarship, however, the Bible has come under rational scrutiny, and a number of glaring contradictions have been unraveled. Many people who based their belief exclusively on the inerrancy of scripture were left with only two options: to reject modern scholarship altogether and follow the fundamentalist pathway or to lose faith in the Bible and consider it simply literature, as many liberal theologians have done. This is what happened to a person like Dr. Bart Ehrman, Professor of New Testament Studies at the University of North Carolina. He grew up in a fundamentalist family and attended a fundamentalist Bible college, where he was indoctrinated with the ideology of *sola scriptura*. He then attended Princeton to further his theological studies. During his studies he discovered that the four gospels and the other books of the New Testament have some discrepancies and contradictory narratives about what happened during Jesus' time. That was sufficient for him to lose his faith altogether.[6] That was also the case with Charles Templeton, who lost his faith for similar reasons. He was a close friend and collaborator of the evangelist Billy Graham, and during the fifties the two of them were considered "the two most successful exponents of mass evangelism in North America." Before he died, in 2001, Templeton wrote a book with the telling title *Farewell to God: My Reasons for Rejecting the Christian Faith*.[7]

According to the Eastern Christian fathers and saints, the proper way of relating to Holy Scripture and the Bible is the exact opposite of *sola scriptura*. For them the Bible is a means to help us attain a direct experience of God and not an infallible historical document. The American-born Greek Orthodox theologian Fr. John Romanides, reflecting on this issue and the mysticism of Eastern Christianity's understanding of Holy Scripture, asks: "Is there a single Church Father who identifies the Holy Scripture with the experience of *Theosis* itself? No, there is not one, because God's revelation to mankind is the experience of *Theosis*. In fact, since revelation is the experience of *Theosis*, an experience that transcends all expressions and concepts, the identification of Holy Scripture with revelation is, in terms of dogmatic theology, pure heresy."[8]

I went on to clarify that the fundamentalist understanding of scripture is not limited to Protestants but also to members of other denominations, including Eastern Orthodox themselves. John Romanides laments the tendency among many Eastern Orthodox theologians, oblivious to the mystical understanding of their religion, to become either fundamentalists in their interpretation of scripture or "liberal" like Bart Ehrman and Charles Templeton. For Romanides and Fr. Maximos, both tendencies are off the mark of the authentic mystical legacy of the patristic tradition, which focuses on the direct experience of Divinity.

After further discussion and clarification of the issues, Fr. Maximos signaled for the next question.

A woman in her fifties, who introduced herself as Maria, a professional counselor, spoke in accented Greek. "Your Eminence, can you comment on what I used to hear my parents say when I was young, namely that in our religion it is believed that the sins of the parents torment their children?"

"Did you hear this in church?" Fr. Maximos asked with some humor in his voice.

"Both in church and outside church," Maria replied. "I work with clients who have psychological problems, and I have heard many folks in church who believe that these people are suffering because of sins committed by their parents or even their ancestors. What is the position of the *Ecclesia* on this topic?"

Fr. Maximos nodded and proceeded to answer. "Okay. As far as guilt is concerned, and I mean from a legalistic point of view, human beings are responsible only for their own actions. I cannot pay for the sins of my father, my mother, or my grandfather. According to Holy Scripture, *ekastos peri aftou dosi logon*. It means that in front of God every person is accountable for his or her own actions and for no other. This is very clear. The notion of guilt that you mentioned has been rejected in the New Testament by Christ Himself."

"Then why do so many people believe in this?" Maria asked.

"Perhaps because of heredity, what people understand today about the genetic code, about DNA. A parent who is schizophrenic, for example, may pass on this malady to his or her child. This is simply a biological problem without any spiritual consequences. Unfortunately, as we all know, we can inherit biological problems like diabetes, heart disease, or whatever. From the biological point of view, it is possible for a person to conclude that we do carry the inheritance of our fathers, mothers, and ancestors. This has nothing to do with sin. It has no relevance when it comes to our relationship with God."

"But I thought somewhere in the Old Testament there is a reference to problems extending over seven generations," a young woman went on to say.

"If there is such a reference in the Old Testament, I believe we can only interpret it in the way I just mentioned, as simply biological inheritance and not as the result of moral responsibility."

"This notion of hereditary guilt is grounded in beliefs of Original Sin that entered into Western theology through Augustine," I volunteered.

"Good point," Fr. Maximos said. "This is probably a key difference between the Eastern Orthodox theological tradition and other traditions. So, what is Original Sin? Did Adam and Eve sin and we pay for this sin to this day? Are we to believe that God has not forgiven us all these years? Must we suffer because of what Adam and Eve did in time immemorial?"

Fr. Maximos went on to answer his own rhetorical questions. "The Eastern Orthodox tradition teaches that Original Sin is related not to some legalistic notion of guilt but to the form of heredity of an illness within the very fabric of our human nature.

"As I pointed out in the morning, the Orthodox tradition," he went on, "understands Original Sin as a medical problem, not a legalistic one."

"It's part of our existential DNA," I suggested.

"Precisely. We are not morally responsible for what Adam and Eve did during that primordial time. But their choices affected the entire human race. Christ came into the world to heal

us from this morbid inheritance. That is why we call Him the
Second Adam. He has come to heal us from our inherited predicament by giving us a new birth."

Another woman raised her hand. "I apologize for my Greek,"
she said shyly.

"Don't worry, my English is worse," Fr. Maximos reassured
her.

"Christ claims," the woman continued, "that the only way to
reach the Father is through Him. This is always a question that
is raised among people. What will happen to the rest of the
world, to the billions of people who are not born Christian and
who may not have even heard of Christ?"

This is a question that I am always asked when I speak to a
new audience about my work with Orthodox monks and mystical practitioners. I pretty much anticipated how Fr. Maximos
would handle it with this audience.

"Yes, Christ did say that. At the same time, John the Evangelist
states in the opening paragraph of his gospel that Christ is the
true light that lightens every human being who comes into the
world. That is, all of us as human beings are icons of God, and
we are invited to unite with Him. It means all human beings can
be saved through their conscience. It is not the Gospel that will
save us but our conscience. What does God require of us as stated
in His Commandments? He tells us not to steal, not to kill, not
to lie, to love our father and mother, to love other human beings.
I don't need to read all these commandments in the gospels in
order to follow them. They are an integral part of my true human
nature. Yes, the gospels do remind me of this natural tendency
to follow the commandments that spring from within my own
conscience. They are part of the nature of every human being,
whether he is Christian or not. Therefore, according to the holy
elders of Orthodoxy, all human beings can reach God without

anything other than their conscience. They can attain the natural state of Adam and Eve before the Fall."

Fr. Maximos then said a few more things about the nature of conscience.

"The Fathers state that conscience has the following characteristic: the more you listen and obey it, the more sensitive it becomes and the greater its capacity to reveal more truth. The more you ignore it, and the more you are indifferent to it, the coarser it becomes and the greater its tendency to distort reality. That means that even the most illiterate human beings who may never have heard of the Gospel can have the experience of God, assuming they guard and listen to their conscience, regardless of how refined it may be. Eventually their conscience will offer them experiences that will lead them closer to God. Abraham is a good example. He lived before Moses and the Ten Commandments and, of course, before the arrival of Christ. He was in fact an idolater who knew God only through his conscience."

Fr. Maximos then encouraged the audience to ask further questions. A young seminarian raised his hand. "Fr. Maxime," he said, "can you give to those of us who are not monks a prescription for how to live a more spiritual life in the world?"

Fr. Maximos smiled. "I believe Christ Himself has given us such a prescription. The Gospel is the prescription for our healing, assuming of course that we put it into practice. Remember what Christ taught as the key to salvation, namely the necessity of *metanoia* or repentance. *Metanoia* in Greek does not mean just to repent bad things we have done. I don't know how *metanoia* is translated into English, but what it means is really a fundamental transformation of how we feel and think. It means a radical change of one's worldview from its very foundation and not simply remorse for one's mistakes. This is only a part of *metanoia*.

The sum total of *metanoia* is the acquisition of a mind like that of Christ. It is to see the world in the same way Christ showed us. This is the prescription for our salvation."

The next question was from an elderly priest with a white beard who was wearing the traditional black cassock. He spoke impeccable Greek without an accent, which meant that he was probably a first-generation immigrant.

"Fr. Maxime," he asked, "many people come for confession who are at the turning point of *metanoia* but who, nevertheless, show no real sorrow or remorse for all the things they are confessing about. What do you do as a confessor under these circumstances?"

"It is a fact, dear Father, that when we go through confession ourselves or when we confess others, we experience all sorts of mixed emotions. This is part of our fallen condition. It happens to us, and it happens to everybody without exception. Sometimes, as a result of a minor incident, we experience deep repentance. Other times, because of a major problem, we may experience nothing. These are phenomena and symptoms, as I said, of our fallen state, of our existential illness, which we carry within ourselves. They are what the Fathers call 'alterations of the soul.'[9] Nevertheless, we must not be discouraged. We must continue our participation in the mystery of confession and *metanoia* if we are to see results.

"Let me give you an example from medicine. Let's say someone is diabetic. He has no pains anywhere. He is not aware of his problem, and consequently he dies. Another person who also does not feel anything but who knows that he must go to a doctor for regular checkups will eventually come to understand his situation and take appropriate measures that will save his life. Likewise, I would urge people to participate in the mystery of the confessional even if they don't feel anything. By their doing so, God will gradually clear the way for deeper spiritual experiences. In other words, when people say, 'I don't see any point in going for confession because I don't feel anything,' even though their thinking seems logical, it is false. If you cease going for confession, you may lose the opportunity for real transformation and spiritual experiences that the confessional can provide. As we say in Greek, your appetite comes only as you begin to eat.

"Let's say someone is suffering from anorexia," Fr. Maximos continued. "He can't even touch the best of dishes. If he forces himself to eat something, then gradually he may get his appetite back. On the other hand, if he gives up eating altogether, he will die. Likewise, I invite people to push themselves to the mystery of confession even if they don't see any immediate results or feel anything in particular. God is always present to help. At a minimum, the shame they may feel in going to confession is significant for their spiritual development. God will notice their small contribution, and He will eventually offer them His Grace."

Fr. Maximos paused, waiting for another question. "I am puzzled by what the Fathers of the Ecclesia say about the Jesus Prayer," Teresa commented. "They claim that when we pray, the mind, or nous, must be on the heart. I don't understand what that means."

"I appreciate your puzzlement," Fr. Maximos replied. "This is what the tradition of the Ecclesia teaches as noetic prayer or prayer of the heart. When the Fathers say that the nous or mind must unite with the heart or penetrate the heart, they don't mean this mind and this heart." Fr. Maximos pointed to his head and then to his heart. "They mean that the energy of the human mind must unite with all the psychological and bodily powers of the person. It means that during our invocation of Christ, the whole person becomes integrated as body, mind, soul, and spirit. While the Fall shattered the icon of God inside us, we are asked to reassemble it during prayer and make it into an integral and unified whole again. This way one prays directly to God. This *noetic* prayer, the 'Lord Jesus Christ, have mercy on me' that we repeat, can help us enormously, particularly at the beginning of our spiritual efforts."

"In what way?"

"It is short, inclusive, and not composed of diverse and complex meanings. Therefore, you can easily focus on it. At a certain point, when the mind concentrates on the single meaning of the Jesus Prayer, all meanings fade away, including the words of the Prayer. At that point the mind unites directly with the Holy Spirit. The person remains silent. All thoughts fade in preparing the way for the union of man with God. This process is a manifestation of Divine Grace. Of course, for Grace to be activated within us presupposes our own cooperation and freedom of will. We are expected to struggle up to the point of our capacities. Beyond that point we may be snatched by Grace, which will take us wherever It wishes."

"I have a question, Fr. Maxime," a young deacon asked. "Is the presence of temptations by demons through various forms of *logismoi* [thought forms][10] a sign that our spiritual growth has stalled? Is it a sign that we are not purified inside?"

"No. A person who is tempted by demons and by various forms of *logismoi* could be completely clean. Don't forget that Christ Himself was tempted by demons. The Fathers of the *Ecclesia* taught that thought forms assault all human beings. And on the basis of their spiritual knowledge and science, they taught us that there are five stages in the formation of *logismoi*. They indicated at which point we are spiritually accountable. The first stage is called 'assault,' that is, a *logismos* hits our mind and makes a suggestion, such as 'Take this microphone with you. Steal it.' It does not mean that I have sinned if such a thought crossed my mind. No. I have nothing to do with this. I am indifferent and the logismos fades away. This first stage is free from sin. There is no responsibility on my part, even if I am pestered by thousands of such logismoi."

"Many people are troubled by impure logismoi even while they are praying, and then they feel guilty and stop praying," the priest added.

"We need great care here. This is a mistake. The best way is to ignore such logismoi and not to stop praying. Pay no attention to them and you have nothing to fear," Fr. Maximos declared; then he continued to summarize the stages of the logismoi.

"The Fathers called the second stage 'interaction.' That is, I begin to converse with these logismoi. Should I do it, should I not do it? We engage in a dialogue with the logismos. This is dangerous, and it is wise to avoid such engagements. But still there is no sin here or accountability. The third stage is 'consent.' That's when I begin to tell myself, yes, I will take this microphone. It is from here that a sin starts to emerge which makes me accountable. The Fathers, based on their extensive experiences with such matters, called the fourth stage 'captivity.' The moment I consent, my mind, which is the steering wheel of my life, becomes a captive to the logismos. I cannot resist, and I commit the sinful act time and again. It becomes, according to the Fathers, a destructive 'passion,' the fifth stage in this process of the formation of sin.

"So," Fr. Maximos concluded, "it is important to be on guard against the invasion in our mind of destructive logismoi that undermine our spiritual life. Again, the best attitude, in order to protect ourselves from them, is a healthy detachment and indifference.

"Keep in mind also that the Jesus Prayer we talked about is a very powerful antidote to these types of *logismoi*. It strengthens our *nous*. Our mind is toughened up. When there is an assault, the *logismos* hits it and bounces back. It does not enter the interior of our heart and mind."

Our session ended when someone from the organizing committee came to announce that we were already way past the allotted time for our informal conversation and that dinner was about to be served.

THREE

SYMPOSIUM

Several members of the Greek-speaking group that met with Fr. Maximos at the Boston conference expressed a keen interest in continuing the conversation. Consequently, after the conference a dinner was arranged at a Middle Eastern restaurant in Cambridge well known for its vegetarian options. We reserved a special room where we could enjoy the privacy necessary for a serious engagement with spiritual questions.

There were eighteen people at the oval dinner table. In addition to the eight participants from the previous discussion, there was the group that accompanied Fr. Maximos to America: Niki and Anna, his two sisters; Andreas, his brother-in-law; Fr. Nikodemos, his close associate, who unlike Fr. Maximos spoke good English; and Ioanna, a young Cypriot philanthropist who took time off from her thriving business to join the rest for the pilgrimage. There was also Linda, a Greek-American lawyer from New York who had volunteered to rent a minibus and serve as a driver for Fr. Maximos and his companions during their East Coast sojourn. Emily once again volunteered to serve as an interpreter if needed.

Before we began eating, Fr. Maximos recited a short prayer

that he offered before any meeting where he was expected to give a talk. Everybody stood up, and in a low voice he began: "O Christ, the True Light that illumines and sanctifies every human being who comes into the world, may the brightness of your face become sealed in our souls so that we may behold the Ineffable Light, and guide our steps to follow your commandments through the intercession of your Most Holy Mother and all the saints. Amen."

We had hardly introduced ourselves before the questions began, mostly from those who had just met Fr. Maximos at the conference.

"Fr. Maxime, what did St. Seraphim of Sarov mean when he said that the purpose of the *Ecclesia* is the acquisition of the Holy Spirit?" asked Maria, the professional counselor who, I learned later, was contemplating joining a women's monastery.

After taking a deep breath, Fr. Maximos repeated that the primary role of the *Ecclesia* is to help people come to know God experientially. "The manifestation of God in the life of human beings," he said further, "gives birth to very concrete and definitive fruits, which I mentioned yesterday."

"Do you mean spiritual fruits?" Maria asked.

"Yes. St. Paul explained to us what it means to be possessors of the Holy Spirit. If you remember, in his epistle to the Galatians, chapter five, verses twenty-two and twenty-three, he presents a list of characteristics or fruits of the Spirit. They are, he says, *agape* (love), *chara* (joy), *eirene* (peace), *makrothymia* (patience), *chrestotis* (kindness), *agathosyne* (goodness), *pistis* (faithfulness), *praotes* (gentleness), and *engratea* (self-control) [original Greek words as translated in the Holy Bible, Revised Standard Version]."

"Can the Holy Spirit be confined to nine characteristics?" I wondered aloud.

"Obviously, this isn't an exhaustive list. God's gifts are infinite. Paul simply offers us this tentative list of gifts so that we can examine ourselves and see to what degree they are present in our lives. That is, to what degree we are close to God."

"They are prerequisites of the God-realized life," I noted.

"That's understood. It's as if Paul is telling us: 'Do you wonder whether the Holy Spirit is present and manifest in your life? The procedure to find out is very simple. Take this list of nine attributes, place it in front of you like a mirror, and judge for yourself.' Raise the question in your mind: 'Do I have these qualities: love, joy, peace, patience, kindness, goodness, faithfulness, gentleness, self-control?' If I do have them, or if they have begun to get energized within me, that is fair and good. But if instead of love I discover hatred, instead of joy I find bitterness, instead of peace I am tormented by hostility, then I can conclude that the Holy Spirit is not present in my heart. It has not become firmly established within my existence."

"That means that we all have a long way to go!" Emily interjected.

"Well, to be sure all of us have plenty of work to do until, as the apostle says, Christ becomes a living reality within us and begins to offer the gifts of His Presence."

Fr. Maximos served himself some hummus and continued. "Apostle Paul describes the fruits of the Spirit in the form of a scale, a hierarchy. He lists the highest and most exalted gift first and ends up with the most basic and foundational."

"What does that mean?" said Emily, who has a reflexive aversion to the notion of hierarchy, which has traditionally denoted social divisions and inequalities.

"Think about it," Fr. Maximos responded. "He lists love first, then joy, until, last on the list, self-control."

"Do you think there is a deliberate logic in that sequence?" I asked. I'd assumed it was a manner of speaking, an aspect of Paul's literary style that lacked intention or hidden agenda.

"If we examine this passage carefully, it appears to be intentional," Fr. Maximos insisted. In an earlier conversation with me, he'd postulated that every passage in the New Testament should be seen not as accidental but as deliberately crafted to help people understand the nature of God and show what they need to do to unite with Him. Fr. Maximos repeated that there are no superfluous statements in the sayings of Jesus. Each sentence and parable is deliberate and expresses great spiritual truths and wisdom.

He paused for a few seconds as we all focused on our eating. The vegetarian dishes seemed never-ending.

"Can we go over that list, Father, and explain the meaning of each term so that we can see how they are connected?" Maria asked with some trepidation. Fr. Maximos looked around to see if there was interest in exploring the subject further. He didn't have to ask. Everybody was eager.

"Okay. Let's examine these gifts starting with the last one. You see," Fr. Maximos said lightheartedly, "he, himself, was already at the top, at the stage of love, and could see from up there the lower steps that one must traverse to reach that highest of stages. So let us look at these gifts in reverse. We will start from the base, with self-control, and climb up the ladder all the way to love."

"Are we to assume that Paul considers self-control and temperance as the foundation of all the other gifts?" Teresa asked.

"That's right. You cannot get to the stage of real love directly. You must struggle at the lower stages first and climb until you reach love. Real love does not appear automatically. You must work for it, struggle for it until you get to know what it is all about."

"So, self-control is a prerequisite to all the other steps?"

Fr. Maximos nodded. "That's what we said. Temperate persons do not crave to taste everything, to use everything and everybody for their own pleasure and comfort. They exercise restraint in the face of temptations, be they food, sex, wealth, fame, power, or worldly pleasures of all sorts."

"But how can one cultivate self-control? Modern social life is not helpful in this regard," I pointed out. I had in mind the founders of sociology, who were concerned with the rise of what they considered unrestrained egoism and individualism that followed the breakdown of the old medieval, communal order. They feared that human beings left to themselves tend to generate desires that run out of control, rendering social life problematic if not impossible. Therefore, through "moral education," human beings should be given clear guidelines and limits as antidotes to insatiable desires. It is an old concern, going all the way back to Confucius.

Fr. Maximos was not a sociologist. He saw the problem of moral guidelines not from the vantage point of maintaining a smoothly functioning society but from that of personal salvation. So the method he espoused for the cultivation of self-control was not for sociological reasons but rather for spiritual and existential purposes.

"To develop the capacity for self-control and mastery," he went on, "you must work on yourself. You start the spiritual life from the most elementary level, taking charge of external things."

"You can't start your university career before you complete elementary school," Fr. Nikodemos interjected.

"Right. This is what often scandalizes young people who come to the Church for advice. They don't like rules and regulations. They don't like 'don't do this, don't do that' rules.

"When I was a young boy," Fr. Maximos continued, "I wasn't sure what I had to do in order to be a good member of the *Ecclesia*. I wrote down in an exercise book all the commandments of God. Then I added whatever other commandments I could find from the New Testament. Based on those commandments, I made a list of what I assumed I was allowed to do and what I was not allowed to do. I wrote down, for example, that I should not spend time in coffee shops, that I should not do this, not do that. I remember I wrote down in the form of a question whether playing billiards was sinful or not! I would then write down, 'No, it is not.'" We laughed with Fr. Maximos about his early spiritual dilemmas.

"It was bad enough that I imposed these rules on myself, but I also imposed them on a few friends in the neighborhood, kids like myself, whom I pretended to place under my 'spiritual guidance and protection.' But when my mother discovered my exercise book, she tore it apart."

After telling us a few more humorous stories from his childhood, Fr. Maximos went on to explain that the commandments, which God gave to humanity through the great prophets and through Jesus, were not legalistic, moral principles. In order to understand what this implies, he said, we must always keep in mind the fact that we are created in the image of God and that our "natural state" is to be in constant contemplation of our Creator. It is, he said, the equivalent of a lover who is constantly thinking about and contemplating his or her beloved. The Fall, he continued, disrupted that state of constant communion with God. Instead of remembering God, our attention shifted to the things of Creation, to objects. The sole purpose of spiritual struggle is to reestablish our connection with God and begin functioning again the way God made us "in the beginning."

"Temperance and self-control, therefore," Fr. Maximos went

on, "is to help us in such a way as to liberate our hearts and minds from the objects of our enslavement so that we may return our gaze to God."

"What do you mean by 'things of this world,' Father?" Maria asked.

"Material possessions, career, success, ideological fixations, everything that steals the heart. The result is one: our passion for God is transformed into the passion for created things of no ultimate and eternal value, be they power, fame, politics, smoking, sex, money, and so on."

"This is the meaning of idolatry," I added. "We worship our own creations."

"Yes, precisely."

"Is fasting a way to overcome idolatry?" Maria asked.

"The objective of fasting and all other rules instituted by the *Ecclesia* is to help us liberate our hearts and minds so that we may be refocused once again on God. There is nothing inherently bad about drinking milk or eating meat or olive oil for that matter [almost half the days of the year at various intervals Orthodox Christians are asked to refrain not only from meat or meat products but also from all kinds of oils, including olive oil]."

"Yet people often turned these practices into absolute rules," Teresa pointed out. "They turned them into ends in themselves."

"This is tragic," Fr. Maximos said. "People are often more obsessed about fasting in itself than about the purpose of fasting, which is to master our desires, overcome our egotism, and open our hearts toward God. For those of us who are serious about the spiritual life, such practices simply help reorient our minds toward that which is ultimately real. They are not ends in themselves.

"Very much like the lover who cannot think of anything other than the beloved," Fr. Maximos continued, "is the person who is flooded by the love and memory of God. This is what we truly crave. If our minds are totally absorbed by our work or by our cars or by our hobbies or by the relentless pursuit of worldly pleasures or whatever else, there will be no room for the love of God."

"So then," I pointed out, "whatever distracts us from the memory of God is a form of idolatry, of sin."

"That is exactly what sin is," Fr. Maximos emphasized. "The practice of temperance is to free us from the tendency to sin, to be distracted from our ultimate objective. Temperance encompasses the entire spectrum of our actions."

"But how can we live then in this world of created things that we find ourselves in?" Teresa asked.

"Use the things of this world, but don't let them use you. Don't become possessed by them."

"We fill up our emptiness with all sorts of obsessions," I interjected, "be it power, fame, politics, smoking, gambling, sports, food, sex, television, moneymaking, and so on."

Fr. Maximos laughed as he remembered something. "Someone once asked me, 'How come you monks don't smoke?' I replied that we don't have a need to smoke and suggested that she should phrase the question differently. Why do people smoke in the first place? It means something is lacking in their lives and they become captives to this destructive habit.

"Elder Paisios used to say," Fr. Maximos continued, "that those who take narcotics can be liberated from their addiction when they taste a more powerful narcotic, and by that he meant Christ. When you discover what you truly desire, then you have no need for substitutes. Then you become truly liberated. You become master of things rather than their slave."

"Sometimes, in their attempt to exercise temperance, certain people behave in a way that is incomprehensible to those of us who live in the world," I said, alluding to the extremes that some hermits resort to in order to free themselves from "the world."

"Yes. Their ways are incomprehensible to us who live ordinary lives. There is, for example, a hermit who spent a lifetime in a cave overlooking a beautiful gorge," Fr. Maximos added. "He never allowed himself to gaze at the beauty around him because he did not wish to have his heart and mind get distracted from his focus on God."

"This is really bizarre," Michael, the young seminarian, complained.

"Well, from our point of view, it is. The reason I am telling you this is to emphasize the lengths that some hermits would go to in order to maintain their exclusive focus on God. I certainly do not recommend it."

Fr. Maximos laughed in his characteristic way as he thought of something else. "When I was abbot at the Panagia monastery, a very nice woman brought us freshly baked cookies. 'I made these for all of you here,' she said, 'so that when you sit on your balconies and are overtaken by melancholy you can have some with your coffee.' 'But, my dear,' I replied, 'we don't have time to drink coffee on our balconies. We have other important things that we must do. We don't have time to be taken over by melancholy!'"

Fr. Nikodemos, who had been mostly quiet, added that he remembered that incident; he had been a monk at the Panagia monastery at the time. Then Fr. Maximos, in a more serious tone, went on to say that the ways of hermits, and monastic life in general, may be extreme, but they highlight for us certain axioms of the spiritual life. "We must not allow anything of temporal value to steal our hearts. Every time we direct our hopes toward earthly things we make a step backward on our journey toward God."

"How can we start?" Maria asked. "I mean, how can we practice temperance and self-control?"

Fr. Maximos ate a piece of stuffed tomato before replying. "The proper way is to start with simple things, like being critical of your thoughts and actions. Let us say that a thought tells you you should do a certain thing, say buy a new television set. Examine it. Ask yourself, 'Do I really need it?' If you think you do, fine. Go ahead and buy it. But ask that question first and explore what your real needs are."

Fr. Maximos continued, as if thinking aloud, "People become fanatical about their political ideologies. They transform a transient thing into something absolute. For us only God is the Absolute."

"Some people today blame religion for all the ills of the world, claiming that religion breeds fanaticism and intolerance," I pointed out.

"A real Christian cannot be a political or religious fanatic," Fr. Maximos added drily. "Not only must you accept people different from yourself but you also must love them unconditionally. Always question your judgment. Even Paul had to search for Peter in order to ask him whether his experience on the road to Damascus was real and not a hallucination. Authentic spiritual life unavoidably makes us humble, not fanatical."

"You are teaching a very different Christianity, Fr. Maxime," I said. "The fundamentalists would hit the roof with self-righteous indignation at what you profess."

Fr. Maximos smiled and continued. "Let me repeat, the foundation of the spiritual life is self-control and temperance, just as St. Paul advocated. This implies an ability to restrain our desires. That's where we must begin our spiritual struggle. We need practice. How can we become compassionate, charitable, and loving if we can sacrifice nothing of ourselves?"

"Is that why the first commandment of God to Adam and Eve was to avoid eating from the tree of knowledge?" Michael asked.

"That's what the elders say. The commandments of God are the medicines that He offered us for our cure. Honoring the commandments liberates us from the slavery of our passions and unbridled desires. When God said, 'Thou shall not eat from that tree,' it was a commandment to exercise temperance. That is why before starting His ministry Christ fasted for forty days and forty nights. It was to show that the first step in the spiritual life is to take mastery over your desires."

We took a break as the waiters collected our empty plates, only to replace them with a fresh round of tasty dishes, all vegetarian and appropriate for Lent.

When the commotion of passing food around had ended, we continued.

I opened the discussion. "The word *temperance* or *self-control*, Fr. Maxime, usually brings to mind restraint in sexual matters and alcohol. I believe the elders have a much wider notion in their minds when they mention that term." I was thinking of the temperance movement in the United States during the early part of the twentieth century, which was started by pious Protestant women with the purported aim of saving young men, migrants from the rural areas to the cities, from visiting saloons and houses of ill repute.[1] It ended up with the discredited Prohibition Act and the emergence of the likes of Al Capone.

"We are asked to develop temperance over all our passions, bodily and psychic," Fr. Maximos replied. "It is a psychic passion, for instance, to have an exaggerated view of yourself and to demand that your views and wishes must always prevail."

"It is possible, therefore," I said, "that one can have mastery over bodily passions but be completely dominated by psychic passions."

"Definitely," Fr. Maximos confirmed. "You can easily find people who are temperate, who have mastered their physical desires. They eat moderately or very little. They are modest in the way they dress and so on. It is much more difficult to find temperate people who have mastered their psychic passions. It is very difficult to find people who are not egocentric, cunning, proud, and vain, people who do not insist that their opinions and wishes always prevail over those of others. That is why physical exercises like fasting and prostrating in front of icons are beneficial for the spiritual life but are not ends in themselves and certainly not sufficient. Reverence, or the struggle against the more subtle passions, is much more important toward real liberation."

"I suppose one can start from where one is," I reasoned.

"Naturally. People ask me how to begin their spiritual struggle. And they will tell me, 'Look, Father, I have never had any relationship with the *Ecclesia.*'" Fr. Maximos leaned back in his chair. "So what am I to advise them? Such people may not be ready to engage in a more subtle struggle with their lower passions. I suggest that they start to do simple things: Go to church regularly, and during the morning and before you go to sleep read a simple prayer, even if you do it mechanically. Try to fast sometime. Try to be a bit more modest in the way you dress and the way you live in general. When people are liberated from such simple fixations, then it is easier for them to turn their attention to higher things, toward God."

An ambulance passed by, its siren briefly interrupting our conversation. "Do you know that we have the potential to have our hearts and minds stuck on something utterly trivial, like a nail or a pen?" Fr. Maximos said. "Even a single pen can enslave us and prevent us from turning our focus wholeheartedly toward God."

To illustrate the point further, Fr. Maximos told us about what the great Elder Ephraim of Katounakia, a man renowned for gifts of clairvoyance and prophetic vision, once did.

"Elder Ephraim visited us at our *skete* once. He needed to write a letter, and our own elder offered him his pen. He drafted the letter and, as he was handing the pen back to our elder, said, 'Hmm . . . what a beautiful pen you have!' You understand that a minor thing like a pen is of great value in a place like Mt. Athos. It is not always easy to find them. Our elder replied, 'Take it, Father. I have another one. Anyway, I go to Thessaloniki on occasion, and I can get more. You, on the other hand, never leave the Holy Mountain. So please take it.' Elder Ephraim reluctantly accepted the gift, placed it in his pocket, and left. His hermitage was two hours away on foot. You must have heard how difficult it is to walk on Mt. Athos. The elder had to hike along rugged mountain paths. It was six in the afternoon when he left. But at midnight we heard knocks at the door. It was very strange to get a visitor that late. We opened the door, and what did we see? Elder Ephraim. He was holding the pen. He said, 'Please take it back. This pen cut me off from God. I felt that Grace had abandoned me.'

"Just imagine. He walked another four hours back and forth to return the pen, which he felt had interrupted his prayerful state."

"This is hard for us to accept," Maria pointed out. "Psychologists would define such behavior as pathological."

Fr. Maximos, who knew Elder Ephraim well, waved his hand dismissively. "What actually happened was that when he went back to his hermitage and began praying, he felt that he could not concentrate. The pen was on his mind, distracting his focus."

Fr. Maximos scanned the table, looking at our puzzled faces. "This is an example of what it means for a great saint to lose his concentration and connection with God. It is insufferable. So for Elder Ephraim the answer was simple. He had to get rid of that which obstructed his relationship with God. It is not accidental that Christ said, 'Whoever loves himself more than me, even his own life, cannot be my disciple.' In other words, God asks us to cut off every relationship. Not to hate ourselves, not to reject ourselves, but to liberate ourselves from self-absorption, from our narcissism. It requires great courage to be liberated from the bondage of this world so that we fear nothing."

Fr. Maximos was fond of referring to a story of John Chrysostom, fourth-century patriarch of Constantinople who later was canonized as a major saint of the Church, both of the East and of the West. He was persecuted by the wife of the then emperor for being critical of her abuse of power and exploitation of the poor and weak. When John was warned by friends to stop his sermons against her on the ground that she had the power to harm him, he scoffed at their advice, replying, "Only John can harm John." Fr. Maximos would bring that up as an example of a person who fears nothing except damaging his relationship with God.

"This is what temperance offers us," Fr. Maximos continued, "to free us from the objects of this world, from our prejudices, our superstitions, our fixations. The conscious practice of self-control can liberate us from the grossest things all the way to the most subtle ones, such as our ideas and cherished beliefs.

"When a person is liberated from egocentrism through the practice of temperance," he went on, "there comes the second fruit of the Holy Spirit, which, according to St. Paul, is gentleness, a product of humility. You see, temperance and self-control give birth to humility, and humility paves the way to gentleness."

"I'm not sure I understand what you mean, Fr. Maxime," Michael interjected.

"Look. When you attain mastery over your thoughts, wishes, and desires, when you cease to be opinionated, then you begin to experience humility. You are no longer invested in things. And the first flower of humility is gentleness, just like the first thorn of pride is anger."

When someone asked whether anger is an evil emotion, Fr. Maximos explained that it is possible to be angry in a positive way, without sinning. Sometimes, he said, it is necessary to express anger in order to "put things in order," for the sake of a higher good. He claimed that anger is a natural property of the soul. But it is given to us to resist evil and to be used for good purposes, such as a mother reprimanding her child when the mother has only the child's welfare in mind. Fr. Maximos's notion of anger without sin was an anger without ego being invested in it.[2] "Saints do get angry but only to energize the power of God within themselves so that they resist sin. There are times that you must resist, like when your friends press you to do something that goes contrary to your conscience."

Fr. Maximos then talked about two hermits who wondered how it felt to be angry. They tried to set up an experiment so that they would provoke each other. But they failed. They did not know how to get angry. "When you reach the stage of gentleness, which is a by-product of temperance, there is no room for things that have the power to generate anger and confusion within you.

"So," Fr. Maximos continued, "we must first struggle to attain our liberation from being slaves to material things, including ideas and ideologies. And I must say that enslavement to ideas and ideologies is much more serious than enslavement to things."

"In what way?" Teresa asked.

"As I said, you can easily find people who are temperate over external things. They are modest in dress, eat little, and have mastery over physical pleasures in general. They may even appear like ascetics. However, these very people may be slaves to their ideas, to their opinions, to their political beliefs and ideologies. They are rigid and unbending in their views about this and that subject, and they get angry if somebody disagrees with them or contradicts them. They demand that others support their views and desires. They engage more often than not in monologues, expecting others to defer to their brilliance."

"You have just described Adolf Hitler!" I interjected. "He had all those characteristics and among other things was a vegetarian. You meet people like that all the time. They also sound like some of our public figures. Hitler was the archetype, an extreme case."

"Yes, ideologically rigid people are quarrelsome and fanatical about the rightness of their opinions," Fr. Maximos said. "Sometimes people who suffer from such passions can reach the point where they are ready to kill or be killed for the sake of sticking to their positions. They cannot remove themselves from their desires and can never give up what they want to believe in."

"Their opinions are change-proof," I noted. "We often celebrate such people as great heroes. Can we include religious martyrs in this category?"

"No. I don't mean our commitment to God. I mean to be enslaved to opinions and beliefs that have to do not with our salvation but with the affairs of this fallen world."

"Yet," Fr. Nikodemos noted, "your enemies in Cyprus have accused you of being a fanatic, a fundamentalist."

Fr. Maximos grinned and sighed. "Yes, they did say that and much more. It is fashionable today to accuse people of the *Ecclesia* of being fundamentalist fanatics and the like. They accuse me specifically of being the leader of the fanatics." We laughed at his wry tone.

Fr. Maximos alluded to accusations he has faced since his arrival in Cyprus from Mt. Athos, in the early nineties. His detractors accused him of "brainwashing" young people to such a degree that they would give up careers and prospects for a married life and join him as monks and nuns in secluded monasteries. The local Communists were particularly vitriolic against him. They accused him of being a purveyor of "false consciousness." As far as the Communists were concerned, Fr. Maximos embodied the well-known Marxist aphorism that religion is the "opium of the people." For them he was also an apostate. His own father, who died in an accident when Fr. Maximos was young, was an active member of the local Communist Party and a relentless opponent of the Church. Fr. Maximos as a young boy had to attend church secretly and against his father's wishes.

"That is okay," Fr. Maximos responded. "But I ask the question, can we attach the label of the fanatic to someone who undergoes in an authentic and genuine way the pedagogy of the *Ecclesia* as dictated by Christ? Can a Christian be a fanatic?"

"Be careful. There are plenty of those around, Fr. Maxime!" I warned, half seriously.

"But I mean an authentic, genuine Christian. I think it is by definition impossible."

"How so?"

"From the very moment that someone is a fanatic, he is into delusion."

"You mean he is not following in the footsteps of Christ?"

"Exactly. Such a person is outside the spiritual teachings as set down by Christ and the great saints who followed in His footsteps. The entire therapeutic pedagogy of the *Ecclesia* is built on the practice of humility. To follow Christ means to have the capacity to coexist with other people who may be radically different from you.

"This does not mean," Fr. Maximos hastened to add, "that you give up your own faith. No, you are absolutely committed to your faith and your relationship with God. At the same time, however, you allow the other person to be, to exist. You wish neither to oppress nor to wipe out the other person simply because he does not share your beliefs."

"Some Christians would love to do just that," I noted.

"Christians in past ages and present—" Emily began.

"I understand what you are about to say, Emily," Fr. Maximos interjected. "This is not the problem of Christ or the *Ecclesia* as a spiritual hospital. It is the problem of flawed human beings."

Fr. Maximos took a drink and continued. "I am reminded of what Elder Joseph the Hesychast wrote in a little booklet about this matter. The title of his essay was 'Delusion.' In it, he clearly identifies delusion with fanaticism. The fanatic is under the spell of delusion. The person who is monolithically dogmatic, absolutistic in his views, and dismissive of others who profess different opinions is under the spell of *plani*, of delusion."

"Religious people often consider such characteristics as virtues," I pointed out. "I mean, to be dogmatic and absolutistic. Alas, this has been the tragic reality of much of the history of the Church."

"Yes. In fact such people may follow the teachings of the Church exactly. They may fast, they may study the scriptures day and night, they may go to all-night prayer vigils, they may be generous and charitable, they may follow everything to the letter, they may diligently study the word of God and pray continuously."

"Where do you see the problem then?" Michael asked.

"Such people often turn such practices into absolutes and get attached to them. They lose sight of the reason that they engage in these practices."

"This is an unavoidable problem for every religion," I said. "Rules and regulations, and various religious practices necessary for the preservation of religion, become ends in themselves as people lose sight of why those rules were set up in the first place."

"Exactly. People become intolerant toward others because others don't act and behave like themselves. They are not pious like themselves, they don't pray or go to church every Sunday. According to Elder Joseph, such fanatical attitudes are forms of delusion. Spiritual persons, says the elder, are whole persons. They do not have gaps inside them. They are perfected in Christ. They act having Christ as their model. And Christ was never a fanatic. Christ would not quarrel with those who disagreed with Him. Human beings who are on Christ's footsteps will present their views simply and modestly, without trying to convince anybody. Christ never got into fights to impose His teachings. Furthermore, whenever He realized that the other was not receptive, He simply remained silent."

"In the same way He responded to Pilate," Maria commented.

"That's the classic example. He recognized that Pilate was not open to His teaching. Christ did not marshal His divine powers to knock down Pilate's views in order to convince him. Christ told His disciples that to them was given the privilege to get to know the mysteries of Heaven, whereas to the rest the teachings were given in the form of parables. The possibility of knowledge, in other words, was given only to those who had a thirst for knowledge and who were ready to accept the word of God. To others, God would not reveal His Truth."

"But why not?" Maria asked.

"He certainly was not rejecting others. It was out of love that he wouldn't reveal His Truth."

"I don't understand."

"When you hear God's word and you reject it, you are more responsible."

"So ignorance is bliss in such a case."

"Of course. If you know the difference between good and evil but you choose evil, you are more responsible for your transgression. It is the same if you know God's ways but you choose to reject them. God in His great mercy, therefore, will not expose us to His ways if we are not ready to accept them. Once again, that is why Christ never tried to convince anyone. Neither Christ, nor the gospels, nor the saints, nor the *Ecclesia*, properly understood, could possibly produce fanatical human beings."

"I wish that were the reality with the Church. Alas, there are plenty of fanatics all around," I said, shaking my head.

"Yes. These are phenomena that are related to the spiritual immaturity of individuals, not of the *Ecclesia* itself. The *Ecclesia* should not be judged on the basis of such spiritually ill and un-developed individuals. It should be judged on the basis of those who have been healed by its pedagogy. A hospital cannot be evaluated by the number of sick persons taken care of inside its walls. Can we say that because a hospital houses sick people, it is sickly and useless and must be closed down? Wouldn't that be absurd? You judge the effectiveness of a hospital by the quality of its doctors and the number of sick people who have been re-stored to health, not by the number of patients who reside there. That's how we must see the *Ecclesia*, as a healing institution, with all of us as its inmates. It is the presence of the saints among us that authenticates its therapeutic efficacy."

We had yet another break as a couple of waiters swooped in to clear the table. While they were preparing for the next course, I thought of an incident related to Fr. Maximos that had impressed me. One of his close associates was Thanos, an environmental architect who was for a while a professor of architecture at the University of Slovenia. Upon graduating from high school in Limassol, he had moved for his higher education to Slovenia. Fr. Maximos and Thanos had been friends since their high school years. Upon Thanos's return to Cyprus with his Slovenian wife and two children, he became one of Fr. Maximos's key advisors on several of the bishopric's architectural projects. Both Emily and I became friends with Thanos since he and Emily shared a passionate interest in environmental sustainability. Because Thanos was in regular contact with Fr. Maximos, I often relied on him to arrange our meetings. That's how close they were as friends and collaborators.

But Thanos was also a self-confessed atheist. He told me that he believed only in science and things that "can be proven." Furthermore, he found that members of the clerical establishment, with the exception of Fr. Maximos, were corrupt and reactionary. Yet his atheism did not affect their friendship and collaboration in the least. Thanos stressed to me that he was attracted to Fr. Maximos not only because they knew each other from their teenage years but also because he found Fr. Maximos "authentic." The elder's selfless lifestyle and extensive community work resonated well with Thanos's leftist political leanings, vegan culinary habits, and ecological commitments. He asked Fr. Maximos early in their relationship whether his atheism would jeopardize their friendship and cooperation. Fr. Maximos replied that he did not mind, assuming that Thanos himself

accepted Fr. Maximos as a man of faith. When a Greek Orthodox bishop from an Asian country visited Fr. Maximos and the
three of them had lunch together, the guest, upon discovering
Thanos's atheism, was very surprised. How was it possible, he
asked, that the two of them were such close friends considering their radical differences in regard to faith? Fr. Maximos
replied by eulogizing Thanos as a man who exemplified many
of the fruits of the Holy Spirit, such as humility, temperance,
detachment from material things. He said to the other bishop,
"Thanos has all the qualities of a real Christian. Our only difference is that he does not know as yet that God resides inside
him." I wondered myself how long Thanos could associate so
closely with Fr. Maximos while remaining a committed unbe-
liever.

After the tea, Middle Eastern sweets, like baklava, and fruits,
like apples and oranges, had been served, we resumed the conversation.

"Fr. Maxime, why do you suppose St. Paul placed the fruit of
faith at the bottom end of his hierarchy?" Michael asked.

"This is an important point. Paul did not place faith at the
top part of his hierarchy but in the bottom triad, namely faith,
gentleness, and self-control," Fr. Maximos replied, extending three
fingers of his right hand. "Why? Because, the apostle claims that
a time will come when faith will be transcended. It will take
place when we have direct contact with God. Faith will no longer be necessary, and only love, the ultimate stage of the spiritual hierarchy, will remain."

"Faith then is just a step on our way to God? I never thought
of it that way!" Michael said.

"Many people in the Church do not understand this fine point,
and they emphasize 'blind faith' and the like as ends in themselves. No injunction that God ever gave to us demands 'Believe

that I am God.' Nothing in the New Testament states or implies the importance of blind faith. Instead we are asked to love God our Lord. The person who simply believes in God is still far from the ultimate goal, which is to unite with God in love. This is the great difference that we need to understand."

"How then is faith, as a fruit of the Spirit, linked to the other two spiritual fruits that you spoke about?" Michael asked again.

"It is like a chain. Only the person who has freed himself from the things and meanings of this world and who has penetrated into the grace of humility can truly have faith. You cannot have faith when you are an egotist."

"Why not?"

"Simply because instead of believing in God, you believe in yourself," Fr. Maximos replied. "Do you remember Apostle Paul's words that avarice is idolatry? Why? Because the avaricious person has faith only in his wealth and possessions. Of course it is not just avarice that is a form of idolatry but all the passions that enslave us to the things of this world.

"This reminds me of a story in which an abbot asks a hermit how he should go about intensifying his faith. The hermit replies, 'How can you intensify your faith, Father, when your cellar is full of cheeses, wines, and all sort of provisions?' What he tried to convey to the abbot was that instead of investing his faith in God he had invested his faith in material possessions. It is as if the abbot had convinced himself 'I am now secure because my cellar is full of foodstuffs.' Or 'I am secure because I have money in the bank, I have a good house,' and the like.

"I remember an uncle who had returned from South Africa and was bragging to me about his three houses and the money he had in the bank. He calculated how much he should spend every month given his investments. He felt very happy and content as he looked forward to a comfortable early retirement.

The poor man died from a heart attack soon after he told me about his wonderful fortune. His wealth was inherited by his brothers.

"In the Gospel, Christ called the person who invested in material things in order to feel secure insane. Such a person places all his faith in things that are chimerical and vain. A person who has such an attachment to material things cannot have faith in God."

Fr. Maximos paused and then continued. "Another Athonite story comes to mind. A hermit placed a lock on his cell to prevent thieves from stealing what little he had. In those days there were thieves roaming around Mt. Athos. At night he was attacked by demons and beaten up. He then realized that it was not the lock that could protect him but his faith in God. To punish himself for his lack of faith he vowed to sleep for six months with the door unlocked and with the key in the lock."

"But we are not hermits, Fr. Maxime, and it is unlikely that any of us here will be aware that we are being attacked by demons," I said, prompting some laughter.

"Well, these stories are written to offer us examples of what perfect faith really means. Naturally, we cannot live like hermits. When we hear such stories, however, we gain courage in our struggle for perfection. I have repeated many times that we must struggle within the parameters of our own limitations and capabilities. Nothing more and nothing less."

"I assume that by faith you mean trust and not belief, right?"

"Of course. When I say I believe in God, it does not mean that I believe that there is a God. Whether I believe it or not, God does exist. It simply means that I have total trust in God's Providence. Once you have this trust in your heart, you fear nothing, absolutely nothing.

"The Fathers of the Church," Fr. Maximos continued, "taught

that there are two types of faith. The first is simply belief that there is a God as revealed in Holy Scripture. You must reach this stage in order to arrive at the second stage, which is the faith that we call *theoria*."

When I began my exploration of Eastern Orthodox spirituality, several years back, I was fascinated to notice the difference between the way science uses the word *theory* and the way the Fathers of the *Ecclesia* understood the same word. *Theoria* in Greek literally means "seeing God." It is composed of the word *Theos*, meaning "God," and the verb *oro*, meaning "I see." Theory as understood by conventional science is a method to develop knowledge of reality. For the Fathers of the *Ecclesia*, ultimate reality is God. Therefore, the aim of the spiritual practitioner is to reach the stage of *theoria*, the stage where one can see God, that is, to be connected experientially with what is ultimately and truly real.

Philip Sherrard, a contemporary Orthodox theologian and philosopher, explains that real knowledge of anything must be based on the presupposition that at the very foundation of the world there is a Divine Reality that can be apprehended only with an organ that transcends both our senses and our reason. Otherwise, whatever we consider as knowledge is nothing other than a series of transient illusions.[3]

"This second type of faith," Fr. Maximos went on, "is not some kind of abstract belief. *Theoria* is the faith that is born out of a direct experience of God."

"The problem is, how do you get there?" Maria asked.

"It's the most difficult task and the only one worth pursuing," Fr. Maximos said. "It is the result of many years of trials, adventures, temptations, and of the way we respond to the difficulties of life. God appears at the end of an exhausting patience when everything looks dark and desperate."

"The dark night of the soul," someone murmured.

"It is the state that Christ reached in the Garden of Gethsemane," Fr. Maximos continued. "It is the ultimate boundary of one's existence. It is at this point that God reveals His Presence. After that ultimate borderline point, everything changes. You move about within a different reality, and you begin to live a different life. You transcend human things, temporal things."

I had a feeling that Fr. Maximos was speaking from personal experience, although he would never admit it. He always presented his views as reflections of the teachings of the holy elders.

"God," he continued, "is now present in your own life, and worldly things are no longer relevant or desirable."

"But how is this second type of faith born in a human being?" Michael asked.

"This is exclusively in the hands of God. It is not the product of human effort. However, as a rule it happens to people who may even have only a small dose of good intentions in moving toward that direction. If a human being slams the door to God, then nothing will happen. It is like being inside a house so firmly sealed from the outside that not even a single ray of sun may go through. Outside, the sun may be shining, but you are inside the house in absolute darkness. If you drill a hole in the wall, then a ray of light will enter. If you drill two holes, then you allow two rays of the sun to enter. If you remove the roof, then the inside of the house will be filled with light. If you step outside yourself, then you will be filled with light. That is how faith works. God exists inside us. It is in Him that we move and live and have our being. From God's perspective, everything is already perfected."

"Yet why don't we believe?"

"Because we are all firmly closed off from the rays of the

sun. When our hearts become receptive to faith, then God will offer His light in accordance with our readiness to let it in. Unquestionably, God cannot cause an injustice to any human being."

"How then can we cultivate faith?" Michael asked again.

"By spiritually exploiting everything that comes our way, positive or negative. If a difficulty comes our way, or even a tragedy, we should use it for spiritual advance. We should do the same with whatever good fortune comes along. Furthermore, spiritual work takes place within us with prayer and study. At the beginning these two are extremely necessary. We cannot progress spiritually if we do not pray."

"Even if we don't know how to pray?"

"Even if you don't have a clue how to pray," Fr. Maximos replied categorically. "Even if you don't understand what you are saying, and even, I daresay, if you don't believe in the one to whom you are praying. Prayer is your dialogue with God and the study of the word of God. The study of the Gospel and the words of the saints is much more important than the accumulation of knowledge about spirituality."

"How so?" Teresa asked.

"Because holy books are written through divine inspiration, our souls commune with the Spirit that is embedded in these holy writings. They are food for the soul, for our entire being."

"And this happens regardless of whether we are aware that it happens," I noted.

"That's right. So from our vantage point, spiritual advance presupposes prayer and study," Fr. Maximos repeated. "By living within the *Ecclesia*, we undergo its therapeutic pedagogy and participate in its mysteries. We are then gradually led to the experience of the Christ who is within us. At first this work takes place without us realizing what goes on. But if we persevere, at some point a switch will turn on and we will be filled with light.

"The person who lives inside God," Fr. Maximos continued, "lives immersed in the Light. Such a person has no trace of darkness inside him. He does not experience confusion or turmoil. And even when he falls and commits a sin, through *metanoia* (repentance) his balance is restored. The fall does not kill or destroy him. God, as the great Healer, is ever present, offering His fruits of faith, gentleness, and self-control that will lead this person toward his perfection.

"Well, enough for tonight. I think the people here are waiting for us to leave. It's already eleven thirty," Fr. Maximos said.

"But we have not discussed the other fruits of the Spirit," Emily pointed out. She then hurriedly read from her notebook. "We still need to talk about goodness, kindness, patience, peace, joy, and finally love."

"Well, Emily, you need to be patient, peaceful, and joyous!" Fr. Maximos joked. "But when and where? Alas, we are leaving soon. That conversation will have to be postponed for some other time."

Eleni, the businesswoman who had decided to get a graduate degree in theology and who'd been quiet all evening, suggested that we continue our spiritual symposium the following evening at her house in Brookline. All of us accepted the invitation immediately, and Fr. Maximos could not refuse. Fortunately, he and his companions were to remain one more day in the Boston area for sightseeing and for Anna, his sister, to consult with a specialist about a health issue concerning her teenage son.

FOUR

FRUITS OF THE SPIRIT

Eleni's spacious two-story brick house, surrounded by a well-groomed garden and facing a small park, was near Boston University. I knew the area well thanks to a visiting professorship I'd had at BU in 2004.

While driving Fr. Maximos to Eleni's home, I shared with him some of my cherished experiences at BU. I parked the car for a few minutes in front of the administration building on Commonwealth Avenue to show my friend the sculpture commemorating the life of Martin Luther King, Jr., who had received his doctoral degree in 1955 from BU. Coincidentally, and I daresay ironically, the late Archbishop Makarios of Cyprus, who presided as the first president of the Republic of Cyprus between 1960 and 1977, also studied at BU for two years during the late forties. I could not hide from Fr. Maximos my admiration for King, what he stood for, and his role in the civil rights movement, and my unflattering view of Archbishop Makarios for his disastrous role in the recent history of Cyprus. Whereas Martin Luther King, a Baptist minister, followed Mahatma Gandhi's method of non-violent resistance to promote justice for the black minority in America, Archbishop Makarios in 1955 opted for a violent overthrow of British colonial rule with ghastly consequences for both the Greek and the Turkish Cypriots. The ultimate outcome of that unchristian misadventure was the invasion and partition of Cyprus by the Turkish army in 1974. I once told Fr. Maximos, tongue-in-cheek, that his own presence on Cyprus was to restore the spiritual honor of the Cypriot Church tarnished by Makarios's politics.

When Fr. Maximos asked about King's legacy, I elaborated on the role of black ministers in sustaining their communities during the dark days of slavery and segregation and the leadership roles they have played since then among their fellow African Americans.[1] I felt that I was offering Fr. Maximos a crash course on contemporary American history as I had studied and experienced it since the early sixties, when I arrived in America. I left him with a question to ponder: "What if Makarios had met Martin Luther King and become friends with him and adopted nonviolent resistance as the method to free Cyprus from British colonial rule?" Fr. Maximos smiled without offering a response.

Everybody was present when we entered Eleni's home at five in the afternoon. She offered us some refreshments as we settled into her comfortable living room. Not wasting any time, I opened the conversation by reminding Fr. Maximos of our unfinished discussion about the nine fruits of the Spirit as listed by Apostle Paul, namely love, joy, peace, patience, kindness, goodness, faithfulness, gentleness, and self-control. "So far," I said, "we have covered the last three: self-control, gentleness, and faithfulness. We were about to begin discussing the next two stages, goodness and kindness."

Fr. Maximos nodded. "According to the Gospel, goodness is an attribute of God. Remember when someone teasingly addressed Jesus as *Didaskale Agathe* [Good Master] and Jesus replied, 'Why do you call me Good?' He went on to declare that only God is good. That means that the truly good person is someone who has no trace of evil in his heart. Let us say it is someone who in the depths of his being is totally purified and clean. When the Holy Spirit is fully activated within the person, there emerges an ultimate form of *Catharsis*."

"So goodness restores a person to his primordial state as an icon of God," someone pointed out.

"Correct. Every human being has Christ within his or her innermost being. Therefore, a person who is truly good is free from explosive emotions and psychological rough edges. The Christ within becomes manifest in his or her life."

"Fr. Maxime," I interjected, "wouldn't you say that being good and free from violent emotions would depend to a great extent on the type of family you grew up in and your social background?"

"Of course it does. Favorable conditions can facilitate the activation of the energies of the Holy Spirit. But this is not an absolute rule."

I had asked the question having in mind the tendency of religious people to overemphasize free will as a factor in shaping a person's fate in contrast to the sociological way of thinking, which shows convincingly how social environment plays a central role in human development.

"There are cases, however, showing that the Holy Spirit works in very unexpected ways," Fr. Maximos pointed out. "There are examples of criminals and robbers who became truly good persons in the way Jesus meant it, that is, icons of God. For example, Abba Moses the Ethiopian was an exemplary model of the good person. Yet in his earlier life he was really bad. That robber was transformed as a result of a simple episode in his life. He climbed over a wall to enter a women's monastery with unholy intentions. Yet his heart was touched by the way the nuns treated him. That was the moment of Grace."

"This is hard to imagine," Eleni said, shaking her head. "How can you explain such a conversion, from a criminal to a saint?"

"Apparently there was a crack in his heart through which the Grace of God found a way to enter. He became a hermit and a totally transformed human being. He had redeemed himself and was completely freed from his past life. These are mysteries that we cannot explain with our reason. It is said that before his conversion he once got into such a rage that he slaughtered with his bare hands the entire flock of sheep of a poor shepherd. That is the kind of reputation he had. After what happened to him in that monastery, he underwent deep *metanoia* and ended up becoming one of the celebrated saints of the Church."

"This is very difficult for people to understand or even accept," Eleni said again. "It violates their sense of justice."

"I appreciate that difficulty. But I have experienced such cases myself, time and again. I have witnessed how people can be drastically transformed as they undergo the pedagogy of the *Ecclesia*. It is truly an amazing miracle to see a person with so much accumulated evil in his heart being gradually transmuted from charcoal into gold. The Grace of the Holy Spirit penetrates such a person, extracts the stench from his heart, and cleanses him."

Fr. Maximos went on to say that *metanoia* has a beginning but no end. It is a process of becoming good within God's eternity and divine mercy. That is, *metanoia* is not a static state but a dynamic turning point on one's eternal march toward union with God. There is no end point in our continuous learning and growth in love and wisdom.

Fr. Maximos then narrated a personal learning experience he had while serving as the *protos* (governor) of Mt. Athos in 1992. He was young at the time and zealous to be successful as governor. There was a difficult issue that he had to resolve. Somehow, he told us, he was a bit harsh on some people. "I felt I was right, but I was somewhat austere. Then an elder approached me and said, 'Father, please sweeten your words.' This sentence stuck in my mind. It is something that they often say on Mt. Athos: 'Sweeten your words a bit, Father.' This incident had a lasting effect on the way I approach people. If you are to criticize somebody, don't marinate your bitter words with vinegar, making them even more bitter. Plunge them instead into honey."

"But who can ever do that?" Michael mused.

"Only the person who has cleansed his heart from egotism, the truly good person," Fr. Maximos replied. "But in order to attain goodness, you must go through the furnace of genuine *metanoia*, which means that you must learn humility, self-mastery, and faith in God. *Metanoia*, you see, is a very painful process. But it is this pain that will separate the dirty part of yourself from the pure and clean ones. That's when a person becomes truly charismatic in soul and body. His entire being becomes beautiful, irrespective of how he appears externally. He is at ease and comfortable with himself and brings comfort to others. He is good, just as God is good. The charisma of goodness emerges as one of the fruits of the Holy Spirit."

Fr. Maximos went on to comment on the next fruit of the Holy Spirit, which according to St. Paul is kindness. "In the Greek original, Paul refers to kindness as *chrestotis*, with the Greek *e* in the *chre* and not with an *i* as it is in *Christotis*, meaning 'being anointed by Christ,' or 'becoming Christified.' *Chrestotis* with an *e* means something different. It means usefulness. It seems that what the apostle meant is that the person becomes useful."

"Excuse me for interrupting you, Fr. Maxime," I interjected, "but when I first heard you talk about *chrestotis*, I went to the New Testament, first in the Greek original, where it is spelled *chrestotis*, as you pointed out with an e, and then I looked into the

King James Version, which translates it as 'gentleness,' and then to the Revised Standard Version, which translates it as 'kindness.' Which is correct?"

"They are all correct. I believe that a gentle and kind person is also a useful or helpful person. I'll explain shortly. But thank you for clarifying these differences in translation. I'll start with the assumption that the actual interpretation of the word chrestotis implies being useful in the sense of being helpful. So chrestotis means several things. It is important to penetrate the meaning of these words so that we can know what St. Paul probably had in mind when he used that term.

"So to repeat, a chrestos person is someone who can be accommodating, easily pliable in three ways: in the hands of God, in his relationships with other people, and in himself."

I noticed confused looks on everybody's faces. How does one become useful or pliable in the hands of God? Fr. Maximos explained. "The God-centered person does not put any resistances, doubts, or fears into his relationship with God. He surrenders to God and has no anxieties as to what will happen the next day.

"I remember when I was a child," Fr. Maximos went on. "I did not want to pray to God and say, 'Thy will be done.' I would say to myself, 'What if God wants something of me that I don't want myself? Isn't it better to ask God to do what I want Him to do?' That's how I thought as a boy. I did not know at the time that God never violates the will of a human being and that He never wishes anything which is not good for us.

"So the useful or pliable person is not afraid of God. He surrenders to God in absolute trust. At the same time such a person is not fearful of his fellow human beings. He is not afraid of himself. He does not have a bad relationship with himself.

Spiritual work helps us to familiarize ourselves with ourselves. It helps us to establish a good working relationship with ourselves. Such work cancels out phobias and resistances and at the same time cuts down the distance between us and other human beings. When spiritual work is done properly, it offers human beings the gifts mentioned by Paul, which render them truly free."

"But isn't fear part of the human condition, like the fear of death?" Teresa asked.

"No. Fear of death, or any fear for that matter, does not belong to an authentic human existence."

In light of all the tragedies and evil in the world, I found Fr. Maximos's statement remarkable.

"In reality," he explained, "all fear boils down to the absence of love and trust in God. We do not surrender to God because we are afraid. I am certain that many of us would be reluctant to say, 'Okay, God, tell me what You want me to do and I will do it.' Few of us would be ready, for example, if God wished for us to go and live in the depth of a jungle full of wild animals. I am not sure I could do such a thing myself. But the truly liberated human beings are not afraid. They move about in total freedom, which is the result of being 'useful' or chrestoi."

"Surely such people are rare, to be useful to others and kind to themselves," Emily pointed out.

"Unfortunately, yes. Our biggest problem is ourselves. I remember how a wise eldress once advised a nun who was difficult to get along with. That nun created problems in the monastery and, as a result, felt guilty. One day, she went to her eldress and told her of her intention to leave the monastery so that she would no longer be a source of tension and division. The eldress advised her to stay put and work on herself. 'Besides,' she said, 'wherever you go you will carry yourself with you.'"

"So what's the moral of the story?" Emily asked.

"The moral," Fr. Maximos replied, "is that the source of all your problems is really yourself. That should be the starting point of your spiritual work. Get to know who you are. Get to know yourself. Get to know your weaknesses, your mistakes, your shortcomings. Do not justify your actions, but be a fair judge with yourself, without panic or angst or any pathological guilt feelings. Do not get disheartened because you discover evil inside you. Just examine yourself the way you are. That way, you can work on those aspects of yourself that need fixing. As you consciously work on yourself, as you work on your weaknesses, plunge into prayer and study. The destructive passions will then begin to recede, and gradually you will become more at ease and more familiar with yourself."

Fr. Maximos was silent for a while to give us time to ponder what he had been saying. He then continued with a rhetorical question. "Do you realize that our best friend is ourselves? We don't have a closer and more intimate friend than ourselves. We are with ourselves all the time. This may seem to you paradoxical, but many people consider staying all by themselves a veritable hell. They cannot be by themselves, not even for a moment. So the first person you must befriend is yourself. You will then be able to see yourself with great love and compassion.

"I remember how impressed I was when I first met Elder Paisios. In his case, there was a total harmony between mind, body, and spirit. There was common purpose and synergy among the three working together to reach God. There was no rebellion of one against another, of the body against the spirit. The body did not hate the soul, and the soul did not hate the body. There was a perfect symphony, a spiritual union of all three. I also recall the words of a saint, that there are spiritual rewards in spending time by yourself."

"What are they?" Eleni pressed on as I felt Fr. Maximos hesitating to reply.

"Over and beyond the fact that you enjoy God's presence in your heart, you also enjoy yourself. You come to realize what a beautiful human being you are. And you have to see yourself in that state before you can see others in the same way. Without this awareness of yourself as an absolutely beautiful being, when you see the other person in all his or her grandeur, you will experience jealousy.

"Someone might say, 'You know, I have seen a very nice, good person, a beautiful person, a beautiful woman.' He may be sincere in saying that without any trace of cunning in his heart. Yet that very same person may experience at the same time a hidden trace of envy.'"

"This is strange," Michael said. "How can you have no trace of cunning and still be envious?"

"A person who is envious is simply someone who has not realized that he also has beautiful characteristics and qualities that others may not have. He assumes that he has nothing and that all the good and lofty traits are found in others.

"When we relate to ourselves in a healthy way, then we may notice and appreciate all the good gifts that we have been endowed with without feeling inadequate, which expresses itself as narcissism. When we perceive ourselves that way, always with humility, then while contemplating our human condition, our mind becomes focused on God, our Creator. We will then see ourselves functioning with the same perfect harmony as the music produced by a great orchestra. Why is it so? you may ask. It is so because God, who has made us in His Image, is harmonious. He is neither superfluous nor deficient. Everything is balanced within God. We are also, therefore, perfect in the depths of our being. When we look inside us and discover no acrimonies or upsetting emotions, then we realize the beauty of God's Creation. Then we establish within us a good relationship with ourselves. We become useful vessels of God's Grace, and we are no longer enemies to ourselves. We then know who we are and become friends with ourselves.

"Many centuries ago Abba Isaac said, 'Find peace within you and there will be peace in Heaven and on Earth.' Similarly, St. Seraphim of Sarov a century ago said, 'Acquire peace within you and a thousand people will become peaceful.' When you reach a state of harmony within yourself and become friends with yourself, then, simultaneously, your environment, Heaven and Earth, will become your friends. For such a person there are no enemies, no 'impure' people. Everything is pure to those who are pure."

"Some may misunderstand such a person and call her naïve," I remarked.

"They just don't understand what is actually going on within such a person," Fr. Maximos replied. "The well-balanced individual can see beyond the externalities of fellow human beings, even if they are, say, thieves or scoundrels. Human beings are by nature good because that is how they were made by God. That is why such persons can love everybody, regardless of who they are or what they do. I am always impressed by the farsightedness and perspicacity of the great elders that I have known. They can see in a human being the reality beyond the externalities, and they, therefore, are capable of loving everybody without exception."

"Do you mean by perspicacity a form of prophecy?" Eleni asked.

"No. Prophecy is a more developed and important gift.

Perspicacity is one of the first and simple gifts of the Holy Spirit, which allows the person to see through you and read your soul, as it were." I understood Fr. Maximos to mean that such a person is gifted with heightened intuitive abilities to understand others.

As an example of what he meant, Fr. Maximos went on to tell us of an experience he had on Mt. Athos when he first encountered the legendary Elder Ephraim of Katounakia, who had a reputation for possessing not only perspicacity but also many other, more "advanced" gifts of the Spirit.[2]

"As I recall, it was in 1976, during my second visit to Mt. Athos, when I decided to visit Papa Ephraim at Katounakia, that rough and inaccessible region of the Holy Mountain. I was eighteen and a half years old, and I went along with classmates of mine who had been there before. I was very reluctant to join them because my first visit to Mt. Athos wasn't pleasant. But that's another story. I was really afraid of what I would encounter. And those blessed friends of mine insisted on going to that remote part of Athos, which hovered over those terrifying precipices. I pleaded with them to at least stay at a regular monastery. But they were fixed on going to Katounakia, where the hermits lived. On the way, they shared some truly wild stories. A certain university professor went to see Elder Ephraim, and the moment the elder set eyes on him he began to tell him his sins. They also gave the example of a visitor whom the elder supposedly kicked out of the room. Stories like that continued until I became petrified with fear. I implored them, 'Isn't there a more normal human being to go visit?' I felt as if my soul was going to come out of my body! Walking on those rocky mountains wasn't easy. I had heard of that other terrible place on Mt. Athos, the Karoulia, where people had to go down with chains because the caves of the hermits were not accessible in any other way.

"So I went to Katounakia fearful and trembling. My great anxiety was that Elder Ephraim was going to spill out all my sins in front of my classmates. That would have demolished me. On top of everything else, my friends told me that Elder Ephraim was very tall, like a giant, and that his face shone like the sun. In my imagination I had already built him up into an extraterrestrial being who would know everything about me and humiliate me in public. In reality, Papa Ephraim proved to be a very charismatic elder. Because of my fears, I remained at the end of the line to get his blessing. He was the way they had described him: tall, with a shining face, filled with the grace of the Holy Spirit.

"The first in my company introduced himself. 'Father,' he said and kissed his hand, 'I am Nikos.' The elder simply said, 'Welcome, Niko. Please sit down.' Another one introduced himself: 'My name is Aristoteles.' 'Welcome, Aristotele. Please sit down.' The third said, 'I am Kostas,' and kissed his hand. 'Welcome, Kosta. Please sit down.' God almighty, I said to myself. He is not saying anything to anybody. I was worried he was waiting to unleash all his wrath on me. Fortunately, the one who followed Kostas offered the elder a box of *kourambiedes* [popular sugar-coated pastries]. We wanted to bribe him so that he would not be so rough with us. The elder gave him a severe, dismissive look, and I saw my friend's hands trembling. Elder Ephraim asked, 'What are these?' My friend mumbled '*Kourambiedes*.' '*Kourambiedes*!' the elder repeated and shook his head disapprovingly. And then he said severely, 'Do you know what place this is?' My friend replied with a barely audible voice, 'Yes, Father. Katounakia.' 'We don't eat *kourambiedes* at Katounakia. Throw them out the window immediately.' My friend froze. We did not expect such a reaction. So with trembling hands he rushed to throw them out the window. I thought, Now he will throw us all out the window. I was the last one who went in. I made a bow in front of the elder and kissed his hand. As I did that he grabbed my hand and declared triumphantly, 'Ahaaa! Finally we caught the thief!' "

Once our laughter subsided, Fr. Maximos continued his narration. "I could barely stand on my feet. I thought I was going to faint from fear. I was perspiring profusely even though it was the heart of winter. He looked at me with a penetrating look, turned his head, and said 'Hmm . . .' while looking at the others. 'This one,' he told them, 'is from our lineage.' 'Oh,' I replied and sighed with relief. 'Father, are you by any chance from Cyprus?' I asked. I was so naïve. The elder raised his hand and replied, 'You are asleep! You are asleep!' "

Fr. Maximos did not elaborate other than to say that from that day on Elder Ephraim became one of his dearest elders and offered him spiritual instruction during his years on Mt. Athos. He also mentioned that, during that first meeting, Elder Ephraim told him details about his life that he could not have known through ordinary means. This confirmed for Fr. Maximos Elder Ephraim's reputation, that he was richly endowed with gifts of the Spirit.

"Elders like him, even though austere at times, are capable of loving everybody unconditionally precisely because they can see the other person in his natural state, beyond the external characteristics of personality," Fr. Maximos explained. "That's who the late Elder Ephraim really was, not the fearsome person I imagined him to be before I met him. Elders like Papa Ephraim are capable of loving even the worst among us because they know that human passions are acquired and not natural to the individual soul. What they see in every person, regardless of their sinfulness, is the presence of the Christ. Therefore, they love everybody the same way that God loves everybody."

"You had mentioned before that holy elders love even demons," I noted.

"Exactly. They love them just as God does. In their very nature, demons are good. Only their intentions are evil. After all, they are fallen angels. They were created to be good."

"This is very difficult for people to fathom," I said, noticing that hardly anyone in the room could relate to what Fr. Maximos was saying.

"I understand that, but God does not discriminate in his love and, therefore, loves everybody and everything unconditionally," Fr. Maximos stressed. I understood that the principle he wanted to convey was that God's love is embedded in all of Creation, unconditionally. He had said to me before that many people get scandalized when they hear that. But God, for Fr. Maximos, cannot not love every being regardless of their current fallen state.

"Once again," Fr. Maximos continued, "the person who has a good relationship with himself or herself also develops a good relationship with others and with his or her surroundings. When a person learns to have a good relationship with others, he also has a good relationship with God. That state of being in the world leads a person to real freedom and liberation without a trace of anything that diminishes him as a personality, be it fear, cunning, self-centeredness, or malice. This is the person who is *chrestos*, or useful, kind, and gentle. He or she does not create difficulties for others and does not feel oppressed by others."

"In short, she is easy to get along with. This is what you mean by useful, or *chrestos*," I noted.

Fr. Maximos agreed. "The opposite of the *chrestos* person is the vexatious and sour person. He is like a thorn, like vinegar. Wherever he finds himself, he generates strife and problems. If he happens to be an employer, he is like a tyrant. If he is an employee, he can't get along with others, causing havoc for everybody."

"We find such people everywhere," I mentioned. "Including in the Church."

"Particularly in the Church," Fr. Maximos added with a laugh. Then he recalled a classmate of his at the university who was constantly fighting with his teachers. "He was wild. One time he was talking about a professor with such hatred, saying that he was going to drink his blood, that he was going to take his eyes out and the like."

"And he was a theology student?"

"Yes, he was trained to become a priest. I tried to advise him. 'My dear Kosta,' I said, 'why don't you imagine your professor as your spiritual elder? Obey him as a form of a spiritual exercise.' His response was 'What did you say? I will cut his head off first!' "

Fr. Maximos never tired of repeating the message that whatever difficulties we encounter in life we must use as opportunities for spiritual growth. "Do you have a difficult supervisor?" he asked a group of teachers once. "Incorporate it within the context of your *askesis*, your regular spiritual practices. It is very important not to see the other as an evil person. Don't see him or her as the enemy and you as the good and innocent victim. Do not see him as Nero and you as a martyr. Try to see the other as yourself and accept him in that spirit. Turn your household, your environment, your job, into arenas for spiritual exercises.

"To become *chrestos*, you must realize that it is an ongoing spiritual exercise in your daily life. Do not seek special circumstances and favorable conditions. Start from wherever you are, from your office, from your work, from anywhere. Learn patience. Learn to incorporate your difficulties within the context of your daily spiritual practice. Think of your marriage, for example, as a challenge in order to transcend yourself. That's the only attitude that you must have if you want your marriage to last and bear spiritual fruit.

"It's the same with monasticism when you are asked to transcend yourself. If within marriage or monasticism you insist on doing what you want, the result will be catastrophic. If you don't learn to carry your cross during your daily life, then you are losing the thousand opportunities that God creates for you at every moment so that you can become perfected as a human being.

"The Gerontikon [a series of books about the lives of great elders] is full of examples of simple practices that have led many to become giants of virtue. Abba Agathon prayed to God, 'Please, God, help me do Your Will today so that I can say that at least for one day I did what You asked of me to do.' And what do you think he did? Nothing different than what he usually did. He didn't say, 'Let me sit down and pray from morning till night.' No. He asked, 'What kind of work do I have today?' He then told himself, 'I have to go to the flour mill to grind my wheat.' He loaded his sack of wheat on his shoulders and went to the mill. Incidentally, when I first went to Mt. Athos, they still had those types of mills. There were neither machines nor animals to turn the millstone. It had to be done by hand, by the monks. It required a lot of hard, physical labor to grind the wheat. The moment Abba Agathon was ready to spread his wheat, another arrived and pleaded with him to let him go first because he was in a hurry. Abba Agathon replied, 'Gladly.' The other person said, 'Well, since you are here, can you give me a hand to move the stone?' 'Fine.' They finished the grinding and the other person got his flour and left. Then as Abba Agathon was about to unload his wheat, another person came, and it happened all over again. Then two more came along asking him for the same thing. Night came, and Abba Agathon was still unable to grind his wheat. He put it on his back and returned to his hermitage. This was considered by the monastic tradition as an example of perfect spiritual work. Abba Agathon did not complain. He did not get upset. He did not say, 'Okay, fellows, you are from this area. I came from afar, from the desert. Let me grind my wheat.' Such examples demonstrate that these hermits were blessed not because of prolonged states of fasting and prayer but because of simple acts of kindness that could be done by any one of us."

"This is comforting," Eleni said. "It means there is hope even for us living in the world."

"This is the lesson from these types of stories," Fr. Maximos stressed.

I mentioned that, in light of what Fr. Maximos said, it was interesting that many people who have had near-death experiences claim that this is exactly what they learned. What they experienced during the "life review" stage of the near-death experience was that little acts of kindness truly count more on the spiritual scale of growth than great worldly achievements and the acquisition of trophies.[3] Fr. Maximos then pointed out that great success in life can often be a trap that takes us away from the spiritual path because, if we are not careful, it will propel us toward narcissism.

"Stories from the lives of hermits like Abba Agathon," Fr. Maximos went on, "are didactic for those of us who live in the world. Hermits like him know how to transmute everyday encounters and challenges into steps that lead to God. For them a spiritual life does not simply mean fasting, praying, reading sacred books, or going to church. Such elders are graced with the fruits of *chrestotis*. They are useful vessels in the hands of God, useful to themselves, and useful and full of sweetness and kindness in their relationships with other human beings."

There was further discussion about the gift of *chrestotis* before we had a short break. When we reassembled, I suggested that we move on to the next spiritual gift. "Coming from the bottom up, Fr. Maxime," I said, "you have spoken so far of self-control, gentleness, faithfulness, goodness, and kindness or *chrestotis*. We're left with patience, peace, joy, and love."

"Fine. Let's continue with patience." Fr. Maximos nodded, grinning. "God is infinitely patient. He does not do things in a hurried and rushed way."

"For example?" Teresa asked.

"Okay. Here is a simple example. God could have created the world in a split second. Yet it took Him six days, cosmic days, that is. He requires that we also be patient. It takes nine months for us to grow as human beings in our mothers' wombs. And then we need time to become fully functioning adults. There is need for a great deal of patience while a person becomes more mature."

"So everything exists within an evolutionary process of patient change," I pointed out.

"More or less. Of course, change can also happen suddenly, but that's another story."

"If we could come out of our mothers' wombs as fully functioning creatures, we wouldn't be able to become fully human," I said. "We need time to grow, to learn a language and become socialized beings. So we can say that patience and endurance are great virtues because they are in harmony with the way that God and the universe work."

"Well spoken. We mentioned earlier that the fruits of the Spirit are the signs that characterize a healthy person. The human individual as a fallen creature is sick, split up, and distorted as a result of his passions and sins. Then enters God, like a good physician, and restores him to health. The signs of his restoration are the fruits of the Spirit as listed by St. Paul."

"It's surprising to me how patience is a more advanced gift than faith," Emily remarked.

"Yes, it is. More precisely, faith gives birth to patience."

"How?"

"Because the person who has faith in God cannot get panicky. God never worries about missing the train, missing an opportunity. We, as human beings, are always obsessed about running after opportunities in case we miss something that we desire or miss an event that's unfolding."

"Just watch the stock market to get an idea of what Fr. Maximos is saying," I suggested.

"God moves within a state of absolute security. He does not have any phobias, does not panic, is not under pressure—if we can use such anthropomorphic metaphors to describe God, that is."

"So the person who has the Holy Spirit within her acts and moves like God," Eleni commented.

"The person who has the Holy Spirit experiences security in his or her heart. Such a person fears nothing, because in reality there is nothing to fear."

"Stress and anguish provide the bread and butter for psychotherapists," Emily pointed out.

"What I said does not apply to the types of psychiatric phenomena related to anguish. I am referring to ordinary people who are otherwise psychologically healthy but suffer stress and anguish from the circumstances in their lives."

"So the patient and forbearing person is the one who, in spite of circumstances, lives without anguish," I pointed out.

"Right. Such persons are freed from any fear. The world may be falling all around them, but they fear nothing because their being is anchored in God and that is how they measure their lives. They are not afraid of failure. Success and failure are part of life. When such persons fail, they accept their failure. When they succeed again, they accept their success."

"They face both success and failure with detachment," I added.

"Yes, of course with detachment. Their lives are not grounded on anything ephemeral."

"What if they are atheists?" I asked.

"There are no atheists, as we normally understand this term."

"What?" I said.

"The Gospel calls the persons who do not believe in God 'foolish.' At the same time, there are people who believe in the existence of God and yet are in reality atheists."

"It sounds like an oxymoron. How can one believe in God and be an atheist at the same time?" Michael interjected.

"Fr. Maximos smiled and went on. "A real atheist is a person who has no real relationship with the Spirit of God. The Holy Spirit is not active in his or her heart. Such a person may appear externally as deeply pious, going to church every Sunday, doing all the things that one is expected to do as a Christian, but his or her heart is completely shut off from the energies of the Holy Spirit."

"No trace of the presence of the fruits of the Spirit," I added.

"This is the real atheist. God is absent from his or her life."

Fr. Maximos then elaborated on the fruit of patience and forbearance.

"The saints are fearless because they have a direct connection with God's Spirit. Consequently, they can endure everything with peace in their hearts and without a trace of anxiety."

"I suppose that is why we hear in church that God is 'ever present, and fills all things,'" Maria commented.

"Right. Only the Spirit of God can fill up a human being. You know, God has this attribute: whether His Presence in our existence is in small or large quantities, we feel fulfilled and completed."

"God's Presence does not leave any gaps for the generation of angst and unfulfillment, which are so characteristic of many contemporary intellectuals and philosophers," I said.

"Yes. A person feels completely rested in God's Presence. But it is important," Fr. Maximos continued, "that he does not become spiritually lazy. He continues to progress with even greater zeal and intensity within the Grace of God. Grace itself pushes the person to taste this love that emanates from the depths of our human existence."

"Angst is the consequence of the fact that people want to do things on their own and in a hurry, relying solely on their own devices and reason," I said. "This creates pressures and doubt, concerns that they may not succeed, that they may not do things on time."

"This is our ordinary human predicament," Fr. Maximos responded. "All such states of mind and feelings disappear once God's Presence is activated in our life. A person finds inner peace without becoming indifferent to others. He is compassionate and suffers with those who suffer but confronts everything the way God confronts the problems of this world."

"All that sounds marvelous," Teresa interjected. "But the question is how do we reach this state of forbearance?"

"Forbearance is a child of all the other fruits of the Spirit that we have talked about. We are human and we are in a hurry. We lack patience. How can we get transformed from being small-minded and fainthearted to being patient and forbearing? As you can imagine, it is not easy. It cannot be accomplished from one day to the next. And it cannot be done by declaring that as of today we will become patient, forbearing, and bighearted."

"So how do we go about it?" Eleni inquired.

"You start with faith in God as the ultimate reality that governs the world and with the conviction that nothing can happen without God allowing it to happen. Something that happens may be bad for you, disastrous or whatever. Do not be afraid. God will never abandon you. He promised that much to us. That is the reason we must never accept whatever threats are hurled at us."

Fr. Maximos then mentioned the way in which Jesus responded to Pontius Pilate when Pilate told Jesus that he had power to free him or have him crucified. Jesus' response was that the Roman proconsul had no more and no less power over Him than God allowed him to have.

Fr. Maximos never ceased repeating that our greatest enemy is our ego, what psychologists would call "narcissism," and that we can work on that ego as we go about our daily affairs. He then mentioned Abba Dorotheos, an early Father of the *Ecclesia* who instructed his monks on how to confront their desires so that they might undermine their egotism. "He taught them simple exercises. If for example they were hungry and curious to find out what the cook had made for the day, the abba's advice was to resist that urge. Or if somebody came along and asked them for a favor, even if they had no interest in going out of their way to do the favor, they were advised to do it anyway. Fr. Maximos then went on to say that if you read the patristic writings, you will see how a person can sanctify every event of daily life, no matter how trivial and insignificant it may appear.

"You see," Fr. Maximos continued, "by unconditionally accepting our fellow human beings with all their flaws, our hearts gradually begin to open up. We become easygoing people. People of God have this characteristic. They accept and comfort others. Patience, as a fruit of the Holy Spirit, is a direct attribute of God Himself, who leads us to the discovery of our real identity, that is, that we are icons of God. But in order to comfort others, we have comforted God within our hearts first. We have found comfort in God, and as a consequence other human beings are comforted by our presence. Abba Isaac the Syrian said that faintheartedness is the mother of Hell."

"How so?" Maria asked.

"Fainthearted persons constantly have something to worry about, to be fearful of, to become anxious about. They torture themselves and others. On the other hand, people in whose hearts the Holy Spirit is activated follow the middle way. They have harmony and balance within themselves. When we reach this state, we confront even our own shortcomings with magnanimity and generosity." Fr. Maximos then spoke of the "complex of perfectionism" as a form of spiritual malady and underscored the wisdom of accepting ourselves with all our limitations.

With those last remarks we had a break for dinner, generously prepared by our hostess. Fr. Maximos, however, did not have a break. As I have witnessed many times before, he was immediately surrounded by several of the guests asking him further questions. Some of them sought advice on personal problems.

Our hostess had to free Fr. Maximos by asking him to offer a blessing for the food. When that was done, we followed his lead to fill our plates with an assortment of delicious vegan dishes, prepared according to the dietary rules of the Great Lent, no meat or meat products.

FIVE

REAL PEACE

It was past eight when we finished dinner. I was eager to resume our discussion because I wasn't certain whether we would be able to go over the entire Pauline list of spiritual fruits before Fr. Maximos's departure the next day. Playing the role of unofficial coordinator, I asked the guests to take their teacups and move back into the living room so that we could continue the conversation.

"The next fruit of the Spirit to discuss," I said to Fr. Maximos as I looked at my notebook, "is peace, a very relevant topic given what is going on in the world!"

Fr. Maximos nodded. "Everybody talks about peace nowadays, everybody wants it, but where is this peace? At Jesus' birth the angels promised 'Peace on Earth,' yet peace is yet to come. Were they lying to us?

"Jesus Himself," Fr. Maximos continued, "made those cryptic remarks that have often confused us. I'm referring to his words 'I did not come into the world to bring peace but the sword.'"

"He declared correctly," I noted.

"It is quite clear, therefore, that when the Gospel speaks of peace, it should not be understood as the absence of war," Fr. Maximos concluded. "What is implied here is inner peace."

"I hope that's not suggesting that we should not strive for world peace," Emily interjected.

"Of course we must strive for world peace. This is a given," Fr. Maximos clarified. "But before we can become real peace-makers, we must bring peace into our hearts. This is the meaning of peace according to the Gospel."

"Christ did bless the peacemakers," Emily said.

"True. But we need to ask what essentially is the nature of peace that Christ referred to, that the angels chanted, and that the evangelists wrote about." Fr. Maximos sipped from his tea-cup. "Paul himself states clearly that Christ is our peace."

"I suppose he made that statement based on his firsthand experience on the road to Damascus, a direct contact with Christ or the attainment of Christ consciousness," I suggested.

"Yes, if you wish to put it in those terms. The opposite state of being is confusion, anxiety, fear, conflict. In such a state of mind, a person torments both himself and others. When Christ penetrates the heart, then we attain real peace within us."

"Can you be more specific, Fr. Maxime?" Maria asked. "What exactly do you consider the key attributes of a peaceful human being?"

"A peaceful human being is someone for whom the parts of his inner world function in total and beautiful harmony. Every-thing works with marvelous precision in the same way that different instruments are harmonized in an orchestra to produce a magnificent symphony."

"But what does it mean in practice?"

"As I have repeated many times, a human being is created as a harmonious whole because he is an icon of God. As the scriptures tell us, peace is the indwelling Spirit of God. Peace is an attribute of God, and a human being, made in the image and likeness of God, has the natural capacity to function in the same way. It is the Fall that has caused the disharmony which has been tormenting the human race. The challenge that confronts human beings is to reassemble their shattered divine image so that they can function harmoniously and peacefully once again."

"Harmony between body, mind, and spirit leads to inner peace," I interjected.

"Yes. This is the peace that human beings truly need, whether they realize it or not."

"But how can we get to that kind of peace?" Eleni lamented. "That's the troubling question."

"It takes an ongoing, gradual effort for us to reassemble ourselves in that state of harmony. I have said many times that this can only be achieved if we place at the foundation of this work our relationship with God. Otherwise, our labor most probably will be in vain."

"Isn't it possible for nonbelievers to attain this harmony within themselves through other means, such as humanistic psychotherapy?" Emily asked.

"If we take the teachings of the holy elders as our guide, the answer is no. When God is absent and everything is built on strictly human foundations, then, according to the elders, we are entering into delusion. According to them, the basis of *plani*, or delusion, is self-sufficiency, which breeds pride and egotism."

"Is it delusional to have self-confidence?" Emily asked again.

"A healthy self-confidence is good. I am talking about the exclusive focus on oneself without any acknowledgment of our ultimate foundation in and dependence on God. It is like trying to attain *Theosis*, or union with God, without God."

Fr. Maximos went on to emphasize that the lack of inner

peace emanates from our egocentric passions and unbridled desires. Furthermore, he pointed out that all external wars, violence, and social and interpersonal conflicts spring from our inner states of disharmony. For him, therefore, achieving freedom and justice must begin with an arduous effort to attain inner peace. Revolutionaries who fight for justice do not understand that, no matter how noble their cause may be, if they don't start by changing themselves, they will create worse conditions than what prevailed before.

"The Spirit of God always unites people, whereas the opposite of God divides and separates them," Fr. Maximos added. "Conflict and disunity between people, separation, quarrels, wars, battles, and the like are not attributes of God's Spirit. On the contrary, the Spirit of God assists a human being to be united with everybody."

"Most people believe that it is external circumstances that do not allow people to be at peace with one another," I pointed out. "For example, in Cyprus the absence of real peace between the Greeks and the Turks is blamed on external forces. Elder Paisios used to say to Cypriots who visited him that if they wished to find peace with the Turks, they should start with themselves and not look for external enemies and other excuses."

"Well, he was right, as you well know. This is the standard position of all the Fathers of the *Ecclesia*. The person who is united with God, who has peace within himself, is united with all of humanity, even those who dislike him. After all, there are people, rightly or wrongly, who do not like us for whatever reason. Likewise, there are people whom we may dislike ourselves, which of course damages us spiritually."

"But is it really possible to be united in peace with such people?" Michael, the seminarian, asked.

"Absolutely!"

"How?"

"We can be united with all of humanity through prayer. The Christian hermits show us that this is possible. They are physically separated from everybody, and yet through Grace they are united with the world as a result of ceaseless prayer."

"You mean we should imitate the hermits?" Eleni wondered.

"Yes, in terms of praying for others, particularly those whom we have difficulties with. Let's say someone does not like us for this or that reason. Say we have done something to that person so that he or she, justifiably, does not wish to have anything to do with us. Or perhaps we are completely innocent. What do we do under these conditions? Consider it a given that the strongest bridge between us and the other person is prayer. Prayer is like those hooks that fishermen throw with ropes to pull boats to the dock. Even if the other person may profoundly hate us rather than simply dislike us, through our prayer his hatred may melt away."

"Wouldn't it be better if we just left that problem to God and went about our business, avoiding contact with such a person?" Maria asked.

"That is not what Christ tells us to do," Fr. Maximos replied. "It is possible, of course, that the problem may be exclusively with the other person and you may be completely innocent. Let us say that the other person, for some strange reason, has an issue with the sheer fact that you exist. Your mere presence irritates him. Can you then ignore him and feel comfortable with such a situation?"

"Well, what can you do?"

"Christ in the Gospel tells us what to do. When you are about to make an offering at the altar and you remember that a brother has something against you, you must first go and talk to him and only then return with your offering. If another person has something against you, even if you are completely innocent, you must cease your offering. You must first talk it over with the other person while keeping in mind that it is also your problem, your own wound. The other person is your brother, and by merely thinking of you he gets into turmoil. You cannot ignore it."

"What can one do under such a condition besides pray?" Teresa asked.

"You must do everything possible to lift the burden off the chest of the other person, irrespective of whether you are totally innocent or not. It is understood, of course, that you need a lot of courage to do that. It is not easy."

"Would you say that the prudent way should be to remain silent and avoid that person as much as possible?" Teresa asked.

"No. As I mentioned before, this is not the spiritual way of confronting such a problem. It is not the way of the Gospel. The way of the Gospel asks us to consider our brother's or sister's problem with us as our own challenge. It therefore asks us to become engaged in order to resolve the problem.

"It is important to keep in mind," Fr. Maximos continued, "that the perfect way of approaching the other person in such situations is with prayer. It may require many years of systematic prayer for God to inform the other person's heart that we truly love him and have nothing against him. We must take upon ourselves this responsibility and say, 'I am to be blamed for this situation also.' The very fact that I exist makes me responsible. I am a culprit in the other person's emotional turmoil. Had I not existed, this problem would not have existed. Therefore, I am responsible."

"This is very harsh and hard to digest, Fr. Maxime," Maria complained.

"But that's the way of the Gospel, the way of the saints. You begin to pray with tears and pain for the good of the other. You pray in such a way that gradually Grace may visit and soften the heart of the other person by bringing clarity and understanding to his mind."

"Do you think this will help the other to understand his or her mistake?" Maria wondered.

"No. We should not ask God to help the other person understand his error. That would be egotistical. We must pray to God to help our brother understand that he should not harbor in his heart such feelings, which are harmful to him. It is irrelevant to us whether he loves us or not. It is not for our sake that we pray. We pray because we love our brother, period. We do not wish to see him suffer spiritually and psychologically by feeling that our very existence is a problem for him."

There was silence for a few seconds as everybody pondered this extraordinary task. "Do you realize," Fr. Maximos continued, "that we can implement this form of action even for the departed? We have examples of holy elders, both ancient and contemporary, who, after sorrowfully praying for years for the souls of departed people who were separated from God, guided those souls to the Kingdom of God."

Nobody raised the question of how that could be verified, but given the spiritual culture of Eastern Orthodoxy, the answer could only have been that such states can be authenticated by the saints themselves, who are graced by the Holy Spirit.

"These saints," Fr. Maximos went on, "took upon themselves the burden of Hell of those departed and imperfect souls, and by doing so they have become true imitators of Christ. Because of their prayers, the Holy Spirit was activated, approaching the souls of these people and guiding them away from their hell.

"So it is important to realize that if our brothers do not have peace with us, we cannot be relaxed with our conscience by saying, 'Well, I have done whatever I could. He does not wish to see me, or talk to me, or love me. What can I do? I am indifferent. Let him do whatever he wishes.'

"No. You should do everything you can to approach that person because there is one thing you did not do. You did not pray with tears for the sake of your brother or sister, for the soul of that person who suffers even thinking of you, rightly or wrongly. The person who has God inside him cannot accept the other person suffering spiritually and remain indifferent."

It was clear to me that Fr. Maximos was speaking from experience. Ever since he had arrived in Cyprus, several members of the higher clergy had done their best to force him to return to Mt. Athos. But by putting his teachings into practice, Fr. Maximos led several of his former enemies to come to at least respect him and tolerate him, if not to accept his presence on the island.

"Once a year we celebrate the life of St. Parthenios, a great saint, endowed generously with many gifts of the Spirit. One of the incidences in his life was his attempt to free a young woman of demonic possession. The demon asked him, 'If you chase me out of her, where do you expect me to go? Allow me to at least enter somewhere else, like into a herd of swine as Jesus allowed.' Then the saint replied, 'Come inside me.'" Fr. Maximos abruptly interrupted his narration: "Incidentally, no one should do that, okay? Otherwise he will enter inside you and stay there!"

"Don't worry, Fr. Maxime. I'm sure none of us in this room has any intention or inclination to invite a demon inside us," I said to laughter.

"Good. Well, St. Parthenios was a great saint, so the moment he told the demon, 'Come inside me,' the young woman was freed from her possession and the demon disappeared. The demon growled, 'I am burned!' You see, he could not enter the temple of God. The saint was God's temple, and no demon could enter there. This is the greatness of a saint like Parthenios. He did not send that demon anywhere else. Instead he was willing to put himself at such great risk in order to save the other person," Fr. Maximos concluded.

I mentioned that contemporary people do not believe in the reality of demons, which according to Fr. Maximos is the greatest achievement of the devil today, that he has convinced most of the world that he does not exist. As a rule, academics would dismiss such stories as taking place in people's imaginations, without any basis in objective reality. But the experiences of the saints throughout history are filled with demonic possession and exorcisms. In Fr. Maximos's experience, the devil and his mischief are as real as the miracles attributed to the Holy Virgin.

"Let me share with you a personal experience that relates to what we are discussing here," Fr. Maximos said. "Some years ago, I gave a talk in Nicosia to a sizable audience. A man whom I had never met before approached me and said that he needed a kidney transplant. 'Father,' he said, 'can you please announce to your audience that I need a kidney? Perhaps someone could offer me one.' I was taken by surprise and did not know what to tell him. I replied, 'Do you really think this is possible? Who would want to give up one of his kidneys?' He said, 'Tell them about my blood type, and those who match mine could stay behind so that we can discuss a possible donation.' I felt very perplexed and uncomfortable. He said, 'Well, what kinds of Christians are they who come to your talks?' I then realized that all of us, including myself, would be in a difficult spot if someone came and requested one of our kidneys. What would I do if he asked me for one of my kidneys?"

We smiled nervously as Fr. Maximos continued. "Thank God

my blood type was different from his, so I was off the hook. I was really scared that we had the same blood type. You see, I should have to be willing to give him my kidney if I wished to practice what I preached. I then wondered whether we really have the capacity to be in a state of oneness with others. Are we ready to sacrifice ourselves for others? When we hear of all the disharmonies and discords that our fellow human beings go through in their everyday lives, do we experience that sacrificial love the saints speak of? This is a very rare phenomenon."

Fr. Maximos was absolutely convinced that prayer, when done sincerely and with total love and focus, leads to the intervention of the Holy Spirit by bringing peace and healing to human beings. And this inner peace can then be translated into external peace, social and political peace. He would repeat time and again that unless peacemakers find peace within themselves, their pursuit of external peace, more often than not, will bear no tangible fruits.

"Let me give you another example from personal experience," he continued. "A young high school teacher who had just been hired told me she had difficulty keeping order in her class. A rough and unruly group created pandemonium every time she entered the classroom. The poor woman trembled every time she faced them. I asked her to write their first names on a piece of paper and give it to me so that we could mention them during liturgy every day. I asked that she also pray for those teenagers. I assured her that she was bound to see a marked improvement in their behavior. After some time she contacted me again. She said, 'You know something, Father? Those youngsters who created so much havoc have mellowed!' I replied that they had mellowed because she was praying for them.

"I told her," Fr. Maximos went on, "that as a result of her prayers, the Grace of God had visited their hearts and softened them up. Prayer had brought peace to the classroom. When we fail to pray for fellow human beings who cause problems for us and instead blame and condemn them, or complain about them, their behavior more often than not will deteriorate. In reality, our toxic feelings become demonic energy sent to them. We are, therefore, responsible for the others when they become worse than before. The more spiritually aware we are, the greater the responsibility we share for their condition. The others may not be spiritually aware. Perhaps they have never heard of the Gospel. Perhaps they don't live spiritual lives and are not aware of or sensitive to the spiritual laws at work. But what about us, who presumably are aware? What do we do? Do we face the other person according to the teachings of the Gospel? Or do we rationalize by saying, 'He condemns me, I condemn him; he slanders me, I slander him; he rejects me, I reject him; he ignores me, I ignore him; he curses me, I curse him,' and so on. That's not the way to stop the work of Satan.

"I am reminded of a story in which Satan appears in front of an abbot and has a conversation with him. Satan tells the abbot, 'All day long I cause havoc among your monks. I make them quarrel among themselves as they work the fields and begin the other tasks you assign them, and I am close to destroying them. Unfortunately, during the night they manage to damage the traps and nets that I set up for them.' Then the abbot asks him, 'How do they do that?' And Satan replies, 'Every night they do prostrations and ask forgiveness of each other.'

"Those of you who have been at a monastery will notice that at the end of the *apodypnon* [a short prayer service after dinner], all the monks fall on their knees and ask forgiveness of each other in case something happened during the day that may have offended them. Then the abbot blesses them and they go to their cells.

"In a monastery one is not allowed to have negative feelings toward anyone. If you have a complaint, you are expected to go to that brother, make a deep bow, and ask for forgiveness. That is how the traps of Satan are destroyed, rendering him incapable of causing divisions among us."

"Is this, perhaps, the secret that has allowed monasteries to last for thousands of years whereas other communal arrangements tend to have very brief life spans?" I asked.

"Well, of course. A community that quarrels all the time will eventually be destroyed. But let me return to where I started. For us to be in discord with another person is not the other's problem. It is our problem. Others may not want us, but we must be spiritually united with them because we know we must love one another. If others do not like us, we are nevertheless obligated to love them and feel sorrow that our very existence and presence is problematic for them. That is how we construct bridges with other human beings. That is how we should approach other human beings if we wish to help them at their very essence. When we condemn others, they might become worse."

"How do others know that I condemn them?" Michael interjected.

"Condemnation, blame, and slander are satanic energies that are transmitted in the heart of the other person. As a consequence of such transmissions, he or she becomes worse. If he has only one complaint against you, he will soon have five or ten. Likewise, when you pray for the other person, and it is unlikely that he will know that, his heart fully accepts your prayer."

"What if his heart is not receptive?"

"It does not matter. His heart may be like a rock full of hatred against you. It doesn't matter. Prayer can crack rocks, even granite. You just pray and you will see how the other person will be affected. Consider it a given that it is absolutely impossible to pray for someone without affecting that person. Your prayers can never be in vain."

"Is it possible that in one in a million cases this axiom may not work, that prayer may not have any effect?" Michael persisted.

"Well, if you put it this way, it may be possible," Fr. Maximos replied with a smile. "Perhaps praying for demons is the exception to the rule. You know, saints do pray even for demons, and yet they seem to get worse. They never repent."

"They wouldn't be doing their job if they did," I interjected, prompting laughter.

"Whatever it is, they are the truly unrepentant," Fr. Maximos replied. "A human being is not a demon. Regardless of his or her spiritual condition, there are always cracks inside that can allow the good to come forward."

"But what if such a person does not respond no matter what you do and how much you pray?" Maria wondered.

"Then you are the exclusive beneficiary of your prayers. But again, it is really impossible to pray for someone without that person benefiting on some level. This is a spiritual law. What it boils down to is that you must become like Christ. This is the ideal human being who is united with everybody in peace. Therefore, when peace is absent, we should not waste our time trying to find the problem in others."

"Unfortunately, Fr. Maxime," Eleni said, "this is extremely difficult. It would require extraordinary spiritual strength and maturity to maintain such a mind-set."

"Well yes! But this is the ideal to strive toward. Instead of praying for the other, we normally use our logic or common sense. In such a situation, our logic is, in reality, our enemy. Our logic tells us, 'Don't you see that she slanders you without you doing anything against her except pray for her well-being? In spite of your good intentions, she does her best to ruin you.' Your logic has good points. Yet the Gospel asks us to go beyond our logic. This is the meaning of *metanoia*, to radically change the way we feel and think. Your logic tells you, 'You are justified in not talking to her since she does not talk to you; you are right in not loving her since she does not care for you; why should you benefit her since she slanders you?' and so on.

"This is what common, worldly logic tells us to do," Fr. Maximos continued. "The logic of the Gospel, on the other hand, says: 'You are right, she does not love you. In fact she hates you. You must pray even more, love her more.'"

"This is impossible," someone moaned.

"Yes. It is very difficult. I say all this, but I don't even know if I put these things into practice myself. It is a mighty struggle to kill your ego, to reject yourself. But is this not what Christ asks of us, to oppose that worldly self of ours and embrace the message of the Gospel?"

"This kind of talking may be nice, but how can we reach such heights of spiritual attainment?" Eleni complained.

"Well, as I've tried to show you in this discussion, it is a gradual process. We cannot become saints from one day to the next. It is an ongoing struggle. We can succeed if on this spiritual path we continuously keep Christ in our hearts and minds and contrast our behavior with His. We should always compare our choices and actions with those of Christ. Ask yourself the question 'How would Christ have responded in our situation?' Judge yourself by comparing yourself with Christ, our Divine Archetype. It is the only way we should behave if we wish to become perfected human beings.

"So when we examine ourselves and discover that our behavior is similar to that of Christ, we can rejoice," Fr. Maximos continued. "Otherwise we should humble ourselves. Never justify ourselves. Whoever tries to justify himself or herself will never reach *metanoia*."

"How does one humble oneself?" Maria wondered.

"Thank God there are plenty of opportunities in our everyday life to humble ourselves! The more difficulties we have in life, the greater the opportunities for humility."

Teresa sighed. "Easier said than done."

"We are impatient and often interpret opportunities offered to us by Providence in worldly, self-centered ways. We seek justification in a worldly manner. Had we really learned humility, we would not witness the disintegration of our families. We wouldn't have the social and political problems that we now face.

"We, not others, cause the problem," Fr. Maximos insisted. "It doesn't matter if others create problems for us even if they are the worst human beings possible. What matters is our own inner state of being. If we do not find peace within ourselves, even if we live among angels, we are bound to create strife and conflict between ourselves and others, either as individuals or as groups."

Fr. Maximos then reminisced about an encounter between Elder Paisios and a hell and damnation theologian, an Old Calendarist (a follower of the Julian calendar) zealot. He wished to condemn people who did not abide by the old calendar to Hell and eternal damnation, a habit of mind that naturally caused him problems in his relations. "My dear," Elder Paisios told him in exasperation, "if I am to go to Paradise and find you there, I would rather go somewhere else! The way you carry on, you will create havoc wherever you go."

After our laughter subsided, we paused for more tea and pastries.

"Let's now talk about joy, the next to the last fruit of the

Spirit that St. Paul mentions in his epistle," Fr. Maximos began. "I don't need to repeat that God's fruits of the Spirit are in reality infinite. Joy is the reality at the very depth of our being," he declared.

"Well, that's a bold statement, considering all the misery and unhappiness in the world," Emily said half jokingly.

"I mean the true joy that only God can offer. You see, right from the beginning, God created human beings in order to be joyous. He created Paradise for them. Human beings are created for joy. That is why Paradise is described in the scriptures as a place of bliss and pleasure, of happiness and contentment."

"We are created for pleasure and joy, but all we experience is pain and suffering," Teresa complained.

"This isn't part of our true nature. Humans cannot find rest in pain, no matter how much we philosophize about it. It was after the Fall that pain entered into human existence."

"Is this why after the Resurrection, upon meeting the first group of women, Christ saluted them with the word chairete [be joyous]?" Eleni asked.

"Well said. God brought an end to the sorrow of human existence and revealed the joy embedded in God's very nature, not the worldly form of joy and pleasure, of course."

"What do you consider the difference between worldly joy and God's joy?" Michael asked.

"Worldly joy is of course joy, but it cannot be compared with the joy that God offers to the human soul. There is a gigantic difference. Worldly joy is temporal. Let us say I have won the lottery and I am filled with joy. It is an event that happens outside myself. I accept the stimulation of the external event and I feel happy. My joy, however, lasts only for as long as this event lasts. When the external event comes to an end, my own inner joy also comes to an end."

"These external events that bring us joy are always tenuous and threaten to come to an end," I pointed out, having in mind the string of losses that we unavoidably experience as we advance in age.

"Yes. Life does not promise us an unending source of joy, regardless of what we do. Let us assume we live a utopian existence," Fr. Maximos went on. "Let us assume that all the circumstances and events in our lives are so beautiful, so ideal, so perfectly positive, that happiness is part of our everyday reality. Yet in spite of that happiness, an event will, like Damocles' sword, always threaten to destroy everything, the lurking nightmare of our inevitable death. Death eliminates this worldly joy."

"Time is our enemy. Every moment that passes brings us closer to our end," someone muttered.

"The joy of this world is threatened by death, and anything that comes to an end cannot ultimately bring joy to the human soul," Fr. Maximos continued. "Anything that has a terminal date cannot offer real comfort to human beings, who are created in the image of the infinite and eternal God. A human being can be truly joyous only within that which is absolutely his, the eternal joy that characterizes God Himself. A human being feels rested and joyous when those things that cause joy are sealed with the mark of eternity. Anything that is sealed with death cannot provide lasting happiness because we know that one day it will be gone. Divine joy, on the other hand, is a condition that is dormant at the very depths of human existence."

"Sometimes we panic in the face of our mortality," I pointed out. "We repress the fear of death and do everything possible to forget that our life's clock is ticking."

Fr. Maximos nodded. "Human beings would do anything to eliminate the vagaries of time."

"Wouldn't you say, Fr. Maxime," I asked, "that this is a natural reaction?"

"Of course! We are not created for decay and death. Anything of limited duration creates this insecurity in us. During funerals you hear the most ridiculous speeches. You hear people addressing the dead, 'Go in peace and we will remember you forever.' But who is going to live forever to remember the dead person?"

"Why then during the memorial services do we chant, 'May her memory be eternal'?" Emily asked.

"It is only God who will remember her forever. People will remember us for as long as they are alive. But after they are gone, what becomes of the memory?"

"A hundred years after we die no one will remember us," I pronounced.

"Much less than that. Do we remember people who died fifty years ago? I wasn't even born then. It is God who will remember us forever. It is God who offers us this sense of eternity, this security, the absolute certainty that even death, our ultimate adversary, does not bring about our annihilation and oblivion. Through the experience of Christ, it is death that is annihilated. That's when real joy enters into our lives.

"The joy of God is not a joy like the joy we experience in this world, and if we start comparing them it is like light and darkness. It is the contrast between something imperishable and that which is perishable. When one has a taste of God's joy, then all the joys of the world are transcended, annihilated. They cannot dazzle you. How could the moon dazzle you when you have seen the light of the sun?"

It was intuitively apparent to Emily and myself, since we had both known Fr. Maximos for many years, that his wisdom was not based only on reading the works of the great elders of Christianity. We were confident that his own direct experience was the chief source of his charisma as a speaker and as a conversationalist. Undoubtedly his close apprenticeship with some of the leading saints of Mt. Athos, such as Papa Ephraim of Katounakia and Elder Paisios, played a major role in bringing forward these spiritual gifts.

"The joy of God is not dependent on stimulations related to external things," Fr. Maximos continued. "It is everlasting and unalterable. That is why it gives birth within the heart of the person to this certainty of God's presence that no one can take away."

"There might be a problem here," Eleni interjected. "One may wonder how such joy is possible considering that there is so much suffering all around. Is such a person detached and indifferent to the pain of others?"

"This is a mystery and a paradox. The man of God is continuously joyous while at the same time, as the Holy Scriptures say, he partakes in the sorrow of all human beings. This happens because his joy is not disconnected from *agape* or love. Such a person can experience deep sorrow for the suffering of others, but at the depths of his being there is the joy of God's Presence that sweetens the pain of humanity."

"Such a person has radically different sensibilities on how to address the problems of human existence," I added.

"Absolutely so. Such a person is in a continuous state of joy regardless of what happens around him. No thing and no one can captivate his heart. After all, the source of joy is Christ Himself. That's why the salutation to the myrrh-bearing women of *chairete* after the Resurrection is truly an evangelical message."

Fr. Maximos went on to explain the importance of the Resurrection as a joyous message, that there is always the Resurrection and a joyous reunion with God after the cross everyone must bear. Elder Paisios told a rebellious young radical who came to visit him: "Here on Mt. Athos we believe not in revolution but in Resurrection!"

"It is possible that all around us everything is dark and gloomy but our hearts are filled with joy," Fr. Maximos went on. "I don't know whether you have seen people dying. I have seen people who were radiant with joy as they were about to die. They won over death, like the case of Fr. Theophylaktos [his name literally means 'one who is guarded by God'], an old monk from Mt. Athos. 'Grandpa, are you afraid?' I asked him. "No,' he replied. 'I continuously recite the Efché,' the Jesus Prayer. It was as if he was on his way to his wedding party. His face was shining as he passed away. And I have seen others who lacked this connection to God in their lives and their endings were real tragedies."

"How is this joy of God born within the heart of a person?" Michael asked.

"According to the teaching of the elders, it starts when a person begins to strive spiritually and tirelessly to implement the commandments of God. He will encounter fatigue and many difficulties along the way. But there will also be a gradual emergence in his heart of the first rays of God's joy, which will offer him further inducement to continue on this path."

"How?"

"As a person makes the effort to spiritually unite with God, there emerges in his heart further desire and energy for spiritual awakening."

"I suppose the vision of God can help one to transcend his human limitations," I added.

"Right. This reminds me of an old hermit who used to regularly pass by our monastery carrying provisions on his back for other hermits and monks. He was very poor, lived in a shack, and was always hungry. I would ask him, 'How are you today, Father?' His reply was always 'Hungry!' I was in charge of the kitchen during that time, and I would give him food to eat. His task was to carry provisions for the other monks by walking hours on end. I asked him why he didn't let others do the rounds instead of taking up their heavy load for himself. His answer was 'Oh, since I'm going to Karyes [the administrative center of Mt. Athos, where there is a grocery store], I don't mind bringing some provisions to the others. They have work to do, whereas I am just taking a walk.' In fact, the reason he was doing those regular rounds, walking for hours, summer and winter, was for the sake of others. Old as he was, he always carried a heavy load on his back. Yet he was always joyous, radiating with happiness. You could see it on his face. He never complained. When asked how he was doing, he would reply *Doxasi O Theos* [Glory be to God]. He was never angry and was always smiling. When he died, we noticed that his feet were in terrible condition, skinned to the bare bone."

"Somebody unfamiliar with the culture of Mt. Athos might think he was psychologically unbalanced," I suggested.

"Nonsense. He was neither a fool nor mentally handicapped. He simply radiated the Grace of God. The paradox of the Gospel is this: through the suffering of the cross there emerges life and joy. Through hard and tiring labor there comes rest. Through a relentless and tiring spiritual labor, by dying daily so to speak, a person finally finds true joy."

I pointed out that what Fr. Maximos was describing was a general axiom about the nature of pleasure and joy. You cannot experience pleasure without experiencing pain first. You cannot enjoy food until you are hungry. You cannot enjoy water without thirst. You cannot experience joy without first going through suffering.

"We live in a world of polarity," I said, "of plus and minus, hot and cold, pleasure and pain, angels and demons. Good and evil seem to be equally balanced in this fallen world."

"And that is the meaning of the cross," Fr. Maximos added. "It prepares the way for the Resurrection, for true joy. It means that I go through life carrying my cross with joy."

"The cross by itself is a symbol of torture, fit for criminals in that Roman period," someone pointed out.

"Yes, but Christ sanctified that symbol," Fr. Maximos added. "Christ transforms the cross into joy. Our pains, trials, difficulties, and tribulations of all sorts are not good in themselves. But these problems can be transmuted so that they yield rich spiritual fruits. It is Christ who transforms what is bitter into what is sweet, darkness into light."

Fr. Maximos concluded by repeating that human beings are created for joy, not pain and suffering. It is our fallen state that subtracted joy from our hearts, plunging us into pain, sorrow, insecurity, fear, and angst about our impending death. It is illusory, Fr. Maximos would argue, to try to overcome these problems by focusing exclusively on pursuits that are ephemeral. These pursuits cannot give real rest to the human soul.

"The only path to real joy," he concluded, "is through the reestablishment of our absolute relationship with God, with a direct experiential connection with the Divine, the presence of God in our hearts. Our hearts then become receptive chalices that accept the fruits of the Holy Spirit, this absolute and inexpressible joy that springs from within us as we strive to abide by God's commandments, that is, to love God and, by extension, every other human being. It is our very nature which dictates that we cannot attain real ontological joy outside of God."

Our conversation lasted past eleven. Alas, we had to terminate it without exploring the last of the hierarchy of gifts as outlined in St. Paul's famous epistle. "We'll have to do that some other day," Fr. Maximos said, smiling as he stood up. He and his companions needed rest before their drive to New York early the next morning.

Articulating the feelings of the rest of us, Eleni lamented that she couldn't foresee when she would have the opportunity again to hear Fr. Maximos's discussion on *agape*, love, the last of the Pauline spiritual fruits. I tried to mollify her disappointment by promising to tape a future discussion with Fr. Maximos on the subject and mail it to everyone who had been present at this impromptu symposium. What I could not promise was the date of that future conversation. I assumed we would have it during a future visit to Cyprus, where I planned to continue my research apprenticeship with the Athonite elder.

SIX

FOGGY LANDSCAPES

During the last thirty years, summers in Cyprus have been growing warmer while the yearly rainfall has been steadily and alarmingly declining. With the advent of the new millennium, temperatures of 100 degrees Fahrenheit during July and August have made life particularly uncomfortable for the advanced in age and for workers laboring outdoors. For the ecologically conscious, the twin problems of global warming and serious environmental degradation have become a recognizable threat for the long-term viability of life on the island. The sparse rainfall and the absence of serious planning to deal with the chronic water shortage forced the government in 2008 to severely cut supplies to households and farmers. It also made it necessary during the summer months of that year to import water from Greece, which was transported to Cyprus at a cost of tens of millions of euros.

Those were the conditions we faced upon our arrival in Cyprus in early June 2008. We were staying in Limassol, the major coastal city, where we reconnected with friends and relatives, adjusted to habits of water conservation, and found relief from the heat by swimming in the sea. In the meantime I had made plans to meet with Fr. Maximos after his return from an extended trip to Greece and a pilgrimage to the Holy Mountain of Athos.

"The heat will be unbearable again today," Emily said as we listened to the weather report over breakfast. "Let's go to Kourion and take Vladimiros with us."

I was in agreement. Emily went to the phone to see whether our octogenarian friend could join us at our favorite remote beach, twenty minutes west of Limassol. Vladimiros happily accepted, and in half an hour we picked him up.

"Thank you for thinking of me," our tall, stately friend said, smiling broadly. Wearing shorts, a blue baseball hat, and a white T-shirt, he squeezed himself into the front seat that Emily had offered him. "It's good to leave the house in this heat." Air-conditioning is not as widely used in Cyprus as one might expect.

Vladimiros was a celebrated novelist of short stories and a retired journalist. His wife, Elena, a renowned poet and writer of children's stories, had just flown to Athens for a series of tests to determine the nature of some suspicious shadows that had shown up in recent scans of her lungs. The excursion to the coast was a welcome distraction from his worries about her and a temporary relief from the heat. A good-hearted and gregarious man, he always enjoyed the company of friends. These encounters routinely became stories in his novellas.

During his long life, Vladimiros had made many close friends, most of them already gone. We had known him and his wife for many years from our visits to the island and shared many common interests, in local and international politics and in the world of letters. Emily, in particular, with a background in literature, was very close to both Elena and Vladimiros.

We decided to take the more scenic route rather than the newly constructed four-lane highway. We preferred the old road because on it, after passing beyond the harbor, the morbid as-phalt and aesthetically unappealing cement buildings come to an abrupt end. Vineyards and citrus groves, protected from the wind by cypress trees, extend all the way to Kourion. That en-tire area was designated agricultural land, and so far developers, who for decades have pillaged the coastal areas, had been kept at bay. The whole Fasouri region, as it is called, happens to be in-side the jurisdiction of the British sovereign bases. When Cyprus attained its independence from Britain, in 1960, after eighty-two years of colonial rule, a ninety-nine-square-mile area was des-ignated to remain permanently under British sovereignty. The Brits adamantly refused to allow "development," not necessar-ily out of love of the environment but out of fear of terrorism. Protection of the environment was a happy by-product of the presence of a British military base nearby.

The Fasouri area was a swamp when a couple of enterprising Israelis migrated to the island. At the time the State of Israel had not yet been established and Cyprus was still under British colonial control. The Israelis drained the swamp and turned the mosquito-infested area into a fertile oasis.

As we reached the start of Fasouri, where miles of country road are covered by a thick canopy formed by the branches of cypress trees that grow on both sides, Vladimiros lamented the health problems that he and his wife faced as they grew older. "Getting old is not easy," he said, sighing. "Most of my friends are gone and my eyes are failing me. I still see, but I can no lon-ger read." He took a deep breath and continued. "For a writer, this is a terrible condition to find yourself in." As he said that I thought of Jean-Paul Sartre, the French existentialist philoso-pher who upon losing his eyesight declared that life no longer had meaning for him since he could not read or write.

In spite of the problems with his eyesight, however, Vladimiros was able to write in broad strokes with a pencil. Then he would give his handwritten novellas to a typist. But for reading he had to depend totally on Elena, who was considerably younger.

"As a writer I've always tried to give my readers a sense of optimism about life and about the future. But increasingly I find myself unable to do that," Vladimiros said.

"But why?" Emily reacted as she leaned forward to rest her arms on the backs of the front seats.

"I foresee nothing positive ahead of me that could give me any hope. I am into my eighties and getting foggy-eyed. What kind of future can I see ahead?"

We remained pensive for a few seconds. Vladimiros had just published a collection of short stories aptly titled The Foggy Landscape, which dealt with the problems aging people face. I felt sad and, fixing my gaze on the shady road ahead, tried to digest the distress of our friend. To sooth his angst, Emily suggested that reaching the eighties could also be seen as a great privilege and good fortune.

"Think of all the amazing experiences that you and Elena have had together for over forty years and how masterfully you transmuted those experiences into delightful novels and short stories," Emily said. She had diligently read everything they had written. Vladimiros and Elena had earned several prizes for their literary achievements and were friends with leading artists and writers in Cyprus, Greece, and elsewhere. "How many people can look back and take as much comfort in what they have accomplished with their lives as you?"

"A twenty- or thirty-something can only hope to live as long as you have and have such a rich background of experiences," I added. "For a young person, life ahead is not a guarantee but only a possibility. For you, it is an actuality. Think about that.

Think of how many young men and women die in wars that they themselves did not start. How many people can be assured that they will reach eighty-two years of age?"

While saying those words I had in mind the work of Viktor Frankl, the Viennese psychiatrist who after surviving Auschwitz invented a school of existential psychotherapy that he called "logotherapy," or meaning therapy.[1] I ventured to practice a bit of logotherapy with Vladimiros by elaborating on Frankl's life and work, hoping to help him lift his spirits.

"But at my age it is hard to think otherwise," Vladimiros said, shaking his head. "Everything will come to an end soon. How could life be meaningful for me from now on?"

"What makes you think everything will end?" I asked with a shrug, pretending I had no anxieties about marching into my sixties. I slowed so we could better enjoy the beauty of the scenery around us.

"When Socrates," I went on, "was sentenced to death, he faced his accusers by declaring, 'I will soon go to my death while you will go on living. Who is better off only God knows.'"

"But Socrates believed in God," Vladimiros replied, grinning.

"Yes, he believed what all the world's religions have taught, that death is not the end of everything but the beginning of something new."

I stole a look at our friend. He appeared unimpressed by my line of reasoning. After remaining silent for a few seconds, he shook his head.

"I cannot accept that I could exist without my senses. The bottom line is that I am losing my eyesight, and soon I will be losing my other senses. When they are gone, I too will be gone. I will become zero," he said with a tinge of bitterness. He was a man who, in spite of difficulties, loved life with passion and his wife with an even greater intensity. One of our fears was how he would be able to live if Elena were to go before him.

"Do you really believe that?" I grimaced. "That we exist because we have five senses? That's it?"

"What else is there? When my brain is gone, I am gone. There is nothing after that except oblivion. This is the depressing fact," Vladimiros replied.

I felt compassion for Vladimiros's difficulty accepting the inevitability of growing old and exiting this life. I had noticed this over the years with many aging friends who lived completely on secular assumptions about the nature of ultimate reality. When death would come up in a conversation, they would nervously change the subject, as if it were taboo. For example, Leonard, an academic mentor and friend of mine, with an international reputation and eighteen scholarly books on psychology to his credit, dreaded dying. I remember when he reached his eighties, every time I called him to inquire about how he was doing, his reply was "Not good." When I would press him to explain, his standard answer was "But do you know how old I am?" When he reached eighty-nine, right after his wife died, Leonard became utterly depressed. He died a year later, fearing what he considered to be the inevitable obliteration of his being. He would not consider seriously any suggestions that life may continue beyond the grave. Like most academic psychologists, he viewed such notions as wishful thinking, or infantile fixations and projections. Like Vladimiros, Leonard was a gentle and extremely intelligent man but a believer in the exclusive sovereignty of physical science as the arbiter of all claims to truth. Like Vladimiros, Leonard had internalized thoroughly the syndrome of modernity, as I discussed it in Chapter 1. There was no way I could convince him otherwise. He had spent most of his life as a professor in a high-powered Ivy League university. Alas, there is no room for psyche and spirit within the corridors of mainstream academic psychology.

I have come to realize that nihilism is often the consequence of a modern worldview that has eliminated all traces of a spiritual foundation for the created cosmos. Many contemporary, secular philosophers have concluded that the world and humanity itself are a cruel joke, a freak accident, as Bertrand Russell would have us believe. Such notions have become the unquestioned and implied worldview of many leaders in the academy, in elite mass media, and in the arts. No wonder then that so many gifted people are plagued by depression and joylessness. Both Emily and I feel privileged that we have met people like Fr. Maximos who affirmed for us a radically optimistic and joyous understanding at the heart of our existence, an understanding that makes you want to share it with the rest of the world.

I remember reading a recent article about the life and work of Woody Allen, the celebrated film director, comedian, actor, and amateur saxophone player, and his fear of facing his own mortality. His case is representative of the cultural elite mindset. Age seventy-two and a declared atheist, he spoke of staying awake all night long, terrified of "the void" and the "indifference" of the universe that had obsessed him since his early life. "I can't really come up with a good argument to choose life over death," he stated. Making films offers him no rewards other than distraction from his fear of death. After his having lost many of his friends, as we all do as we age, his perception of time changed because he came to the realization of "how brief everything is" and how "meaningless" life is.[2]

Few people are as conscious or as self-disclosing as Allen is about the personal consequences of unbelief. I have known many colleagues who spent their entire lives hiding their beliefs from themselves and from others until the fatal heart attack hit. This realization led Ernest Becker to write *The Denial of Death*,[3] about the tendency most of us have to suppress the fact of our mortality by creating "immortality projects," be they the books we write, the films we make, the wealth we amass, the respect we try to earn as members of our communities, or the "noble causes" we espouse. As another psychologist friend of mine who believes in God but not in personal immortality once said to me, "I will become immortal through the genes that I pass on to my children." Notwithstanding his belief in God, he too believed in personal "oblivion."

Vladimiros was neither an actor nor an academic psychologist like my late friend Leonard, but like so many contemporary writers and intellectuals, he was a nonbeliever schooled in the Marxist worldview of historical materialism and the belief that only the physical universe is real, religion being a form of superstition destined for oblivion with the attainment of the communist utopia. Thanks to a scholarship during his younger years, he had studied philosophy and aesthetics at a Bulgarian university during the height of the Cold War, when Bulgaria was within the Soviet orbit. Vladimiros learned Bulgarian and Russian and mingled with the leading writers and poets of the Eastern Bloc. Upon his return to Cyprus, carrying the stigma of Communism, he joined the local Communist Party and worked as a journalist for the party's newspaper. Later on, during the Gorbachev years of the Soviet Union, and because of championing the democratization of AKEL, the local Communist Party, Vladimiros, along with other "progressives," was summarily expelled for undermining the party.

Although no longer a Marxist-Leninist, Vladimiros retained, if not an aversion to religion, at least a deep skepticism about its key premises. The catastrophic role that the local church had played in the political problems of the island only reinforced his negative predisposition to religious claims or beliefs. This was in spite of the fact that his paternal grandfather was a priest and his parents were devout churchgoers. Vladimiros was a true child of the Enlightenment. He believed in the perfectibility of humanity solely through the application of human reason and scientific knowledge. For a moment I thought of remaining silent, as I usually consider prudent with doctrinaire materialists. But Vladimiros was not made of such cloth. I admired his open spirit and his readiness to listen to contrary views. Those were attitudes reinforced by his two-year tenure in New York as cultural attaché of the Cyprus mission to the United Nations during the early nineties, one of the happy periods in their lives, as both Vladimiros and Elena often told us.

I felt compelled to offer an alternative verdict on the nature of ultimate reality. "Allow me to disagree with you, Vladimire," I said as we approached Kourion. "I have the exact opposite view about this matter. I believe God is the ultimate reality, and I don't believe that death is the end of everything. I do not believe we human beings become zero after death. In fact, all indications point in the opposite direction, toward a new beginning."

Vladimiros looked at me with surprise, as if he couldn't believe what he was hearing. I could only imagine his thoughts: how could a university professor believe in such medieval notions? In fact, Elena told Emily a few days later that Vladimiros had told her with disbelief that "Kyriacos believes in the things he is writing about!" He assumed that my writings about Christian mystics had been strictly academic exercises or a form of investigative reporting. He assumed I was basically a secular intellectual like himself with an instinctive aversion to anything religious.

I turned off the main road and headed toward the beach. We

passed a forest of eucalyptus trees on our right and a strawberry farm on our left. Half a mile farther on, we turned onto a narrow road that ran west by the sea. Mercifully there were no tourist developments on the beach except three low-key, traditional, unobtrusive restaurants that the British allowed to operate. For all practical purposes the area remained undeveloped, a park by the sea without being formally declared as such. That is why we loved the place. It reminded us of our youth, when all around Cyprus one could enjoy such pristine settings. A hundred meters north from the beach, the cliffs rose sharply, similar to the majestic coastline of the eastern coast of England. Adventurous hang gliders used the top plateau as a launching platform. Several of them hovered above us like enormous eagles with colorful wings.

The area of Kourion was part of an ancient kingdom that had been destroyed by an earthquake during pre-Christian times. In fact, at the top of the plateau near the launch site, an ancient Greek amphitheater had been discovered and renovated. Open-air performances of classical and modern plays and concerts took place there during the summer months.

We parked at the third and most remote and humble-looking restaurant. Under thatched umbrellas and with a bottle of cold local beer, Vladimiros waited for us as we enjoyed a brief, refreshing swim. After our lunch of fish and salad, followed by a cup of Turkish coffee, we resumed our conversation on life, death, and life beyond the grave.

"So what made you into a believer?" Vladimiros asked with curiosity.

"Look, Vladimire," I replied, "over the years I realized that the worldview we have inherited from the nineteenth century is no longer tenable. It just doesn't make sense. I mean the view that only concrete matter is real and that only that which is accessible to our physical senses is true."

"But what were the reasons that turned you into a believer?" Vladimiros insisted.

I thought for a second and then went on to say that among other things it was my exposure to the mystical teachings of all the major religions; the emerging new understanding of science beyond the mechanistic model of the universe, the new paradigm that radically challenges the Newtonian assumptions about how the world works; the scientific studies related to death itself, particularly the accumulated literature on near-death experiences; the evidence on the nonlocality of mind and the so-called shamanic state of consciousness; and, most important, my personal encounters during the last twenty-five years with living Christian mystics, hermits, and saints.

"That's a long list," Vladimiros noted. He sipped his coffee. "How about a specific example?"

With Vladimiros I knew that I had to offer a response outside the traditional ways that he was familiar with, growing up within a Christian Orthodox culture. Obviously, that exposure had not prevented him from becoming an agnostic, if not a diehard atheist. In other words, I could not persuade him of the reality of life beyond the grave by resorting to Revelation, the end of the world, virgin births, judgment day, resurrection of the dead, and the second coming of Christ. For rational intellectuals, such arguments reinforce their beliefs that there is nothing to mainstream religion other than propaganda and imaginative mythologies. Vladimiros could take seriously only an argument that did not oppose scientific thinking and rational discourse.

"Okay. Let's start with all the world's religions, not just Christianity," I responded. "It is a very impressive fact that the mystics of all the world's religions, in spite of their great diversity of beliefs, are in agreement that the physical, observable universe is only a very small part of a wider reality that cannot be apprehended by our physical senses. All the religions agree that there is a reality that includes and transcends the natural world and that this reality can be approached and experienced through mystical ecstasy. It has been called by various names: God, Brahman, Allah, Yahweh, the One, the Absolute, the Great Spirit, and so on."

"Also, most of the great sages and philosophers hold a similar view on this issue," Emily added.

"Exactly," I went on. "With the exception of leading nineteenth- and twentieth-century philosophers like Marx, Freud, Russell, and Sartre, most of the world's sages—Socrates, Plato, Aristotle, Plotinus, Kant, Hegel, Shankara—based their philosophies on this fundamental assumption about the fabric of reality, that is, that the physical universe is not all there is. But it is the mystics who offer experiential validation of this fact. It is the mystics from the various religious traditions who set down ways to approach and come to know this transcendent Reality."

"What are you referring to?" Vladimiros interjected with a quizzical look.

"The Hindu sages, for example, invented the various yoga systems, such as Bhakti, Gnani, Raja, and Karma. In tribal religions you find the ecstatic experiences of traditional shamans. Anthropologists in fact discovered what they call the 'shamanic state of consciousness,' an out-of-body experience, which has been scientifically studied as a radically different form of consciousness than any other state, such as waking, sleeping, being hypnotized, et cetera.

"In ancient Greece," I continued, "there were the mystery

schools like those of Pythagoras that influenced Plato and Socrates, who himself had mystical experiences.

"In Christianity, which interests me the most, there is the Hesychast tradition of Mt. Athos, the spiritual methodology of inner silence (hesychia) practiced by hermits and monks since the early years of Christianity. In the Christian Orthodox tradition, for example, God will reveal Himself to you only when you cleanse your heart of egotistical desires and passions. Once this is done, the struggling soul may experience what the Fathers of the Church call the 'Uncreated Light of God.' It is an ecstatic experience that transforms the person totally. It has nothing to do with cerebral, intellectual knowledge."

"How can you have trust that what they report is based on reality and not on fantasy?" Vladimiros asked. What I presented may have been new ideas to him, but the question he raised was the standard response of skeptics to such phenomena.

"When you read the reports of people who have had such experiences, you cannot help but be impressed. Obviously, unless you have the experience yourself, you cannot really know. But I believe that the experiences of the great prophets, saints, and mystics have such extraordinary force that, to me at least, it is impossible to dismiss them as mere delusions."

"My problem with religion," Vladimiros interjected, "is that it has done so much harm in the world. So many wars were fought in the names of particular gods, whether in the rise and expansion of Islam, or the Crusades, or the Inquisition, or the current wars in the Middle East, not to mention, of course, the disastrous role played by the Church in our problems with the Turks."

"Yes, this is a legitimate concern. Religious fanaticism has been a problem throughout the ages. But when you compare the violence that has been perpetrated in the name of religion with the violence that has been perpetrated in the name of secular ideologies, you will notice that secular ideologies have been even more unrestrained and savage and the number of human lives lost because of them even greater than those attributed to religion," I replied.

"What do you mean?" Vladimiros asked.

"Look at the twentieth century and the millions who died in wars and revolutions that were motivated by either nationalism or ideologies like Communism and Nazism. The twentieth century, considered the most secular century, has been the bloodiest century in all of history. Think of the Nazis and the Holocaust. Think of Stalin and Mao, of Pol Pot and Cambodia. Together they caused the deaths of tens of millions of people in order to promote their notion of the good society."

Vladimiros nodded as I mentioned Stalin and Mao. I suspected that in his youthful years he had had a different opinion of them. "The sociologist Peter Berger many years ago," I went on, "in his book *Pyramids of Sacrifice*, pointed out this sociological fact that, on balance, secular ideologies have been much more destructive than religious ideologies.[4] So this is something to keep in mind when we point a finger at religion as the cause of all the problems of the world. Perhaps the world would have been much worse if religion had been eradicated from the face of the earth, as some militant atheists would like to see happen today."

I had in mind the current flurry of books by neo-atheist authors, such as the biologist Richard Dawkins and the journalist Christopher Hitchens, who consider the current malaise related to religious fundamentalism as a problem embedded in religion itself. Both of them and a few others have embarked on a crusade to free the world from religion and replace it with pure rationality and scientific thinking.[5]

"I don't deny that religion has often played a destructive role in history," I clarified. "Just keep in mind that most of the problems blamed on religion are only indirectly related to religion."

"But look at the Irish conflict between Catholics and Protestants, or the Cyprus problem between Greeks and Turks, or the fights between Buddhists and Hindus in Sri Lanka, or Jews and Palestinians in the Middle East, the wars in Iraq and Afghanistan, to mention but a few!" Vladimiros exclaimed, spreading his hands. Our conversation was energizing him.

"If we look at these conflicts more carefully, we'll see that the underlying causes have much to do with economic and political exploitation and oppression, like colonialism and neocolonialism, and only indirectly with religion. With the exception perhaps of bin Laden and Al Qaida, the disputes are not about theological differences or about spreading a particular religious ideology or belief. Yes, religion does play a role because it is a powerful force for self and group identity. People are socialized to think of themselves as members of a particular religion." I paused for a moment and then brought up an anecdote about Ireland that an anthropologist colleague, Henry Munson, had once told me. "A masked terrorist stops a pedestrian on a dark side street in Belfast during the height of hostilities between Protestants and Catholics. With pointed gun he asks him, 'Are you Catholic or Protestant?' The frightened man replies, 'Neither. I am an atheist.' Then the masked man asks again, "But are you a Catholic atheist or a Protestant atheist?' "[6]

It was heartwarming to see Vladimiros burst out laughing. "My interest," I continued, "is in the mystical core of these religions. When you look at the lives of all the major figures of the great world religions, you find a different reality. The leading lights of Christianity, for example, whether Jesus himself or Paul, or all the great saints through the ages, preached the peace of the Gospel. It is people's spiritual immaturity that leads to violent conflict. The other day I was interviewed by a local Greek Cypriot newspaper, and I pointed out what Fr. Maximos has said many times before, that had the Greek Cypriots been true Christians and had they implemented the teachings of Christ, we wouldn't be having any problems with the Turks."

"That's for certain," Vladimiros murmured in agreement.

"You know," I continued, "the problem that you have mentioned related to religion is the problem of people's spiritual maturity. I know that you're not a believer, but the majority of people around the world are. Yet as Fr. Maximos told me once, they aren't all of the same spiritual age. There are those, he claimed, who view God as a fearful overlord who can toss them into Hell if they misbehave. People who carry in their minds such infantile notions are the 'slaves of God.' Left to themselves and without fearing Hell, they would do horrendous acts. For this type of people, a fear of God is needed to keep from committing evil acts and harming fellow human beings. You don't kill, you don't steal, you don't commit adultery because of the fear of eternal damnation. These were the people that Voltaire had in mind when he whispered at the dinner table to his literary guests not to talk loudly about their atheistic beliefs because if the servants overheard that there was no God, they would cut everybody's throats!

"The second type of people are the 'employees of God,'" I went on. "Such people do good because they expect to be rewarded by God. They work to earn their place in Paradise. They work for God, they do good deeds, and at the end of the day they expect their divine paycheck. The majority of people are religious in this sense. Let us say they are the religious middle class. Once again, this attitude toward God is not the most mature and authentic.

"The third type, according to the Christian elders, are the 'lovers of God.' These are people who have come to know the true nature of God in His total and unconditional love for all people and all creation. They view all human beings as icons of God, and they realize that the aim of life is to become one with God. These are the most spiritually mature believers. They have come to know God experientially.

"So when we talk about religion, it is prudent to keep in mind these distinctions. You can find lovers of God in all religions, just as you can find slaves and employees. In my opinion, anyone who cares to study the world's religions without prejudice and bias will realize that Christian saints and mystics have more in common with the sages of Tibet and India than with Christian fundamentalists."

"I am curious," Vladimiros said after pondering my words, "about the other factors that made you a believer, like what you called the 'emerging paradigm' in science. What do you have in mind?"

"I mean that an increasing number of scientists are questioning the basic assumptions upon which modern science is built on. In reference to our discussion about why I believe, it seems to me these new set of assumptions support a view of the world that cannot be explained by itself."

"I don't understand."

"Let's take the new cosmological understanding of Creation itself. Since the mid-sixties, the Big Bang theory of the creation of the universe has become the accepted view among virtually all astronomers. As you know, the Big Bang theory stipulates that the universe came into being about 13.7 billion years ago, as the result of a primordial explosion. The entire 100 billion galaxies of the known universe were compressed into less than an atom, and all of a sudden there was an explosion. The dust of particles that were generated created this stupendous and finely tuned system of creation.

"This is the conclusion of leading thinkers today," I emphasized. "For example, Allan Sandage, one of the most influential astronomers of the twentieth century and best known for determining the age of the universe, declared that the Big Bang could only be considered a miracle.[7] And this miracle gave birth to another contemporary scientific understanding of human creation. It has been called the 'anthropic cosmological principle,' meaning that the universe evolved in a way that made the appearance of humanity possible. In other words, the universe's creation and its evolution have as their inner purpose the emergence of self-conscious beings like us. This is a spiritual understanding of Creation.

"Patrick Glynn, in fact, after diligently and systematically surveying all the modern scientific theories about creation concludes that 'in effect, the anthropic principle says that humanity is (apparently) the final cause of the universe. The most basic explanation of the universe is that it seems to be a process orchestrated to achieve the end or goal of creating human beings.'[8] Furthermore, Andrew Greeley, the celebrated professor of the sociology of religion at the University of Chicago, pointed out that 'Glynn's arguments for the existence of God, as the cause of the evolution of the universe leading to the creation of humanity, put the burden of disproof on those intellectuals who think that the question has long since been settled.' That is, that God is dead.

"Do you see what is happening?" I went on. "Modern science is now offering a vision of reality that is radically different from that which was dominant during the nineteenth century and the time of Darwin, that the universe is a machine without any inner purpose."

While gazing at the sea, I remembered reading many years back another article about this topic in *The New York Times Magazine.* The author joked that during the last few centuries scientists had struggled to conquer the mountain of knowledge, only to find at the top a bunch of theologians waiting for them.

"Side by side with these developments in cosmology," I went on, "there were changes coming from scientists studying the subatomic level that is quantum physics. Again, in this mysterious microcosm, scientists discovered that their own minds are integral parts of what they are observing."

"I am not sure I follow you."

"For example, scientists discovered that a particle behaves as a particle when the observing scientist expects it to behave like a particle, and it behaves like a wave if the experimenting scientist expects it to behave like a wave. That means our own consciousness is mysteriously in communication with physical matter."

"Don't forget Masaru Emoto," Emily reminded me.

"Right. That may be another good example of the impact of our thoughts on matter," I said and explained to Vladimiros the work of the Japanese scientist who has provided evidence, controversial to be sure, that our attitudes and ways of thinking and feeling can affect the behavior of water on the subatomic level.[9] Emoto showed that when human subjects sent concentrated loving thoughts over samples of water that were then frozen, the crystals, photographed with special cameras, in the experimental samples appeared markedly different from the crystals of water in the samples that served as controls. The experimental samples showed stunningly beautiful crystallized patterns, whereas the control samples appeared dull by comparison."

"It really amazed me when I saw pictures of Emoto's experimental samples in a presentation he gave at a Montreal conference," Emily pointed out.

"This seems to provide support to the Orthodox ritual of using water for sanctification, particularly during Epiphany," I added as I noticed a faint skeptical smile on Vladimiros's face.

"Emoto's experiments may offer scientific support to such practices," I continued and went on to say that the Orthodox claim that sanctified water is qualitatively different from ordinary water and that it has therapeutic qualities may be based more on fact than on fiction.

"So what do you mean by all this?" Vladimiros wondered.

"It means that on this subtle, subatomic level, our thoughts may affect the way matter behaves. It means that there is an ongoing and unconscious interaction between our thoughts and feelings and the material universe, which we assumed was simply dead matter. Let me put it simply: the universe seems to be permeated with spiritual energy. It does not seem to be a dead machine, as assumed during the nineteenth century, which led philosophers to conclude that 'God is dead.' Richard Tarnas, a leading contemporary philosopher and historian, concluded after a thirty-year exploration that evidence indicates our universe is, in his words, 'informed by a powerful, creative intelligence, and an ordering principle of truly astonishing power, complexity, and beauty.'[10]

"So these changes take place on both the macro and the micro level. We live in exciting times. Scientists are discovering what the ancient philosophers and all the great mystics have claimed, that what is above is also below. Perhaps this is why in the Lord's Prayer we say 'on earth as it is in heaven.' According to some observers, we live at a time that may lead us to witness a new enlightenment, which would dwarf the Western Enlightenment of the seventeenth and eighteenth centuries. It may be the time when the best of science and the best of religion will come together, offering us a radically new vision of reality and,

I should add, a more optimistic and holistic vision. We wouldn't be able to feel depressed or meaningless because our consciousness would be in harmony with the very fabric of the universe, that is, filled with meaning."

"You mean God," Vladimiros clarified.

"Yes. And since I believe like St. Paul that God is the Reality within which 'we live, and move, and have our being' [Acts 17:28], then we as icons of God, as parts of God, are also immortal beings. Death appears to be an illusion. Its sting lacks the power that it has when one believes that this limited world we live in is all there is."

"I wish I could believe in what you're saying," Vladimiros said and shook his head. I was encouraged by his response and continued.

"You see, Vladimire, according to all the spiritual traditions, we are gods suffering from self-inflicted amnesia."

"Gods suffering from self-inflicted amnesia!"

I pointed out that Plato believed that knowledge is in reality *anamnesis*, or bringing forth from the pool of our very being things we already know. "Yes. The aim of our lives is to awaken to our true nature and realize that we have God inside us," I went on. "When that moment comes, we will know who we are, what the true meaning of our existence is, and who God is."

I was certain that such ideas were new to Vladimiros. He did not dismiss what I was saying, as others who are ideologically committed to an atheistic worldview would have done. My feeling was that he had simply been insulated from exposure to such ideas, as most modern intellectuals are.

"What about death?" Vladimiros asked as we decided to take a barefoot stroll along the beach. "What evidence can we possibly have that death is an illusion, as you put it? Just believing in such a notion is not good enough for me."

"You're right. We can never be certain about these realities until we have experienced them ourselves."

"Obviously nobody died and came back to tell us about how things are on the other side," Emily noted.

"Obviously not. However, we can draw certain tentative conclusions based on the reports of great saints and mystics as well as reports of out-of-body experiences and scientific studies related to the near-death experience."

I went on to explain briefly to Vladimiros what is meant by the near-death experience, which became a household concept in the United States when Raymond Moody published his seminal work on the subject.[11] After getting a doctorate in philosophy and then an M.D. in psychiatry, Moody was the first to venture into this controversial field. What triggered his interest were reports of people who were declared by their physicians clinically dead but who for some mysterious reason came back to life. A large number reported finding themselves outside their bodies, seeing their bodies lying dead below, then traveling through a tunnel and on the other side being welcomed by dead relatives and by a radiant being who showed them total and unconditional love. At some point they experienced panoramic reviews of their lives in minute detail and saw how their actions affected other people in both positive and negative ways. Those who had such experiences reported that they felt they went "home" and wished to stay there permanently. It was the Christ-like being who instructed them to return to their bodies because they still had work to do in this life. Most amazing, and what stunned Moody and his coworkers, were the patients who reported knowledge of episodes and events that took place during their near-death state. They knew what was happening on this side of the divide when they were already declared clinically dead. This aspect of the near-death experience cannot be explained through mainstream psychology, raising the question of the existence of consciousness outside the material body. It suggests that our minds and personalities may be independent of the brain, that our physical bodies and brains are only necessary for us to live in this world.

"What is interesting," I told Vladimiros, "is that these people universally lose their fear of death because they realize, as they claim, that there is no death. They are totally convinced about this. Furthermore, most of them have become better human beings. They claim that the major lesson they learned from the near-death experience is that we come into this world in order to learn how to love and to grow in knowledge and understanding."

"Interesting," Vladimiros murmured.

"Very much so. What we see with this development is scientific support of the ancient belief in life after death. Before the modern age we had no way, medically speaking, to 'bring back' people who had a near-death experience. Now we can verify scientifically that a person is clinically dead but also attest that the very same person is having vivid experiences during the near-death experience. The brain is out of commission, 'dead' for all practical purposes, yet the person is fully aware."

"Does this development in medicine give you confidence that there is life after death?" Vladimiros asked.

"It's an important factor that we must consider when we ponder death and human nature," I replied. "In and of itself it doesn't, of course, provide proof of life after death. I don't believe that this can be proven in any strictly scientific sense. But if you connect this evidence to all the other factors that we've examined so far, such as the teachings of the great saints and mystics of history, it provides further support. If nothing else, the near-death experience supports the idea that the mind and the brain are not one and the same thing. So what you said earlier, that you are only your five senses, is simply not true. One can exist, feel, think, have memories, and observe events happening in this world while one's body is clinically dead. It means that we are not our bodies. Some investigators today have coined the term 'nonlocality of mind.'[12] Their conclusion is that our brain is simply the instrument for the expression of our mind and personality. What I am trying to say is this: our ability to think, have memories, be aware as personalities with likes and dislikes, have human relationships, develop whatever skills and knowledge while living in this world is not absolutely dependent on a physical body. The physical body is necessary to allow us to live in this world and to develop our conscious mind and personality. But once the body is gone through death, personality continues to be. This is what I think one could rationally and tentatively conclude based on the indirect evidence we have up to this point of our human experience. In short, we continue to be beyond death. Do you see what I mean?"

"I'm trying," Vladimiros said thoughtfully. "So what do the mystics and elders that you've studied say about what happens to us after we die?" I wasn't certain whether he asked me this question from personal interest or whether he was simply curious about what others believe concerning these issues. Yet I felt that on a deeper level that question came from a genuine interest in what might happen to him once he is gone. "To be frank with you," he said, "when I hear priests talk about Hell and damnation, or about judgment day and the resurrection of the dead with the second coming of Christ and things like that, I am completely put off religion. How can any thinking person today believe in such myths?"

"I understand what you mean," I responded. "I personally

don't believe in an objective Hell that God created to punish all of us sinners. I do believe, however, in a subjective hell."

"What's the difference?"

"In my understanding, God created us for Paradise, not for eternal damnation, as is claimed by many fanatical believers threatening nonbelievers. All the major religions speak of an ultimate end to suffering and of the attainment of sheer bliss from this very life. This is what characterizes the great saints. They have already attained the paradise that is deeply buried within every human being. If we are to use terms such as hell and paradise, I would say only paradise is objectively real."

"Why can't we say the same thing about hell?"

"Because I believe that only good can come out of God. At least from the point of view of Christianity, paradise is real, awaiting every human being who overcomes his or her destructive passions and lowly desires. We ourselves, however, create our own hells, and we will stay there until we overcome our egotism. I believe this is an evolutionary process that continues beyond the grave."

Judging by his expression, Vladimiros hadn't dealt with such questions before.

"I've discussed these ideas in my earlier books. By now I have come to agree with the sages and saints who make the claim that the purification of the soul for the attainment of real paradisiacal bliss continues beyond the death of the physical body. God, being total love and compassion, surely gives ongoing opportunities for all of us sinners to enter His Kingdom. But it is not going to happen automatically. We will have to work for it and undergo real metanoia, a radical change of our thinking and feeling."

"You're assuming that we can think and feel even after we are dead!"

"That's what I've been trying to suggest to you, at least as a rational possibility, given our state of knowledge at this time. I know that this may sound strange to you."

"Yes, that's one way of putting it . . ."

"Well, let me explain. Based on my encounters with mystics from around the world and from my readings in this area, as well as from the information that we have gathered so far from the near-death experience, a consistent image emerges of the soul after death. I mean information over and beyond what traditional religion has been offering us. Now, what I am about to say is speculation based on the tentative information that I believe has been accumulated so far."

"I'm listening," Vladimiros said with interest.

"Nobody can know for certain what happens to us after death. This is the great mystery that led philosophers like Plato to declare that all of philosophy is a preparation for death. But sages from around the world speak with such conviction and power about the afterlife that I, who don't have their experiences, feel compelled to take note."

"So what did you learn?"

"They claim that nothing happens to us after death other than the fact that we no longer have physical bodies. In fact, we are liberated from the limitations of the material body. They say that the laws that govern the physical universe, such as gravity, do not restrain us in the after-death state. Our thoughts and feelings literally create our own reality on the other side. Again, based on what I have read, human beings can instantly be at a place or with someone by simply thinking of that place or that person. I have read about such notions in the work of anthropologists who have done research in other cultural traditions.[13] We do maintain, they claim, our center of self-consciousness and the capacity to think and feel and have memories just as we did while we were living in this life. Our first tendency upon passing over is to construct with our own thoughts, feelings, and desires a world similar to the one we knew on Earth. Furthermore, we try to satisfy our desires the way we used to, that is, eating, drinking, and so on, even though we do not need food or drink in order to exist in those spiritual dimensions. With time and with the help of spiritual guides and angelic beings, we will come to realize this. Furthermore, most of us will be with others whom we used to enjoy being with while in this life, that is, our friends and beloved family members. Again, spiritual guides and angels will be there to help us adjust to our new situation.

We will then begin learning from the experiences of the life we're just lived. We will learn how we helped and how we hurt others. In a sense, hell is a form of self-punishment. God does not punish us. Rather, we punish ourselves with the hellish conditions we have created with our thoughts and actions in this life. In short, we will enter into a hell or a paradise that we have already created on this side of life. Athonite holy men, I was told, enter paradise while they are still living in this world. Likewise, criminal characters will enter a hell that they themselves have constructed and are already in. So at every moment that passes we are at work weaving our future state beyond the grave!"

"In other words," added Emily, who was familiar with this material, "people create their relative hells and relative paradises."

"That may be the case. Just like here, somebody's hell may be somebody else's paradise. If you were, for example, a gambler in this life, you will feel you are in paradise if you find yourself with your buddies in a smoky basement playing poker! For a spiritually developed human being, however, such an environment may be a veritable hell. It is said that some people who have just died will assume that they are still alive. It may take them some time before they realize that they are dead. And by the way," I added with a humorous intonation, "they also say that an atheist will continue arguing that there is no God and no life beyond death."

"So do you yourself feel certain that this is what happens when we die?" Vladimiros asked.

"Of course I'm not certain. I'm simply telling you what I have read in reports of other investigators. We can never know until we get there." We walked in silence along the beach while the sun disappeared behind the cliffs in a soothing array of reddish hues. We then cleaned our feet and got into the car for the return trip.

"I don't think it's possible for us to know what really happens to us after death, other than to have faith that all will be well, as the entire process is governed by an all-knowing and all-loving God, whom, as we progress spiritually, we will come to know and unite with," I said as we traveled back to Limassol. "According to the elders of Mt. Athos, great saints are already there, and in reality 'they don't die when they die.'"

"You forgot to mention what mystics say in regard to hateful people or to those who have committed serious crimes," Emily interjected.

"They claim that those who have done terrible things enter states of hell where they are confronted with the consequences of their actions. These hells are forms of rehabilitation centers or spiritual hospitals. It is in these spaces where human beings will presumably have further chances to continue their journey of spiritual advance, assuming that they undergo real remorse and *metanoia*. Otherwise they will continue to be tormented eternally in their hells with the hateful feelings they carry in their hearts. So this is hell. But it is not something that God created. Sages say that we are creating our own hell every moment by our thoughts, feelings, and actions. And sooner or later, in either this life or the one beyond, we will have to face the consequences of what we do. It is a basic axiom of spiritual life that the universe is governed by laws, on the physical as well as on the spiritual level. In an ultimate sense, Creation is governed by a totally just and loving God, and we will reap what we have sown. How that is done, only God knows."

With some trepidation, I shared with Vladimiros an experience related to the spirit world that both Emily and I had just had while attending the annual conference of the International Institute of Integral Human Sciences in Montreal.

This conference was founded by Drs. John and Marilyn Rossner. John has been a professor (now emeritus) of comparative religion at Concordia University. His wife, Marilyn, was also a professor (also emeritus) of child psychology and a world-renown "intuitive." They decided thirty-three years ago to start this organization for the promotion of a deeper understanding of reality by bringing together scientists who work at the frontiers of knowledge, scholars in a diversity of religious traditions, and various spiritual practitioners. Because of my work, I was invited to participate in their conferences, and so for the last eight years, during which Emily and I have become close friends with the Rossners, we've had the privilege of being exposed to some of the most amazing research taking place around the world, research that I believe may pave the way for an eventual reconciliation between religion and science, as well as the recognition by science that the world of physical matter is not the only world there is and that, in fact, the physical universe is the external manifestation of deep spiritual realities. It was during that conference that we had the pleasure of meeting and dining several times with Dr. Raymond Moody, the discoverer of the near-death experience.

At the last meeting of the IIIHS, I presided over the presentation of Dr. Mark Macy, an electronics and computer scientist who, along with twelve international colleagues, in 1995 founded in England a network for instrumental trans-communication (ITC). Their attempt was to create a communication bridge between Heaven and Earth or, more precisely, as they put it in their website, "between our world and the finer worlds of spirit, using technology as the medium."[14]

"In its most basic definition," Macy said in an interview, "ITC . . . is the use of TVs, radios, telephones, computers, and other technical devices to get information directly from the worlds of spirit in the form of voices, images, and text. . . . ITC is a marriage of technology and the human mind, and it also involves a close rapport with a spirit group, or team of invisible collaborators."

According to reviewers of his books, Macy's work provides some of the first serious scientific evidence that life may continue after the death of the physical body.[15]

"I understand," I told Vladimiros, "that such claims are really outlandish."

"I'm glad to hear that!" Vladimiros quipped.

"On the other hand, we found it rewarding to suspend judgment and see what this scientist had to say. This has always been my approach when investigating these matters. What we observed in Dr. Macy's presentation was intriguing, to put it mildly. He showed pictures, presumably transmitted from the spirit world, depicting life there in extraordinary detail. Macy himself claimed that he had received one particular phone call, which he taped, from a departed colleague named Konstantin Raudive, which lasted nearly fifteen minutes. We were able to hear the tape and the amazing 'information' about the world beyond that his friend presumably transmitted."

I told Vladimiros that Macy was an atheist before. God and afterlife had seemed like wishful thinking to him. But that all changed in 1988, when he was diagnosed with colon cancer. With death staring him in the face, he suddenly had to know what really happens to human beings after they die. He said he could not take it on faith alone. Being a scientist, he needed solid evidence to convince him of something beyond his rational understanding. It was in 1991 that he met a group of researchers in Europe who claimed to be in touch with spirits through technical devices. That encounter changed his life and career forever.

I told Vladimiros that one can dismiss such claims as wishful thinking and charlatanism. But given my experiences with mystics and researchers in these matters, I could not draw such an easy conclusion. Mark Macy's extraordinary presentations were combined with his demeanor, a blend of humility and confidence in his discoveries.

I further mentioned that while Macy was presenting his work I remembered a story I had heard about the late Elder Porphyrios, a monk from Mt. Athos who became a legend as a result of miraculous happenings attributed to him. He died after serving for decades as a priest in a church at Omonoia Square in downtown Athens. One of Elder Porphyrios's disciples in Australia, unaware that the elder had passed away, called him up a month after his death. According to the story, Elder Porphyrios replied on the phone, telling the fellow not to call him again because he was no longer in this life but in Heaven! Mark Macy would say that that was a case of instrumental trans-communication. Modern electronic and computer communication, he argued, makes such improbable phenomena possible. I was further intrigued by what Macy had to say about the spiritual world. I summarized this description for Vladimiros:

"It's been my experience that the spirit worlds are all super-imposed over each other and over our own physical world, separated by vibration, not by distance or space. So essentially the spirit worlds are everywhere, and they range in nature from very subtle and divine worlds beyond form and structure (the realm of angels or ethereal beings) to rather dense and dark worlds (the realm of ghosts and lost souls). Between those two realms are many paradise worlds where most people go after they die to get settled into a wonderful existence free from pain and suffering. As humans and as spiritual researchers, we draw into our lives and into our work spirits from the different realms who resonate with our disposition, attitudes, and feelings."[16]

"Do you really believe in all this?" Vladimiros asked.

"Well, what I find in Macy's work and in the work of other researchers like him is fascinating. It challenges our materialist notions about the nature of reality and who we are. What he says about the spirit world corresponds to the claims that many mystics have made about the world beyond. So perhaps they are onto something. Perhaps their work can give us a fuller under-standing of life and death," I added as we entered Limassol.

Vladimiros remained pensive. When we reached his house, he turned toward me. "Tell me something. What are your views on euthanasia? Why should you continue living if you feel that there is nothing to look forward to except old age, misery, loss of loved ones, loss of your mind and senses? Why not take your own life and get it over with? Don't get me wrong. I have noth-ing of the sort in mind, but such thoughts do cross the minds of many people my age that I've known."

"Yes, I'm aware of this problem," I said. "Older people are disproportionately likely to die by suicide in America, particularly when they lose beloved family members, spouses, friends. In fact, some call suicide an epidemic among the elderly. For an answer I can only resort to the spiritual traditions of humanity, not only of Christianity but of all religions. They universally condemn suicide. As far as Christian spirituality, which I'm most familiar with, is concerned, we come into this world to learn spiritual lessons and grow in love, in the direction of uniting with God. Fr. Maximos never tires of advising that everything that comes our way must be exploited spiritually, be it success or tragedy. Furthermore, killing oneself is taking human life, a mortal sin according to Christianity. In other words, your body is not yours to dispose of at will. It is a gift from God so that you can experience this physical universe. Killing yourself is in a sense murder. Furthermore, mystics claim that those who kill themselves will go nowhere. They cannot escape from the problems that brought them to the point of suicide. The conditions that they were unable to cope with will come back to haunt them in the life after death. In short, suicide is like flunking life. It is preventing oneself from growing spiritually. Incidentally, this is also the consensus of those who go through the near-death experience. They claim that this is what they have learned from that experience.

"I believe those who advocate euthanasia," I went on, "are ignorant of spiritual laws and base their claims on totally secular foundations. For them there is neither spirit nor God in the equation. Therefore, killing yourself is your 'inalienable right'!"

Vladimiros's question would later remind me of an extract I'd saved in my files on the work of the celebrated psychiatrist Carl Jung, who two years before his death, at age eighty-four, in an interview claimed: "Among all my patients in the second half of life . . . every one of them fell ill because he had lost what the living religions of every age have given their followers, and none of them has been really healed who did not regain his religious outlook." In a letter to a prominent Chicago social worker who inquired about the meaning of that statement, Jung explained that the source of our current cultural and collective malaise was the collapse of a spiritual underpinning that has tradition- ally provided direction and purpose to people's lives. That is why we live in what Jung referred to as "crazy times."[17]

I don't know how much we helped our friend that day at Kourion to overcome his pessimism about his old age and the inescapable reality of our mortality. I hoped that the discussion had at least exposed him to an alternative worldview. We were happy, however, to get his phone call a couple of days later an- nouncing that Elena's tests for cancer came out negative. To play it safe, the doctors suggested further examinations and vigilance. We promised Vladimiros that we would ask Fr. Maximos and our friends at the Panagia monastery to pray for their health. I was pleased to hear him say a warm "Thank you!"

SEVEN

BEYOND DEATH

Father Maximos returned to Cyprus from Greece three days after our excursion to Kourion with Vladimiros. The day of his arrival I called and made an appointment to see him at eleven the following morning. I looked forward to reconnecting with him and discussing further some of the ideas on mortality that were the focus of conversation with our aging friend. At nine the next morning, my friend Stephanos called and surprised me with the news that Fr. Maximos was speaking live on the radio. Listeners were free to call in and ask questions related to the spiritual life. I picked up my mini transistor radio and began walking toward Fr. Maximos's office and residence at the bishopric, thirty-five minutes from our apartment and next to the radio station. I aimed to reach his office before Fr. Maximos finished with the radio interview.

I crossed the Zoological Garden, the central park of Limassol, with its carefully trimmed and manicured flora, passed a newly erected statue of Pushkin, a sign of the city's increasing Russian presence, and reached the road that ran along the seashore on the other side of the park. I headed west toward the town center. On my left was the beach, with hundreds of sunbathing tourists, followed by a one-mile promenade with tall palm trees. On my right was the commercial part of Limassol, with its narrow streets, archaic buildings, ancient fortress, and many cafés, taverns, and souvenir shops. Wearing my hat and sunglasses for protection against the blinding Mediterranean sun, I walked holding the mini transistor close to my ear and listening to the broadcast.

One of the callers was a tearful woman whose father had just died. She was terrified by the prospect that her father might already be a permanent resident of Hell. During his life, she said, he'd never cared for the Church, never attended services, and never went to confession or took communion. "My father," sobbed the woman, "died in my arms. He was a good man."

Father Maximos, in his usual soothing way, replied: "God is not unjust. God is good, and you should have no concerns about the fate of your father's soul. God is loving and compassionate and does not wish anyone to be lost in Hell. Be certain of this!"

I could hear an audible sigh of relief from the poor woman. Having come to know Fr. Maximos over the years, I did not expect him to say anything different. He frequently lamented the distorted view that many Christians have of God, as a kind of angry tyrant who takes pleasure in tossing sinners into the burning fires of eternal damnation. I thought of my late father-in-law. A much-loved retired schoolmaster, he was known for his dry sense of humor. Right before his death, at age eighty-nine, he was visited by the local priest to administer the last rites. Before offering him holy communion, the priest asked whether he wished to confess his sins to God. My father-in-law waved his hand, signaling a refusal, and said, "Father, I didn't know I had any quarrels with the Almighty." The priest then offered him communion without confession.

When I reached the office, I was pleased to find there my close friend Lavros, an advisor to Fr. Maximos on environmental issues. Waiting for Fr. Maximos to finish with his radio interview, Lavros and I caught up with personal news.

In a few minutes Fr. Maximos joined us. He looked rested in
spite of his heavy schedule. I mentioned that the theme he had
discussed on the radio coincided with the discussions Emily
and I had had with Vladimiros. Fr. Maximos listened with interest to the points I'd raised to help our friend overcome his fear
of old age. There was a look of understanding on his face, but
he didn't comment on our dialogue. I was uncertain, therefore,
whether Fr. Maximos agreed with my points, particularly in
reference to life beyond the grave.

Any possible clarifications on the matter were put aside as Fr.
Isaac, one of Fr. Maximos's close associates, came into the office
with urgent business. Before Lavros and I left, we made plans
with Fr. Maximos to meet soon and continue our conversation.
I also reminded Fr. Maximos that I needed to hear his views on
love, the last fruit of the Spirit, which we were not able to complete in Boston almost two years earlier. In fact, I had reminded
him of that unfinished conversation on several occasions. I
joked that my book would be incomplete if we did not finish
that dialogue. He nodded with a smile and reassured me that
the Holy Spirit would create the conditions to complete that discussion.

"Well," I said as Lavros and I stood up, "in the final analysis,
the only certainty about our world is that we will die and that
we will never know when."

A few seconds passed without a response from Fr. Maximos.
Then he said softly: "The first statement is true but not the second."

"What do you mean?" I asked with curiosity.

"I have known elders on Mt. Athos who knew exactly the
day and time of their death."

I sat back down. Lavros did likewise, as did Fr. Isaac. Fr. Maximos went on to clarify his cryptic statement. "Let me give you as an example Fr. Joachim, a Romanian elder I knew while I was a monk on Mt. Athos. Fr. Isaac knows about him too," he said.

"One day Fr. Joachim announced to everybody in the monastery that the Holy Virgin had appeared to him in a vision and announced that she would come to take him to Heaven at nine in the morning on Monday. Fr. Joachim looked very happy saying that; he believed he was going to be escorted to Heaven by no less than the Mother of God. But we assumed he was joking. He had a reputation as a humorous monk, and there was no apparent problem with his health. Certainly there was no indication that his time was up.

"If I recall well, he made that announcement on Tuesday after breakfast," Fr. Maximos continued. "On Thursday morning we noticed that he wasn't in church. Naturally, we were very concerned. Fr. Joachim never missed a morning service. We hurried up to his cell and knocked at the door. There was no answer. We knocked again. Nothing. We tried to open the door, but it was locked. We feared that either he was too sickly to respond or, worse, he was already dead. We decided, therefore, to break in. When we finally managed to enter, we found him sitting on the floor, surrounded by lit candles. He was praying in front of a small altar with icons of the Holy Virgin and of Christ. He calmly turned toward us and reprimanded us: 'Didn't I tell you Monday? I said Monday, not Thursday! Everybody out!'

"Monday morning," Fr. Maximos continued, "Elder Joachim died at exactly the hour he said he was going to die. The Holy Virgin took him to Heaven as she promised."

"Some other time, I will tell you the story of how Maria, my wife, died," Lavros said to me. "Fr. Maximos knows the details, so I won't repeat it now. She too knew the exact day of her death from her patron saint in a vision."

This wasn't the first time I had heard of such phenomena. But it was the first time I had heard of cases within Christianity. I had come across such stories in my study of other spiritual traditions. It is said, for instance, that great Tibetan lamas would inform their disciples of the exact date and time of their death. Shortly before the prophesied time, these lamas would enter into a state of deep meditation and remain there until they expired. It is understood that these lamas are not intentionally taking their own lives. In Buddhism as in Christianity, suicide is condemned. They simply knew inwardly when they were about to leave this world, and, like Fr. Joachim, they prepared themselves. Such stories from different spiritual traditions provided, I thought, validation of what Fr. Maximos claimed was true of elders like Fr. Joachim: all human beings die, but it may not be true that no human beings know when they will die. Perhaps the most spiritually advanced among us often do know.

"Elder Joachim," Fr. Maximos added, "had an *osiakos thanatos*."

"What does it mean?"

"A beatific death, a spiritually ideal and desirable death. This is what we say on Mt. Athos when one has a good death."

"A good death! How different," I marveled, "is the Athonite way of thinking about death from the way we ordinary folks approach it. The notion of an *osiakos thanatos* sounds like an oxymoron to ordinary people like us."

Lavros laughed. "This conversation reminds me of what happened to me once at Vatopedi [Athonite monastery]. I was on a pilgrimage there when a funeral of an elderly monk took place. After the burial we assembled at the *archondariki* [reception hall], where, as it is the custom, we were treated to pastries and tea. It was more like a party. Everybody was cheerful. A young and smiling monk approached me and, raising his teacup, said, 'And to yours, Mr. Lavro! May you also have an *osiakos thanatos*, a happy ending!' I was distraught. My face dropped, and I murmured, 'Bite your tongue, Father!' "

"Now that you mention it," Fr. Maximos said as we laughed, "I had a similar experience as a young monk during a funeral in Thessaloniki. I was on a special errand that day outside Mt. Athos and, having some free time, I assisted the priest of the church that I often attended when I spent time in the city. After finishing with the burial service, everybody went to the home of the deceased. Young and inexperienced, I shocked everybody by going around and, instead of offering my deepest condolences, wished them all an *osiakos thanatos*. People looked at me with horror and nervously made the sign of the cross. Others knocked on the nearest wood they could find. I didn't realize what was happening until the priest approached me and whispered in my ear, 'Father, we don't say such things here. You're scaring the poor people!' How could I know that people are so mortified to chat about death?" Fr. Maximos asked with a humorous shrug.

The great elders' total indifference to death came home to me several years back when I was listening to a Greek radio interview with the surgeon who operated on Elder Paisios. The revered elder was brought to Athens from Mt. Athos after his cancer reached an advanced state. It was a matter of hours before his death. What stunned the surgeon was the total tranquillity of the elder despite the excruciating physical pain. Elder Paisios was giving courage to those who visited his deathbed. "Do not mourn me," he told them with his characteristic lively humor, which he never lost. "I have never felt better. After all, I have prepared for this moment all my life, and I look forward to soon being greeted by Christ."

Elder Paisios's fearlessness as he confronted his imminent

death was similar to that of other Christian saints but also to that of great non-Christian souls, like Socrates and the Buddha. I remember how impressed I was as a teenager with the heroic way Socrates spoke about his death sentence in his *Apology*. Then in *Crito*, after he drank the poisonous hemlock, Socrates spent his remaining moments consoling his weeping disciples. Likewise Gautama Buddha, while dying from dysentery after he was unwittingly fed spoiled food, was more concerned with the welfare of others, particularly the person who had accidentally poisoned him, than with his own impending death.

As Huston Smith recounts, "In the midst of his pain, it occurred to him that Cunda [the disciple who had caused his death] might feel responsible for his death. His last request, therefore, was that Cunda be informed that of all the meals he had eaten during his long life, only two stood out as having blessed him exceptionally. One was the meal whose strength had enabled him to reach enlightenment under the Bo Tree, and the other the one that was opening to him the final gates to *nirvana*."[1]

Such examples of equanimity in the face of imminent death go contrary to the way ordinary people like us confront our final exit. In fact, physicians concerned with the emotional state of their terminally ill patients often avoid revealing to them the truth of their situation, and many people die without knowing they are dying.

However, as I had explained to Vladimiros, ordinary people who have had near-death experiences also overcome the fear of death. I remember attending a conference during the inaugural meeting in 1993 of the Office of Alternative Medicine at the National Institutes of Health in Washington, D.C. In addition to conventional doctors and researchers, there were practitioners of alternative therapies as well as people who'd had unusual experiences that could not be explained in conventional ways.

Dannion Brinkley, a collaborator and one of the subjects of Raymond Moody's studies, who'd had two near-death episodes, was telling the audience of about a hundred specialists that after tasting "the other side," not only did he lose any fear of death, but also he could not wait until he was really dead![2] The persuasive conviction with which he spoke left little doubt in our minds that what he was describing to us was a profound mystical experience and not a theatrical performance. "If it were up to me," he said, "I would be there in a minute. . . . I came back to my body kicking and screaming." And "I will exchange ten lives on this side with ten minutes of being there." Of course, skeptics would say that the body may release some type of wonder chemical that makes us feel euphoric before we die and that when a person is resuscitated that chemical somehow shuts off. Perhaps! But people like Raymond Moody, who has studied the phenomenon in all its complexity, do not reduce it to chemistry but consider it an ontologically real happening. And those like Dannion Brinkley who have had such experiences universally reject the idea that they were nothing but delusions caused by chemical changes in their brains.

The attitude toward death of the great saints and sages is, as I pointed out, radically different from how ordinary people as a rule cope with news of their approaching death. It was Elisabeth Kübler-Ross who, during the latter part of the twentieth century, pioneered the study of the death process, a taboo subject until then. She studied the manner in which ordinary people react to learning from their doctors that their illness is terminal. She identified five distinct stages that most of us (not including those who die from accidents), who neither are great sages nor have ever experienced a near-death experience, go through in confronting the news about their approaching death. The first response is typically *denial*. Ordinary people cannot accept that

they will die. The second stage is *anger*. People see their coming
death as a monumental injustice and, if they are believers, grow
furious at God and the world. The third stage is *negotiation*, in
which the person hopes to avoid death by bargaining with God.
The fourth stage is *resignation*, which often leads to depression.
Only a few individuals may reach stage five, which is *acceptance*.
At this stage, the person is no longer paralyzed by fear and anxiety but tries to make the best of his or her remaining days or
hours.[3]

I assume, based on Kübler-Ross's categories, that spiritually
advanced souls find themselves at stage five without having to
go through the other four stages. Or judging from their wel-
coming of their imminent deaths, perhaps they form a stage all
by themselves. Such persons act as archetypal examples of how
to experience an *osiakos thanatos*, a blessed death without fear,
without anxiety, and without despair. I don't know of anyone,
other than a few saints and great sages that I've read about, who
could be identified with an *osiakos thanatos*.

One of the personal questions that Vladimiros asked me during our excursion to Kourion was whether I was afraid of death.
I replied, "Very much so. I am an ordinary mortal." However, I
added that I am not as afraid as I used to be. My change of attitude came as a result of regaining my faith and of being exposed
to the vast literature on death and dying, including the hearten-
ing reports of mystics and scientists who have studied the subject extensively.[4]

What all people who overcame their fear of death had in
common was an unshakable and deep conviction that there is
more to life than the present lifetime. And that conviction was
apparently based on direct personal experience of transcendent
realities.

A few days after our "death talk" with Fr. Maximos, I gave a presentation in Limassol about my work, as my books had just been published in Greek. During the question and answer period I asked my friend Lavros, who was sitting in front with Emily, to relate his own experiences on the Holy Mountain. "Share whatever you want to share," I said without having given him warning that I was going to call on him. It was a spontaneous invitation. Without hesitation he stood up and, facing the audience, related to them the story about the funeral of the elderly monk he had attended. He then explained what Mt. Athos meant to him personally.

"The monks of Mt. Athos," he said, "managed to liberate themselves from the most morbid of fears which all human beings face, the fear of death. Their example and ways of dealing with this fundamental human problem give me great comfort and hope as I approach my eighties."

That night, I sat with Emily on the balcony of our apartment to enjoy the sea breeze and review the points I had raised with Vladimiros and Fr. Maximos.

These concerns, alas, were not academic for us. A string of losses of relatives and friends in recent years kept us preoccupied with issues of life and death. The raw memory of Akis, Emily's brother, who had died the year before at the Nicosia hippodrome when a spooked horse struck him, was still hovering over us. Regardless of how much we can philosophize about death and the afterlife, the loss of a beloved person, particularly when it is unexpected, is deeply unsettling. Fr. Maximos himself broke into uncontrollable tears when Fr. Arsenios, one of his closest friends and associates, who had succeeded him as abbot at the Panagia monastery in Cyprus, died in a helicopter accident on Mt. Athos, of all places.

Had it not been for the spiritual work that we had been doing over the years and our association with Fr. Maximos, the pain of losing her brother would have been, as Emily said on several occasions, ten times worse for her. Thirteen years her senior, Akis was not only a deeply beloved brother but also a second father to her while she was growing up.

After our evening conversation, Emily read a book on permaculture, which had preoccupied her for several years now, while I turned to my reading of Philip Sherrard's seminal work *Christianity: Lineaments of a Sacred Tradition.* I was fascinated with its content, a novel approach to Eastern Orthodox theology that I felt could appeal to any modern intellectual, regardless of his or her beliefs or religious orientation.

Sherrard's life was as unusual as his theological exposition. A lay theologian, he was a convert to Orthodoxy from Anglicanism. His conversion was the result of a long flirtation with contemporary Greece: its language, history, culture, and religion. It began when he served there as a young British officer during the Second World War. A prolific author, Sherrard also translated into English many of the leading contemporary writers and poets of Greece. Most important, along with the Oxford scholar and Greek Orthodox Bishop Kallistos Ware, also a convert from Anglicanism, he translated the monumental *Philokalia,*[5] perhaps as important to the spiritual life of Eastern Orthodoxy as the Bible. Both of these converts have played central roles in making Eastern Christianity known to the West. A regular pilgrim to Mt. Athos, Sherrard spent the latter part of his life on the island of Euboea, not far from Athens, and served as a lay elder to people who sought him out for spiritual counseling.

I felt great attraction to his work because of the breadth of his knowledge and the openness of his vision. Although deeply embedded in Eastern Orthodoxy, he was receptive to the wisdom traditions of other civilizations, thus avoiding the great temptation of many devoutly religious intellectuals and theologians to view the world from an exclusivist vantage point. Furthermore, being a product of the Western Enlightenment while at the same time enmeshed in the mystical tradition of Eastern Ortho-doxy, he, like Kallistos Ware, served as a bridge between the best of the Christian East and the best of the secular West.

Interrupting Emily's reading, I remarked that it was amazing how Sherrard had drawn an outline of the life beyond that was both compelling and consistent with other diverse sources. "Sherrard claims that the soul doesn't remain bodiless after the death of the material body," I continued as Emily took off her glasses. "In fact he wrote that after death the soul possesses a perfectly good body. It still possesses an organized structure through which the soul can act, think, see, hear, and feel."[6]

"That reminds me of views on this subject from other sources, particularly what the folks in Montreal have been say-ing," Emily noted.

"True. But what's fascinating about Sherrard is that such no-tions are proposed by a celebrated Eastern Orthodox theologian. More traditional theologians may have difficulties with such bold statements. Here is more," I said, encouraged by Emily's response.

"At our physical death [there are] little changes for us. We still inhabit, or imagine we inhabit, the same world that we inhabit before our physical death. For the world we inhabit before our physical death is constituted . . . by . . . mental images to which our soul is attached; and this whole psychic complex we carry over with us into the after-death state. And the images that compose it have just as much power over us then as they do now. In fact in some ways they have more power over us then than they do now, because now . . . we can through an act of will prevent some of them from developing. We repress them, whereas then they are free to grow in accordance with their own inner logic."[7]

"Fascinating!" Emily exclaimed.

I continued reading: " 'In our post-mortal state our habits continue, though the means we have for satisfying them are now different. They continue because we are still in the thrall of those images, or apparitions, or fantasies, which fill our soul after our physical death as they filled it prior to this death and which are the progeny of our unpurified ego and our ego-consciousness—images or their corresponding thoughts that are entirely real for us and from which it may not be very easy for us to escape.' "

"Sherrard must have also been influenced by his reading of comparative religious traditions," Emily noted.

"I think it's very clear. One of the things I like about him is that instead of demonizing everything about other religious traditions, as some fundamentalist theologians do, Sherrard has the courage to identify common ground with them. Here's what he says further:

"Hence the importance of our life on earth, since it is in our life we set these sequences or these streams of consciousness in motion. How we are in our immediate post-mortal state, and which direction our life takes then, will depend on what direction we have given it here. The judgment we have in this phase is, in this respect, a self-judgment. . . . In this sense it is true that we make our own hell and our own heaven. If at the hour of our physical death we are still caught up in the world of lies and falsities and evil—still enslaved to that bundle of illusions and deceits which St. Paul describes as 'the body of this death' (Rom. 7:24)—we are in hell. To the degree to which we have freed ourselves, or resurrected ourselves, from the body of this death we receive the blessings of heaven.[8]

"On the other hand," I went on, "Sherrard points out that if we don't overcome our current illusions, we will continue to carry them beyond the grave. 'Those who have died to their false selves during this present life, and who have already experienced their inner rebirth—the uncovering of their higher selves—do not see death and do not die: they are resurrected to the life of eternity, that life in which the here and now of their earthly life has already become their nourishment and their center.' "[9]

"What if in our after-death state we still identify with our lower passions?" Emily interjected. "What does Sherrard say about this? Can we ever hope to escape from this condition?"

"He does address this issue at the end of the chapter 'Death and Dying: A Christian Approach.' He claims that, assuming that in the present life we started liberating ourselves from our illusions and bondage to our false self, we will have opportunities beyond the death of the physical body to continue our spiritual ascent toward full liberation. We will be in a position to actualize our spiritual potentialities. This is what I believe too. Here is what he says further:

> "Provided we do not suffer a relapse, we can continue to actualize these potentialities, can continue to free ourselves from ignorance and self-love in our post-mortal state. It may well be that after our physical death we are in need of further purification, further refining, even though we have died in a state of repentance. But God can never cease from pouring out His grace and we can never cease, on whichever side of physical death we may be, from possessing the capacity to receive it. As

for the eternity of hell, or for whether we can be in the state of hell for all eternity: to be condemned to be in such a state for all eternity must presuppose either that God's grace can never reach it, or that when in hell, although we possess the capacity to receive such grace, we have totally lost the capacity to exercise it. Both these presuppositions represent the worst kind of illusion and absurdity. Also, when we speak of eternity, we are not speaking of a state to which we can apply our categories of time. Hence we are not in a position to say that eternity can last even for a single second."[10]

Emily shook her head. "The man is fearless."

"And sensible," I added as I've always opposed the notion of eternal damnation, which I consider a monstrous doctrine that poisoned the lives of believers for hundreds of years.

"Okay. Enough of death talk," Emily said, standing up. "Time to play some backgammon."

She brought the *tavli*, the backgammon set, to the balcony, and we began tossing the die and slamming the tokens about with a fair bit of taunting. It was part of our relaxation during summer evenings in Cyprus, when we could momentarily leave aside issues of life and death for more trivial but enjoyable matters of victory and loss.

EIGHT

PILGRIMAGE

The following year, we were back in Cyprus to continue my exploration of the mystical tradition of Eastern Christianity. This time we were able to stay for several months thanks to a sabbatical leave from my university. Freed from teaching responsibilities, I planned to complete this book. Emily was looking forward to continuing her project at Agia Skepi (Sacred Canopy), the drug rehabilitation center in Cyprus initiated several years back by Fr. Maximos. For the past two summers Emily, along with Charles and Julia Yelton, a pioneering permaculturist couple from Australia, had worked as a volunteer to set up an edible permaculture forest adjacent to the detox center.[1] Their objective was to create a garden that could serve the therapeutic aims of Agia Skepi. Furthermore, they hoped the garden would become a model for spreading the principles of this new form of sustainable agriculture in Cyprus. They enjoyed the wholehearted support of many committed environmentalists, including our friend Lavros.

We arrived in Cyprus at the end of February 2009, at the peak of spring. Unlike the previous year, there had been rain, and the countryside had finally greened and wildflowers bloomed. I had several opportunities to experience the countryside while accompanying Fr. Maximos on various errands to monasteries under his supervision. Spiritual centers, like the Panagia monastery, Mesa Potamos, and the women's monastery of St. Heracledios, were located either in mountain forests or far from urban areas, surrounded by lush gardens and orchards.

This latest visit to Cyprus, however, not only gave me access to Fr. Maximos but also afforded me the opportunity to visit other regional centers of Eastern Christianity, such as the monasteries of Mt. Athos and the ancient monastery of St. Catherine in the Sinai. My friend Antonis played a key role in my continued exposure to Mt. Athos.

For almost twenty years, Antonis was a regular pilgrim to Mt. Athos, visiting the monasteries with a small group of friends twice a year, in the spring and in the fall. This periodic withdrawal from "the World," as the monks and hermits of the Athonite peninsula call every place outside Mt. Athos, was a necessity for him. He felt emotionally and spiritually uplifted every time he returned from the Holy Mountain. As he put it, "I need these pilgrimages to recharge my batteries so that I can survive the jungle of the business world." On several occasions I joined him and his companions during their spiritual retreats. Each pilgrimage was filled with novel experiences and surprises. Mt. Athos is unlike any other place on Earth.

I did not hesitate, therefore, when Antonis urged me to join his group for yet another adventure to Athos. I too needed to recharge my batteries. Moreover, I needed to gather additional field material to deepen my understanding of the spiritual culture of the Christian East.

When we mentioned our plans to Fr. Maximos, his eyes brightened and he joked that he was jealous of us. Mt. Athos was his true *heimat*, his real homeland, which he was forced to abandon in 1993, when his elders requested that he become a sort of

a neo-apostle to "the World." Fr. Maximos offered us his blessings with suggestions on monasteries to visit and elders to see.
As I began preparing for the journey, I realized how helpful it
was to be part of the Athonite network. Thanks to Antonis's or-
ganizational skills, finely tuned over decades of managing his
hotel and construction companies, I could relax about flight
arrangements, taxi rides, hotel reservations, boat tickets, visas,
and other logistical matters.

A further attraction of the trip was Antonis himself. He was
always eager to learn new things, a quality that made him an
engaging traveling companion. He was never shy to express
what was on his mind, and he brought his pointed questions to
any conversation, whether it was on ways to solve the perennial
political problem of Cyprus or on the miraculous culture of
Eastern Orthodox saints.

Emily was working at Agia Skepi when Antonis picked me
up. In twenty minutes we arrived at his home on the hills overlooking Limassol. "Unfortunately, even if Famagusta is given
back, we won't be returning," he lamented as we entered his
home. "It will be too late for Frosoulla and me to go back. After
so many years, we are established here in Limassol for good."

"I can see that," I said, marveling at their well-constructed
new home. Like Emily, Antonis and Frosoulla, his wife, were
refugees from Famagusta, and like Emily, for more than three
decades their greatest longing had been to return to the beloved
city of their youth. Occupied by the Turkish army since the
1974 invasion of the island, the once prosperous tourist center
has remained a ghost town, fenced off by barbed wire and in-
habited only by lizards, snakes, rodents, and wild cats.

Antonis had walked to the kitchen for a quick bite when Frosoulla entered the house carrying two large paintings by a renowned local artist. I helped her position the artwork on the

living room wall as we chatted about art, their new home, and their fading hopes for a return to Famagusta.

After Frosoulla had joined Antonis in the kitchen, I began perusing their library, which was filled with books not only on subjects related to his work but also on Greek literature, world history, classical philosophy, and Eastern Orthodoxy. Educated at the London School of Economics, Antonis has the passion of an idealist intellectual tempered by the pragmatism of a businessman, a combination that serves him well as an entrepreneur on the island. I picked up a volume from his rich collection of Eastern Orthodox books and sat on the sofa. Across from me a window overlooked the city and the sea. I flipped through the pages, reading various passages.

"Do you like Elder Porphyrios?" Antonis asked upon entering the room and noticing what I was reading, the life and homilies of one of the most remarkable contemporary saints of Greek Orthodoxy.[2]

"Very much so. I think he's one of the most extraordinary human beings of the twentieth century."

"Absolutely. Do you remember what the late Paisios told us about Elder Porphyrios when we visited him?" Antonis was referring to our encounter with the legendary hermit Paisios on Mt. Athos during my first visit there, in the spring of 1991.[3]

"It's been a long time. What do you have in mind?"

"Remember when he said that elders like Porphyrios appear only every two hundred years?"

"I do, yes. In fact, I recall when he joked that Porphyrios is the equivalent of a color television, while Paisios himself was just an old black-and-white TV. You know, Porphyrios reminds me of Padre Pio of Italy. He was also in color." I was alluding to Padre Pio's reputation as the foremost miracle-producing twentieth-century saint of the Catholic Church.

Antonis looked surprised. "It seems that you do believe there are saints outside of Orthodoxy."

"Well, I don't think we can confine God within Byzantium!" I said as I returned Porphyrios's book to the shelf. "In fact I said as much to Fr. Maximos when he once asked me the same question."

"And what did he say?"

"Nothing that I recall. It was while I was driving him to the Panagia monastery. He was very tired that day. He just listened to what I had to say without making any comments and then dozed off.

"I know that most devout Orthodox think that we're singularly privileged by Divine Grace and that only in our own spiritual tradition are genuine revelations, wisdom, and saints to be found," I continued. "But such notions are extremely difficult to sustain in a globalized world. Worse, more often than not they breed religious narrow-mindedness and intolerance. Furthermore," I added, "their claims to a monopoly on Divine Truth and revelation turn modern-thinking people off from the Church."

"What about the Filioque? How do you deal with that?" Antonis asked after a few seconds of silence.

"Not being a theologian, I delight in the privilege of ignorance and irresponsibility," I replied jokingly. "Frankly, I don't hang my faith on such, in my humble opinion, hairsplitting metaphysical controversies, which are understood only by a handful of theologians. I'm not preoccupied with whether the Holy Spirit proceeds directly from the 'Father' or from the 'Father and the Son.' This detail of the East-West theological dispute isn't essential for me. Perhaps it is for others, but I just don't see what all the theological fuss is about. Let's put it this way: I don't spend sleepless nights thinking about it. I'd rather recite the Jesus Prayer."

I continued, "I'm certain that the majority of Christians wouldn't understand or give a hoot about this issue. In fact, I feel certain that most people have never even heard of the word. Now, if you asked me which of the two versions of the controversy do I prefer, I'd tell you I prefer the Orthodox version as it is stated in the Creed, that the Holy Spirit descends directly from the Father. After all, I grew up in an Orthodox culture that nurtured me to view the world in a certain way. I have no doubt that had I been born in Ireland, I would have seen the world through Irish theological lenses and would feel perfectly comfortable with the notion that the Holy Spirit descends from 'the Father and the Son.'"

The Filioque controversy was one of the purported reasons for the Great Schism of A.D. 1054, when the Roman Pope and the Patriarch of Constantinople excommunicated each other. This event triggered the fragmentation of Christianity, beginning with the separation of the Roman Catholic Church from the Eastern Orthodox. Ever since that time, the various expressions of Christianity, whether Orthodox, Catholic, or Protestant, have been demonizing each other.

"Don't you think there are serious differences between the Orthodox, the Catholics, and the Protestants?" Antonis asked.

"Definitely, but in my opinion, they're not due to the Filioque. I could be wrong, of course."

"So then what do you see as the key difference between Western and Eastern Christianity?"

"They differ on how to know God. The Western part of Christianity puts a greater emphasis on an intellectual approach to God, whereas the East focuses on a more experiential and mystical approach. This is the key difference. But I do believe, at the same time, that this is not an unbridgeable theological divide. Both approaches are needed for a clearer vision and understanding of ultimate reality, of God. The ongoing division relates more to history and politics than to theology."

Antonis remained pensive as he packed a few more items. "So it seems you are convinced that Christ can manifest in other cultures and religions," he noted as he zipped his suitcase and placed it by the door.

"Absolutely. I'm a firm believer in the Gospel of John that Christ is the Logos, who is behind all of Creation, and who can manifest in any way He wishes and in any time and place. It is the light that lightens every human being who comes into the world. Don't you agree?" Not waiting for Antonis's response, I went on to quote a passage from Huston Smith, professor emeritus of philosophy at MIT and foremost scholar of comparative religions. A son of missionaries to China and a devout Christian, Smith had stated in a recent interview that, as far as he was concerned, "God is fully defined by Jesus but not confined to Jesus."

I waited for a couple of seconds to see Antonis's reaction, but he remained pensive. I then added, "I would paraphrase Smith's statement and say that Eastern Orthodoxy fully defines Christ but that Christ is not confined within Eastern Orthodoxy."

I went on to relate some of the stories about the life of the Catholic elder Padre Pio, which were as incredible as those about Elders Porphyrios and Paisios: miracles during his life and after his death; amazing healing phenomena, prophetic visions, selfless service to hundreds of thousands of the faithful, and the like. I lamented that Orthodox people hardly know anything about such elders in the West in the same way that Westerners know next to nothing about elders such as Porphyrios and Paisios.[4]

"As you can see, I am by temperament and training a firm believer in intercultural and interreligious communication and understanding," I added.

"Are you an advocate of merging religions and creating something new?" Antonis asked.

"Absolutely not! I'm not advocating what traditional theologians fear, syncretism. I'm against such an artificial merging of religious cultures. In fact, I'd argue for the preservation of authentic spiritual traditions as necessary cultural vessels of divine wisdom. In reference to Christianity, what is needed is real understanding between East and West and between Christianity and other religions. What one painfully notices instead, time and again, is a total misunderstanding and prejudice against not only other branches of Christianity but also other religions. Frankly, I don't think Christ wants us to think and act that way. But that's another story."

"So Christ doesn't discriminate," Antonis concluded.

"Well, I should certainly think not! Otherwise He wouldn't be Christ."

Antonis then asked what I thought of the miracle that many faithful claim happens every year during the Resurrection ceremonies in the Holy Land. He referred to the phenomenon that allegedly occurs during Easter celebrations over Christ's tomb at midnight. Because of the Orthodox Patriarch of Jerusalem's intense prayer while alone and in total darkness, a candle is believed to light by itself. This light, we are told, does not burn like regular fire during the first few moments that it emerges ex nihilo. During the first moments, it is allegedly more like an ineffable bright light than ordinary fire. It is then passed on by the Patriarch to the energized faithful outside the tomb, and they light their candles while chanting "*Christos Anesti ek Nekron*," "Christ is risen from the dead." Orthodox believers claim that the Patriarch does not use any physical means to light the candle and that officials conduct strict searches to make sure that no trick is involved in this yearly paranormal phenomenon.

"I must admit," Antonis said, "that after carefully reading testaments by a score of eyewitnesses, I can no longer just dismiss it as make-believe. In fact, studying about it strengthened my faith in Christ. What do you think?" It was a question I had been asked on several occasions.

"This is a phenomenon that is believed to take place on the physical plane," I said, "the dimension we can perceive with our senses. The recognized authority to authenticate that this is a real physical phenomenon, and not the result of collective hallucinations as skeptics would undoubtedly insist, is natural science. So as far as I am concerned, this is an empirical question that can be investigated by conventional science."

"I don't think they'll allow scientists to study this phenomenon."

"Well then, it will remain on the level of belief and only among the Orthodox," I said wryly. "Don't get me wrong. I do believe in miracles. The creation of the Universe itself fourteen billion years ago is a standing miracle. The mystical experiences of the great saints, as well as of ordinary people, are miracles. Extraordinary healing phenomena attributed to the prayers of great saints can be seen as miracles. I have no problem accepting all the healing miracles in the New Testament. But a specific phenomenon like the spontaneous combustion of candles on a regular basis, at a particular time and place, must be and can be verified by a team of scientists if it is to be accepted as fact by people other than the devoutly Orthodox."

"But do you believe something like this is possible?" persisted Antonis.

"Considering that I am a skeptic by training, I can only keep an open mind and accept it as a hypothesis amenable to empirical confirmation," I told him. "My model is St. Thomas. I demand evidence before I can believe in anything, particularly of such stupendous magnitude. Of course the moment one accepts other dimensions of Reality, as I do, one must keep the possibility open that such extraordinary claims have a basis in truth, rather than dismiss them in advance as mass delusions. I have no doubt, however, that most contemporary psychologists and other social scientists would consider such claims as occurring not in the objective world 'out there' but rather, as a colleague said to me once, in the heads of believers."

I then said that for die-hard skeptics, a phenomenon such as spontaneous lighting of candles would be categorized with the notorious Indian rope trick.

"Indian rope trick?"

"An Indian fakir unfurls a coil of rope in the air, and then a boy climbs up it and disappears. Hundreds of people reported, time and again, that they saw with their own eyes the boy climbing up and disappearing. And their reports were identical. Scientists thought it was a classic case of mass hallucination and decided to study it as such. They brought along video cameras. To their astonishment, they witnessed with their own eyes the same phenomenon. The boy climbed up and disappeared. In horror they then witnessed dismembered parts of the boy tumbling down. The fakir collected them in a basket. He then climbed up the rope himself, eventually coming down along with the boy, both smiling. According to the experimenters, there wasn't a single person among a hundred-plus witnesses, including the scientists themselves, who disputed these 'facts.' "

"But this is ridiculous!" Antonis protested.

"Just wait a minute! When the scientists developed the film, all it showed was that when the fakir threw the rope up, it came right down, and the boy standing next to him had never moved an inch from his side.[5]

"So are you suggesting that the Patriarch of Jerusalem is

doing something like the Indian fakir?" Antonis asked impatiently. "A trick?"

"No, I'm not saying that. Definitely not. In fact, I've seen healing phenomena that were videoed by American researchers in Brazil and the Philippines that were as awe-inspiring as what that fakir did. But in those cases the cameras picked up what the witnesses, including the scientists, were actually seeing with their own eyes. So yes, extraordinary phenomena do happen all the time, but if well-intentioned skeptics, and I don't mean the doctrinaire skeptics, are to take notice, such episodes must be studied and confirmed under controlled experimental conditions. Otherwise, such claims scandalize people, not only the skeptics and followers of other religions but also other Christians who aren't Orthodox and who may suspect the Orthodox of trickery, creating propaganda to put themselves in a position of spiritual superiority over everybody else.

"What we must keep in mind, as the Indian fakir indicates," I continued, "is that our senses aren't always the most reliable guides to reality and truth. I think, by the way, that it's a mistake to dismiss such phenomena as mere trickery. In the case of the Indian fakir, the fact that the camera was not picking up the scene as everybody else saw it was not necessarily proof that nothing was happening. We cannot simply dismiss it as collective hallucination. That fakir was doing something worthy of further investigation, something that raises questions about the nature of consciousness in relationship to matter."

"So how do we know about anything?"

"This is a tantalizing, fundamental question that philosophers and scientists have struggled with throughout the ages, as have all the great sociologists who formed the canon of my discipline."

"What do you have in mind?"

"Well, there are no easy answers. Objectivity is extremely problematic, if not impossible to achieve."

"Why do you say that?"

"Because we always approach reality and truth from our particular vantage point. We see parts of reality and consider them the whole picture. Philosophers and sociologists realized that we have been conditioned since infancy by our culture to think and view the world in certain ways, through 'a glass darkly,' as St. Paul said. We see the world not directly and 'objectively,' as the world is in itself or as God created it, but through the cultural lenses we've inherited. A Tibetan Buddhist, for example, views the world and what might be beyond the world through his or her conditioning as a Tibetan in the same way that a Hindu, or a Christian, or a Muslim will see the world through the lens of his or her own culture. Our tendency is to be absolutely convinced that our way of perceiving the world is the only way, that we are singularly privileged in comparison to everybody else. We just don't know any other way. So we are, by being human, condemned to perceiving reality in biased ways.

"Sociologists have also pointed out," I went on, with the strange sensation that I was lecturing in my course on sociological theory, "that our class background, our ethnicity, our gender, our idiosyncrasies, and even our professional affiliation shapes in a major way how we see the world. We don't perceive the world as if we are disembodied spirits viewing it in purely objective ways."

"I see what you're driving at, but can you be more concrete?"

I paused in thought. "Okay. Let me give you an example from personal experience. When I was an undergraduate at Youngstown State University, I was a close friend with Marios, a fellow Cypriot who, like me, had relatives in Ohio and came to

America for his higher education. At the time he was my closest friend in America. We were of the same age and cultural background. We agreed on just about everything. We perceived the world in almost identical ways. Upon graduation, we moved in different directions. I hadn't seen him for thirty years. We met again last fall, when I returned to Ohio to give a talk. He drove for several hours to come to my presentation and reconnect with me. We were, of course, delighted to see each other and reminisced about our youth. We also shared a common feeling of awe as we saw the then president of the university, whom we'd known well during our four years there, transformed into a statue in the middle of the renovated campus. We soon realized, however, how much we had changed, how much we differed in our ways of seeing the world, how we saw, experienced, and understood America in regard to politics and social problems. My way of seeing social reality was shaped by my training as a sociologist. He was a successful surgeon, and his perception of the world was shaped by his lifelong experiences in hospitals and his status as a highly esteemed doctor."

"So our group membership determines the way we see the world," Antonis concluded.

"That's what sociology teaches us. Here's another example. As our children constantly remind me, they are of a different generation and therefore apprehend the world differently from their immigrant and sometimes 'old-fashioned' father. I grew up in Cyprus and came to the United States in the early sixties. I was shaped as an American by the experiences of the sixties. They, on the other hand, grew up in Maine and came of age in the nineties, in a very different world. So our generations and the kind of experiences that we have undergone also determine the way we perceive and apprehend 'objective reality.'"

"Isn't there an escape from all that so that we can see the world as it is, independent of our opinions and biases?"

"Presumably through science. But as modern critics of scientific knowledge have shown, even science cannot escape from this problem. Science can also be ideological, suffering from similar blinders and biases.[6] So it isn't easy. Objectivity is a goal that we may never reach, yet we must constantly strive toward.

"I firmly believe," I continued, "that the first step toward objectivity is to recognize that we are full of biases and prejudices. That in itself could make us more humble and less dogmatic about our perceptions of how things are. Alas, dogmatism is the source of political and religious fanaticism, which leads to holy wars. There's a tendency among the devoutly religious or ideologically committed to claim a monopoly on truth and wisdom, and to consider others who aren't part of their own community as heathens or demonized adversaries. In extreme situations, this attitude can lead to the wholesale elimination of another group, ethnic cleansing and the like."

"How can we escape from our ignorance and false perceptions then?" Antonis asked as if he were interviewing me.

"The only escape from our ignorance and prejudices is to develop our consciousness by cultivating our capacity for love, compassion, and selflessness."

"But that's what Orthodoxy teaches!" Antonis exclaimed.

"Exactly. We can reach our target, in an ultimate sense, only through Divine Grace, after we have done the hard work ourselves, that is. At the same time, we must keep in mind that God's wisdom is widespread in all His Creation, so that we do not claim exclusive ownership of that wisdom. I like the Orthodox expression of the *Logos Spermatikos*, that the seed of God's wisdom is planted in His entire Creation. This is important to remember.

"So" I continued, "to make a long story short, the closer we come to God, the more we come to know the world as it is in itself, that is as God created it and as God knows it."

"In this case, the saints come closest to understanding the world as it is."

"This is what I believe. It's precisely what mystic Christianity teaches. In order to really come close to God, which also means to know the world as God knows it, we need to start from the stage of *Catharsis*, by freeing ourselves from all egotistical passions that cloud our perceptions and keep us cut off from God. This is the best way to overcome bias and not to assume that simply employing a scientific methodology will be sufficient to know reality. *Catharsis* will be followed by the gifts of the Spirit, of *Fotisis*, and then on to *Theosis*. So yes, the most 'objective' people are those who have attained *Theosis*, that is, the great saints. They are the ones who have freed themselves as much as is humanly possible from the shackles of social and cultural conditioning."

"You're suggesting then that objectivity, the true knowledge of Reality, is a function of one's development of consciousness, or the degree of one's purification from egotism. It is not simply the sharpening of one's intellectual faculties through science."

"You said it well. Let me put it in another way. We say that God is infinite love and goodness; infinite knowledge, or omniscience; and infinite power, or omnipotence. It's like a perfect triangle. These three properties of God that lie at the heart of the Christian tradition are also inside us."

"Well, after all, we were made in the image of God."

"Yes, in the very depths of our being. Holy Wisdom teaches us that all human beings are created in the image of God. But this triangle is in a dormant condition and is manifested in a distorted, skewed manner."

"What do you mean?"

"A person can have a lot of knowledge and power but no love. That means that such a person can cause much havoc to himself and to others. It is a satanic condition, to use a conventional term." I paused in thought. "Here's an example that just came to my mind. Wernher von Braun, the great German scientist, worked for Hitler's rocket program. When he was later asked how he could reconcile the fact that in the past he was helping Hitler win the war whereas now he was working for the Americans to send rockets to the moon, his response was something like 'I am a scientist, not a politician. My job is to send rockets up. Where they fall is not my responsibility.'"

"So are you suggesting that scientists should also be saints?"

"Well, ideally yes. Scientific knowledge is divine knowledge, but when not balanced by ethics and loving wisdom, it can be disastrous. Human beings lived for tens of thousands of years as food gatherers roaming the forests of Africa. Are we sure we can survive another two hundred years with modern science, which may have landed men on the moon but which also built fifty thousand nuclear weapons that can destroy the Earth several times over? So, yes, we are in desperate need for scientists who are also saints, that is, who are free from egotistical passions and realize that their knowledge springs from divine wisdom itself."

Antonis thought for a moment and then added, "It's possible also that one could be advanced in love and have a lot of power but lack knowledge."

"In such a case one can do a lot of harm because of ignorance. Likewise someone who has love and knowledge but no power cannot do much good.

"So," I continued, "we can see that the ideal situation is when a person develops his or her consciousness within the infinity of Divine Providence, when a person moves on in a way that the three divine characteristics that all of us have inside us as potentialities emerge harmoniously, like an equilateral triangle."

"And that must be a never-ending process."

"Precisely. It is so because in reality we are God, and for us Christians, Jesus is our Divine Archetype. That is why Jesus said that what he did we can do and more."

"I see."

We had to interrupt our conversation because it was time to head for the airport. Antonis's cousin Therapon, a mild-mannered hotelier, had just arrived to join us for the trip. His daughter volunteered to drive us.

By 7:00 P.M. we had landed at Thessaloniki, where we met with the two other members of our group, Herakles and Zenonas. Herakles was a stocky, muscular, self-made contractor of heavy building equipment with a rough Cypriot accent, an elementary education, and a disarming good nature, while Zenonas was a retired Athenian accountant in his late seventies. After a two-and-a-half-hour taxi ride, we arrived at Ouranoupolis, the port town bordering Mt. Athos. The following morning we would take the boat to Daphne, the central disembarkation point of the Athonite peninsula. We checked in at a modest family-run hotel, and then all five of us went out for a late evening meal.

Zenonas was the odd man out in our group. A devotee of the "pleasure principle," he showed little interest in spiritual questions. Furthermore, he loved to tell sexy jokes, a tendency out of sync with the Athonite culture of fasting, prayer, and all-night vigils. Zenonas, who had been Antonis's chief accountant for a number of years, had never been to Mt. Athos. He came along "for the fun of it," as he put it, to experience something new and exotic. Antonis wished to expose his former employee and friend to the spirituality of the Holy Mountain in the hope that it would help him as he marched toward the terminal phase of his earthly existence.

After meandering down the harbor's cobblestone streets, we entered a Greek tavern owned by another friend of Antonis. As the weather in Ouranoupolis was still cool, we opted for a dinner indoors, by the fireplace, under the personal supervision of the owner. Since it was Lent, we avoided meat or meat products. Instead we ate octopus, squid, and a variety of vegetable dishes. His cheeks round and rosy, Herakles made certain that our glasses of retsina wine were always full.

Cognizant of the austerities that awaited us at the monasteries, we gave ourselves license to indulge in the local gourmet dishes. During the forty-day fast of Lent, food is to be consumed minimally and only for survival purposes. The focus of monks and serious pilgrims must be exclusively on Christ's Passion and personal purification, or *Catharsis*.

I remember how my loving and devout aunt who raised me would always cook on Holy Friday an inedible lentil soup that was saturated in vinegar. When I was a boy, that dish was a veritable Golgotha for me, the worst food imaginable. I dreaded Holy Friday. We were told that the reason for the morbid dietary custom was for us to partake in Jesus' Passion on the cross, when the Son of Man was given vinegar instead of water to quench His thirst. It was partly because of our lentil suffering on Holy Friday, the culmination of the forty-day fast, that Easter was such a great relief and exuberant culinary celebration.

The retsina and Zenonas's one-liners put us all in the mood for storytelling. Everybody had some unusual yarn, which served as a kind of preamble to the otherworldly stories that one routinely hears upon entering Mt. Athos: teleportation of magnificent icons from one monastery to another, close encounters with lively dead saints, concrete visions of the Holy Virgin, levitating abbots, the disappearance of cancerous tumors, materializations of olive oil in empty jugs, implausible synchronicities, and the like.

I encouraged Antonis to share with us a story that he'd alluded to during our flight but hadn't described in detail. Once Antonis saw that we were genuinely interested, he began narrating what had happened to his late father. "My father used to tell us a story about his youth that stayed with me. In fact, in retrospect I think it had a lasting influence on me, because it triggered my interest in a lifelong quest to understand the meaning of life."

"Which eventually led you to discover Mt. Athos, and in turn, through you, led to my own discovery of the Holy Mountain," I interjected.

Antonis went on. "As a young man, my father, George, who came from a village of fifteen hundred people near Famagusta, decided to migrate to England. At that time, in the twenties, few Cypriots ventured outside the island.

"When news spread in the village that George planned to go abroad, everybody came to the house to bid him farewell. Among the first to come was an old woman named Zisemou, sister of my grandmother. 'My son,' she said, sobbing, 'I learned that you are going *pera* [abroad], and that's why I am here. I want you to do me a great favor, and I promise I'll always pray for you for the rest of my life. My blessings have power because I'm an old woman.' My father replied, 'Aunt Zisemou, if I can do it, consider it done.'

"Then the old woman told him that she had a son named Antonis, who in 1911, when he was George's age, quarreled with his parents and left Cyprus. He joined the Greek army and fought in the Balkan wars. Nobody had heard of him since. It was assumed that he was killed in Turkey. Later on, his parents were informed that he was actually taken prisoner. But he never wrote to them, and it wasn't certain whether he was dead or alive. His mother was convinced that her son was alive because she saw him in her dreams. What my father's aunt wanted of him was to find her son and persuade him to send her a photo of himself along with a letter.

"My father was dumbfounded," Antonis continued as he washed down a bite of octopus with the retsina. "There was no way he could find this relative, since he had no address and his elderly aunt didn't even know in what country to look for him. My father tried to ask her questions, but Aunt Zisemou thought he was teasing her. She just said 'pera.' What else did he possibly need to know? From her point of view, it was natural that any-where outside of Cyprus was pera. My father simply promised her that he would do his best to find her son, realizing that what his old aunt asked of him was impossible.

"Just before his departure," Antonis continued, "my father went to church with my grandfather to get a blessing from the priest. After that, the whole family went to the harbor in Fama-gusta to bid him farewell. As the boat hauled up its anchor, my father leaned over the railing, waving good-bye to friends and relatives. He suddenly heard the weak voice of an elderly woman calling him: 'My dear George. May God bless you. Do not forget to find my son. His name is Antonis Tsangarides.' He looked around and realized the voice was that of his old aunt Zisemou. He waved at her and reassured her once again that he'd do his best to find her son. But before the boat left Cypriot waters, he had already forgotten about old Zisemou and her request.

"They arrived at the port of Piraeus. In the meantime, my father made friends with three other Cypriots who were also migrating to London. They decided to all stay at a cheap hotel until their departure for England. Upon settling into the hotel, they decided to visit Athens. They learned that the cheapest way to get there was by train, so they headed for the station. But they felt that the directions they were given were not helpful. My father's companions asked a couple of pedestrians for directions, but they were ignored. Then my father decided to take the initiative and ask the first person who happened to be heading their direction. He asked him, 'Sir, do you know by any chance where the train station for Athens is?' The stranger grimaced at my father with disdain and replied, 'Mister, if the station was a mule, it would have given you a kick in the butt by now. That's it right in front of you!' Well, the station was only six meters from where they stood. My father murmured a thank-you to the stranger even though he had a burning desire to swear at him. Then he walked toward his companions, who were standing a few yards away. Suddenly he heard that stranger calling after them: 'Hey, are you fellows from Cyprus by any chance?' 'Yes we are,' my father replied. 'Is there someone among you from Famagusta?' My father replied that he wasn't from Famagusta himself but that he knew a lot of people from there. Famagusta at the time had only seven thousand inhabitants. The stranger then asked my father, 'Do you know of a woman by the name of Zisemou?' The moment my father heard that name, a chill ran through him and his hair rose. He asked the stranger, 'Are you by any chance Antonis Tsangarides?' Puzzled, the stranger replied, 'Yes. How did you know?'"

Antonis narrated how his father's uncle began to cry when he heard his mother's story. People gathered around, and the police soon arrived to determine what was going on. Instead of visiting Athens with his friends, Antonis's father stayed with his uncle and heard the story of what had happened to him many years ago. He was captured by the Turks as a prisoner of war. After the war he married a Greek woman from Smyrna. Utterly impoverished, they became refugees in Greece. His uncle explained that he wished to send his mother some money along with a letter, but at the time he had nothing to spare.

"My father accompanied his uncle to a photographer to have his picture taken," Antonis continued. "His uncle then sent that photo, along with a letter and some money, to his mother. Old Zisemou and her son finally began corresponding. But it wasn't until 1952 that my father's uncle managed to save enough money to visit Cyprus. Unfortunately, by that time his mother had died."

Antonis's story prompted the rest of us to share our own coincidences. Everybody had a story to relate, and everybody was aware of the improbability of those coincidences. Such stories baffled even old Zenonas, who admitted to having strange experiences of his own but shrugged them off as accidents, bereft of any deeper meaning.

"Perhaps, Zenonas, such coincidences undermine your belief in unbelief!" Antonis joked while his former employee, a chain smoker, drew in one last deep inhalation from his disappearing cigarette. Zenonas then shook his head with a smile and extinguished the cigarette in the ashtray.

It was past midnight when we returned to the hotel, where I shared a room with Zenonas. He mercifully promised not to smoke in the room. The boat for Daphne was scheduled to depart at ten the following morning.

Based on his many years of experience, Antonis reassured us that we had guaranteed seats on the *Axion Esti*, the famous ferry that for many years had been carrying pilgrims to and from the Holy Mountain. He was confident there was no need to make reservations in advance. The plan was to simply have an early leisurely breakfast by the harbor and then board the ferry shortly before ten and enjoy the two-hour ride.

It was, therefore, a shock when we discovered an unusual influx of pilgrims at Ouranoupolis. There were no ferry tickets left. Furthermore, there was no guarantee that we could find seats the following day or the day after.

Accustomed to having things well organized, Antonis frantically worked his cell phone, trying to contact influential people he knew in the hope of getting us seats on the only boat available that morning. He even sought help from an aunt in Cyprus. The best she could do was to assure him that she was going immediately to light a candle in front of the icon of the Holy Virgin, asking her to intercede so that we could enter Her Orchard, as Mt. Athos is often called. Antonis's face dropped as he turned off the phone. The thought crossed our minds that we might have to abort our trip. In earlier years, there had always been seats for pilgrims. But Mt. Athos was being discovered by an increasing number of spiritual tourists, Orthodox and non-Orthodox alike. Even Tibetan monks had visited the Holy Mountain, as well as Prince Charles, who became a regular patron, spending several days there every summer, apparently to satisfy, like us, his spiritual needs.

And just when our predicament seemed like it couldn't get any more bleak, lo and behold! The prayers of Antonis's aunt bore immediate fruit. Antonis rushed toward us from the ticket office all smiles. "Let's hurry, let's hurry before the boat leaves," he yelled as he waved the five tickets in his hand. His ingenuity had helped the miracle to manifest itself. Apparently another group had canceled their reservations at just the right moment, making it possible for us to take their place.

It was a sunny, calm day as the *Axion Esti* began its fully booked journey. Wearing hats and sunglasses, we sat out on the top deck to enjoy the April sunshine. The boat was transporting mostly men between the ages of twenty and forty-five, although a number of older, black-bearded monks were also onboard. The renaissance of monasticism on Mt. Athos, which began during the seventies, came mostly from the ranks of university graduates.

Looking at them, I thought of Pitirim Sorokin, whose work, as I mentioned in Chapter 1, had fascinated me when I was a graduate student. The Russian-American sociologist predicted in the late thirties that the secular, materialistic phase of Western civilization, what he called "sensate culture," was coming to an end and giving way to a new age of spirituality and religious revival, a move toward the "ideational culture." I wondered whether the influx of young and educated recruits to monasticism was a sign of the times he had intuited. I shared my thought with Antonis, who predictably asked a torrent of questions about the subject. We engaged in a mini conference on Sorokin while the others in our group listened quietly or watched the scenery.

Herakles was feeding the seagulls. He offered pieces of bread in his left palm, his arm stretching out over the boat railing, while seagulls dove down and snatched them up.

"Amazing! There is so much intelligence in nature," Antonis commented. "Why do you suppose seagulls are so clever?"

"You said it," I replied. "There is intelligence in every particle of matter, including seagulls."

We passed by the imposing-looking monastery of Simonopetra, perched on a massive rock high up the mountain, a place I had visited with Lavros on an earlier journey. Farther down there was the monastery of Gregoriou, a place I had also once visited with Lavros. Alas, it was impossible to visit more than a

few monasteries during any given pilgrimage. A lifetime of visits would be needed to do justice to the spiritual and cultural
richness within Mt. Athos's twenty functioning monasteries,
many hermitages, and scores of *sketes*, or small communities of
monks affiliated with the monasteries.

NINE

MONASTIC HOSPITALITY

We disembarked at Dionysiou, the monastery farther down the western slope of the peninsula, a place I had first visited with Antonis ten years earlier. Like the other Athonite monasteries, Dionysiou was constructed centuries ago as a fortress on a cliff overlooking the Aegean Sea. In olden times the monastery, like all Athonite monasteries, had to protect itself from bandits, pirates, and marauding troops. Its walls resembled those of a medieval castle. The massive entrance gate was built with thick hardwood and large iron bars. Because of safety considerations, a centuries-old tradition was established that all monasteries close their impenetrable gates by sunset. We entered the monastic citadel in the early afternoon, a few hours before the closing of the doors.

We planned to stay at Dionysiou for a few days and looked forward to reconnecting with some of the monks we had befriended the last time we were there. As we walked from our disembarkation point to the monastery, which was a half-hour walk up the mountain, I wondered how the many years of continuous prayer had affected the lives of those fathers.

Fr. Lukas was at the gate to welcome us. He was still in charge of hospitality. He warmly welcomed the thirty of us who had arrived that afternoon, offered us the traditional refreshments, and introduced us to the rules of the monastery. He had already arranged who was staying in what cell. Furthermore, he offered his services as a confessor for those who were interested.

The fact that Fr. Lukas himself was from Cyprus and that he remembered us well from our previous visit added to the charm of our reconnection as we gathered in the *archondariki*, the hospitality room. He had also read my book *The Mountain of Silence* and praised it, with some minor critical comments. I was pleased.

In addition to refreshments, Fr. Lukas offered us a brief spiritual pep talk. Responding to a question, he spoke about what makes one a saint. We are all invited, he announced, to sainthood. It is not only our birthright but also the supreme goal of our human existence to get to know God.

Fr. Lukas responded to another question by a pilgrim who wondered about the well-known paradox of great saints who lamented their utter depravity and felt that they were the worst of all human beings. "Though they are so much more advanced spiritually and closer to God than any one of us, saints feel totally humble. Why? Because the closer you come to the perfection of Christ, the more you become aware of your own blemishes. They really mean it when they speak with such intensity about their own insignificance. They're certainly not pretending, nor are they playacting."

I later told Antonis that I found Fr. Lukas now a much more impressive ascetic than the thirty-five-year-old monk I remembered from our visit ten years earlier. He had a more laid-back attitude compared to his earlier zealousness to save our souls and the soul of every pilgrim who set foot on Dionysiou.

"After so many years of spiritual work, one mellows and becomes more tender," Antonis explained. In fact Fr. Maximos, speaking from personal experience, told me on a number of occasions that hermits who spend most of their lives alone in continuous prayer and contemplation undergo an inner transformation that is visible when they interact with others. Regardless of their original disposition, continuous spiritual work softens them. Fr. Maximos claimed that without spiritual practice people who are cut off from human companionship would look more like beasts in the wild than humans. The defining personality traits of most authentic hermits are not austerity and rigidity but their exact opposites: kindness, compassion, and tolerance.

"Do you know the story of Fr. Lukas?" Antonis whispered to me while we drank Turkish coffee outside the *archondariki*, which overlooks the monastery's yard. Since I didn't, he briefed me on Fr. Lukas's career as an Athonite monk.

According to Antonis, Fr. Lukas's father had died when he was eight, and his widowed mother looked forward to seeing her only son married with children, the dream of every Greek parent. He found work in Athens after graduating from the university with a degree in civil engineering. He was on track for a promising career. But Fr. Lukas was yearning for God. He decided to abandon his career and "the World" and become an Athonite monk. His mother, as it is often the case with parents of young monks and nuns, was inconsolable. She believed that her son had been brainwashed and asked help from the then minister of the interior of Cyprus, who happened to be her cousin. The minister dispatched three Cypriot policemen to Mt. Athos to bring the young man back. They believed that Fr. Lukas was on Mt. Athos against his will. When Fr. Lukas realized that the three strangers were not pilgrims but secret police plotting his abduction, he decided to confront them directly and explain his case. After conversing with him for an hour, the policemen understood that even if they managed to take him to his mother,

Fr. Lukas would return to Mt. Athos. Once they realized that he was not being coerced to be a monk, they returned to Cyprus empty-handed.

"At four o'clock there will be a short service and then *trapeza* [dinner]," we heard Fr. Lukas announce. "Then at nine an all-night vigil will begin that will last until four in the morning."

"Splendid!" Antonis exclaimed. "What a wonderful break from the headaches and routines of business."

Zenonas's face dropped. Seven hours in a vigil was for him hardly a reason for celebration. "Come on, Zenon!" Antonis said lightly. "You don't come to Mt. Athos to sleep all night. That's a habit for ordinary living. Here's your chance to experience something different."

The rest of our company were veterans of Mt. Athos and looked forward to participating in the ascetic ways of the mountain. But poor Zenonas was in a state of culture shock, particularly when at *trapeza* we were each given a bowl of plain and watery tomato soup sprinkled with some rice and complemented with bread and olives. It was the heart of the fasting season, and the food barely differed from my aunt's Holy Friday lentil soup. Yet I knew from previous visits that on weekends and in fast-free periods the food served in Athonite monasteries brought joy to even the most demanding palate.

~~~

Not only did we survive the seven-hour vigil but, as on previous such occasions, we left invigorated. Even Zenonas marveled at his capacity to last that long, a common experience for first-time visitors to Mt. Athos. Antonis explained to him that the prayers, the chanting, the incense, and the Grace of the Holy

Spirit energized the molecules of his body so that they could postpone the need for sleep.

As we exited the chapel, I noticed scores of monks, followed by pilgrims, who were all waiting in line to pay homage to a special icon of the Holy Virgin. One by one they would kneel and prostrate before the icon. They then stood up, crossed themselves several times, and reverentially kissed the sacred icon.

"Don't you know what that is?" Antonis asked, surprised. After I confessed ignorance, he informed me that it was the famous Icon of the Salutations. My eyes widened. For as long as I can remember, the Salutations, or *Cheretismoi*, have been part of my cultural identity, equivalent in importance to the Madonna of Lourdes in France or to the Virgin of Guadelupe in Mexico.

It is a tradition in the Greek Orthodox Church that on the four Fridays preceding Holy Week, special homilies of high poetic force and beauty are offered in honor of the *Theodokos*, or Mother of God. The tradition began in A.D. 626, when Constantinople was threatened by invaders. Most of the Byzantine army, and the emperor himself, was preoccupied with fending off Persian invaders at the remote Anatolian borders. Consequently, the capital city of Byzantium was left only lightly guarded. Taken by a surprise assault, it was expected to fall. In those desperate hours, Patriarch Sergius grabbed the most ancient and venerated icon of the Holy Virgin and in a special litany carried it around the walls of the city, blessing and giving courage to the defenders of the *Polis*, as the great city was then called. A terrible storm followed the litany, destroying the boats of the invaders and forcing them to abort their siege. It was considered a miracle attributed to the *Theodokos*. The people gathered at the great church of Agia Sophia (Holy Wisdom) and inaugurated the tradition of the Salutations. Its hallmark was the *Akathist*

Hymn (hymn sung while standing). In a beautiful melody, "The *Polis*" addresses the *Theodokos* in the first person and thanks Her for Her intercession and rescue: "O Champion General, I your City now inscribe to you triumphant anthems as the tokens of my gratitude, being rescued from the terrors, O *Theodokos*. Inasmuch as you have power unassailable, from all kinds of perils free me so that unto you I may cry aloud: Rejoice, O unwedded Bride."[1]

Alas for Constantinople, the *Theodokos* did not intercede when the armies of the Turkish Sultan Mehmet the Conqueror overran its one-thousand-year-old walls in 1453, bringing an end to the Roman Empire in the East, otherwise known as Byzantium.

Mt. Athos is filled with Byzantine relics such as the Icon of the Salutations, I thought, while retrieving my digital camera. But Antonis warned me that taking pictures of the icon was strictly prohibited. Later on, when I asked Fr. Lukas for special permission to photograph the holy relic, he waved at me to follow him. He spoke to a younger, more zealous monk who was in charge of guarding the chapel, and I was given permission to take a few quick pictures. Fr. Lukas then gave me a pocket-size copy of the icon to take along as a souvenir. On its back was a brief description of the icon's historical and spiritual meaning.

The Icon of the Salutations was donated by Emperor Alexios Komnenos in 1375 to St. Dionysios, then abbot of Dionysiou monastery, for safekeeping. To this day the monks of Dionysiou conduct daily supplications to the Holy Virgin, followed by Divine Liturgy at the chapel where the icon is guarded.

Learning about the famed icon of the *Akathist Hymn* and its history coincided with my reading of a recently published work on the history of Byzantium, which I'd brought along. Given Antonis's interest in the subject, I shared with him some of the historian's insights while we sipped tea on one of the monastery balconies and gazed upon the sun setting over the Aegean.

"This should interest you," I said as I read from the book:

"[Byzantium's] ability to . . . defend itself and its magnificent capital was to shield the northwestern world of the Mediterranean during the chaotic but creative period that followed the collapse of the Roman Empire in the West. Without Byzantium there would have been no Europe. During this critical early-medieval period, when the Arabs stormed out of the desert to capture the Holy Places of the Jews and the Christians and the granaries of Egypt, only Constantinople stood in the way of their ambitions. Had the fortifications of the Queen City and the determination and skills of its inhabitants—emperor, court and people—not ensured the security of this defensive system, Islam would have supplanted Byzantium in the seventh century. Having accomplished the conquest of Damascus, Jerusalem, Alexandria and the Persian empire, the Muslims would surely have overrun the Mediterranean empire created by Rome, once they had incorporated Constantinople with its resources and revenues, its shipyards, and commercial networks. In the same way that they progressed along the southern littoral of the Mediterranean into Spain, they would have advanced across the Balkans to dominate the northern shore as well."[2]

"Why do you suppose the Holy Virgin did not save Byzantium in 1453 as in 626?" Antonis asked, not expecting an answer.

"The Byzantines themselves explained their tragedy as punishment from God for their many sins," I replied. "Fortunately for the West, by that time Europe was already on its feet and could have taken care of itself."

We then continued our discussion on the bitter legacy left in that part of the world as a result of the fall of Constantinople. Our three companions joined us in that impromptu conversation. But our tea symposium was interrupted by Fr. Lukas. "The abbot would like to see you," he announced.

The five of us followed Fr. Lukas through a labyrinth of corridors until we reached the cell and office of the person in charge of running the monastery. I remembered Abbot Petros from my previous visit. Our presence in his monastery was of special interest to him since he too was from Cyprus, from Famagusta, in fact. For an abbot, he was relatively young-looking, tall and lean. Antonis, who knew him well, told me later that he used to be a basketball star in Anorthosis, the leading athletic club of Famagusta.

We talked of Cyprus news and the stalled negotiations with the Turks. Then Abbot Petros, sitting behind his desk and surrounded by icons of saints and the Holy Virgin, lamented the spiritual malaise plaguing the Greek world.

"People today are thirsty for spiritual renewal, but they don't know where to look, where the spring is. They flock to secular psychologists and psychiatrists to find answers and meaning in their lives. I am told," Abbot Petros continued while fiddling with his *komboschini* (prayer beads), "that a European psychiatrist who arrived in Greece recently was treated like a rock star. Thousands of people attended his talks on how they should live their lives. At the same time, so many people in Greece today ignore or are ignorant of the rich psychological tradition of the saints, the real psychologists. So they flock to a self-professed atheist for counseling about their psyche! This is truly sad."

"And ironic," Antonis added.

"Orthodoxy has a huge deficit in marketing its spiritual products," I said lightly.

We went on to discuss Greek affairs and the role of the Orthodox Church in Greek society. The abbot then gave each one of us a package of books related to the history and life of the monastery, particularly its leading saints.

"This one," Abbot Petros said as he pulled from his drawer a large, heavy book that was also included in his gift package, "is a commemorative publication on the life and work of St. Niphon. I believe you'll like it." He summarized for us the unusual story of this saint. During the Byzantine period, he was the Patriarch of Constantinople, highly esteemed by the faithful as a holy man. Dethroned by an unscrupulous usurper, he found refuge at the monastery of Dionysiou. Nobody knew who he actually was. He presented himself as a simple monk and ended up working as a mule driver, carrying provisions to the monastery. One night an angel appeared in a vision to the then abbot and asked him, 'Why do you let my Patriarch be a mule driver?' The angel then revealed the true identity of the humble mule driver. All the fathers waited for him at the entrance of the monastery with candles and full ceremonial regalia, giving him a hero's welcome, with chants and prostrations reserved for saints. From a simple monk he became the spiritual elder of the monastery. After his passing, he was canonized as a saint of the Orthodox Church.

The culture of Mt. Athos is replete with such colorful, didactic stories, which help the monks in their spiritual efforts to attain humility. Stories like that of St. Niphon are also reminders of the reality and imminence of Heaven.

After our three-day stay at Dionysiou, we thanked our hosts, made a modest donation to the monastery for their warm hospitality, and at eleven in the morning we boarded the passing ferry for Daphne. We promised Fr. Lukas, who escorted us to the boat, that we would return in the near future. To Fr. Lukas's pleasure, Antonis and Therapon already made plans to return in the early fall.

Our new destination was Vatopedi, on the northeastern side of the peninsula. It is the monastery where I first met Fr. Maximos, in 1991. It was a chilly morning when we boarded the *Agia Anna*, the alternate ferry to *Axion Esti* that takes pilgrims to the monasteries. High winds howled down from the summit of Mt. Athos, causing unseasonably low temperatures. More seriously for our company, the winds created turbulent seas, which made Therapon anxious. His oversensitive stomach could not handle even the slightest sea motion. Fortunately, the wind subsided as quickly as it had started, and the ninety-minute journey proved relatively smooth and uneventful. We were dropped off at Daphne, where, thanks to Antonis's foresight and connections, Fr. Savvas, a taxi driver monk, was waiting with a truck to take us to Vatopedi, an hour's journey on unpaved roads through stunning scenery.

As at Dionysiou, we enjoyed a warm welcome and reunion at Vatopedi with monks we'd come to know over several years of visits. We were offered the traditional hospitality, and we shared news about Cyprus. Many of the hundred or so monks, including the abbot, were Cypriots. We also brought bottles of Commandaria, a special Cypriot port wine for communion. It was a gift sent by Fr. Maximos to his alma mater.

At 7:30 that evening, before another all-night vigil, pilgrims gathered in one of the monastery's reception halls to hear a talk by Abbot Ephraim, a close friend and former colleague of Fr. Maximos. They were the same age, had graduated from the same theology school, at the University of Thessaloniki, and had been guided and trained by the same spiritual elders. They were, in other words, spiritual brothers and classmates.

After a lively welcome, he made a few comments about the importance of periodically withdrawing from the world for spiritual renewal. He then abruptly asked Zenonas to come and sit next to him. It was an unusual and unexpected gesture. The seventy-eight-year-old Zenonas stood up, smiling, clearly cherishing the honor of sitting next to the elder. "Don't you think it's time, my dear brother," the abbot said with a friendly tap on his shoulder, "to reflect on your mortality?"

Zenonas's face dropped momentarily, and then, without responding, he smiled awkwardly. The rest of us chuckled.

"It's important," Fr. Ephraim went on, "that if you are serious about spiritual work, you set aside at least an hour each day for prayer and the study of the lives of saints. The major problem of the world today," the abbot said, is *polymerimnesia*, that is, that people are concerned about too many worldly things. As a result we forget God. We forget that our clock is ticking, that we will die soon, and that we will not be able to carry anything with us.

He went on to talk about the traps of modernity, such as television, cell phones, computers, and the like. "Such inventions are indeed useful and have made our lives easier, but they are distractions. Not long ago, I stayed at a friend's house in Athens, and I was amazed at how many hours they spent watching television."

The abbot also spoke of the historic importance of the Vatopedi monastery, the second largest of the twenty monasteries still in operation on Mt. Athos. He mentioned that in addition to producing many saints of the Orthodox Church, such as the great fourteenth-century theologian St. Gregory Palamas, the monastery is recognized for its seven miraculous icons. He gave us examples of those miracles, such as the production ex nihilo of olive oil, central to the life and rituals of the monasteries. Not long ago, at a critical moment during the heart of the winter, the olive oil of the monastery was severely depleted and the weather would not permit getting to Thessaloniki to renew the supply. Then mysteriously, the jugs began filling overnight.

"The fathers could not find enough containers to put it in!" the abbot exclaimed, spreading his hands. He went on sharing miracles attributed to icons, such as the cure and disappearance of cancerous tumors and other such paranormal signs and wonders.

"The presence of the Holy Virgin is very intense in our monastery," he said. "Just the other day, a pilgrim asked me whether there are any nuns here. Of course not, I told him. The monastery is *avaton* [only for men]. The pilgrim said that he'd had a powerful experience of a tall woman dressed like a nun crossing the yard and entering the church. I explained to him that it must have been the *Panagia* [Most Holy One]. She does appear to pilgrims and visitors on occasion." The good abbot spoke with conviction that these spiritually transformative experiences were grounded in fact, not fantasy.

A middle-aged man from Crete with a thick mustache announced that his visit had changed his perceptions of the monastery. He was enchanted, he said, by the deep spirituality he experienced there and the selfless hospitality and love that the monks had shown the pilgrims.

"The journalists," he declared, "misled us. They present a picture of this monastery that is pretty negative. But what we have experienced here is an entirely different reality."

"The journalists should come here and see for themselves what's happening instead of writing articles without ever setting foot on the Holy Mountain," a man next to him declared. This conversation was based on a flurry of bad publicity that the monastery had suffered, criticisms concerning some commercial dealings with the Greek government.

"I was not planning to comment on that issue," the abbot replied with some hesitation. "But since you raised it, I will have to respond."

He then spoke of the enormous costs to keep a monastery of this size, which once housed several thousand monks, a town unto itself, going. To fix the run-down buildings, the abbot claimed, would require close to 250 million euros. Furthermore, simply to operate such a monastery costs an enormous amount of money.

"More and more people are discovering Mt. Athos, and more and more people want to visit us here. This is just great, and we welcome this trend. We want people to come and experience the Holy Mountain. The fathers," the Abbot continued, "work day and night to cater to the pilgrims and keep the tables ready for the communal meals. They do it with gladness and generosity of heart. But it also strains our resources."

No one needed to be convinced of what the abbot was saying. We had all had direct experience of the extraordinary and selfless hospitality offered to lay pilgrims.

"Just to give you an idea," the abbot continued, "last year, during Paschal celebrations, the monastery had to spend fifteen thousand euros on fish alone."

"Why not charge a fee for those who want to visit?" someone suggested.

"People have asked me this before. But that would violate the spirit of free hospitality. It goes contrary to everything that the

Holy Mountain stands for. So we need, somehow, to raise funds to preserve this fundamental Athonite tradition."

~~~

We remained four more days at Vatopedi. To the chagrin of Zenonas, we spent most of our time in prolonged services and all-night vigils, a way of life on the Holy Mountain during Lent that often sends monks and pilgrims into mystical and life-changing experiences. In between services, we chatted with some of the monks we knew from previous visits. We shared memories of the events that had set the stage for my writings on Orthodox monasticism, a subculture that is treated with scorn if not utter contempt by the more secular segments of Greek society, particularly the intelligentsia.

We left Vatopedi by boat. Just before noon we arrived at Ierissos, the northeast port and picturesque fishing town bordering Mt. Athos. Andreas, our taxi driver, was waiting to take us to the Thessaloniki airport, two and a half hours away, for the trip back to Cyprus. Having ample time, we stopped at a local restaurant for lunch. The driver, a sympathetic and devout forty-year-old man, was horror-struck when we ordered octopus, a variety of vegetable dishes soaked in olive oil, and local organic wine. It was Wednesday. Octopus, shellfish, and olive oil can be consumed only on weekends during the Great Lent. Andreas ate hardly anything. I had a sense that he believed we were compromising our souls by violating the food taboo.

Antonis explained that we took the liberty of breaking our fast for medical reasons. We were much older than he was and needed plenty of vegetables and olive oil to lubricate our intestines for adequate elimination. In fact, Antonis had complained earlier that the strict fasting during our stay on the Holy Mountain had created problems for him. He had swallowed many pills to be able to go to the bathroom.

Our devout taxi driver could not accept this as a legitimate excuse. "We must call things by their proper names!" he declared, another way of saying that our failure to follow the strict culinary prohibitions was unforgivable. It was clear that he was more interested in the well-being of our souls than in the money he would earn from us. Being a good sport and of an otherwise openhearted disposition, Andreas sat patiently, waiting for us to finish our lunch with folded hands and a sad expression. There were no further reprimands about what was on our plates. Nevertheless, it was not easy to enjoy our meal knowing that we had scandalized our hapless driver. Over the years of driving Antonis back and forth to Mt. Athos, Andreas had gained a very favorable view of him. Seeing him violate the fast must have created a dissonance in his mind.

"Help me understand this. The Church allows the eating of olives during Lent but not olive oil! Where is the logic in this?" Zenonas protested.

"There you go again, Zenon!" Antonis said lightly. "You still don't get it, do you? The whole idea is to minimize the amount of food you eat during Lent so that you can train yourself in self-mastery, learn how to fence off temptations by focusing exclusively on God, rather than on your stomach. Olive oil is very good and makes food tasty. You, therefore, eat more. On the other hand, how many olives can you eat? Do you get it now?"

"No. Thank you very much!"

We all, including our pious taxi driver, laughed. The heavy atmosphere lightened.

~~~

"We have a ninety-minute flight to Larnaka," Antonis said as he settled into his window seat next to me on the plane. "Here's our opportunity to talk uninterrupted about Christianity."

"Where should we start?"

"From the beginning."

"Well, sociologists have a different way of explaining a religious movement like Christianity than, let's say, traditional theologians. That is, they would raise the question of how a little-known religious movement, at the farthest reaches of the Roman Empire, could develop from a cult of less than a hundred or so at the start of Jesus' ministry to six million by the time Constantine made it the official religion of his empire."

"Wouldn't you say it was miraculous the way Christianity replaced paganism and the gods of the Greco-Roman world in such a short time?"

"Perhaps one can see it that way, but that's not the way sociologists and historians would explain such a phenomenon. One can argue, of course, that God and Divine Providence can work through historical and sociological forces. Okay. So a historical-sociological understanding does not necessarily displace a belief in divine intervention. The two forms of understanding can complement one another. So let's focus on the historical-sociological level to better understand the phenomenon and leave the rest to Providence."

"Let's start from the very beginning," Antonis repeated as the plane reached thirty thousand feet and the flight attendants began serving refreshments.

"As with any other historical phenomenon, we can have only partial understanding of the factors that brought it about. This is a sociological axiom. We can never have complete knowledge of all the factors that give birth to a historical event.

"Contemporary sociologists of religion, such as Rodney

Stark, have offered us a compelling picture of the social forces that gave rise to Christianity."[3]

"That's what I want to know," Antonis told me.

I went on to summarize for my friend the view of Rodney Stark, a leading sociologist of religion, of the factors that established Christianity as the religion of the Roman Empire, and its far-reaching consequences for the history of the world. I mentioned how Stark, using modern sociological theory, statistical analysis, and research, combined with a careful historical examination, drew some very convincing conclusions.

"Stark showed that, contrary to common belief, Christianity arose not as a religion of the downtrodden but as the religion of the relatively well off. Many established and influential Romans embraced the new religion. Had it been the religion of just the downtrodden, the Romans would have easily suppressed it, seeing it as a class movement that threatened the social foundation of the empire. The Romans were notorious for their brutality in defending their power.

"Most important, Christianity thrived because large numbers of people were disillusioned with paganism. The gods of Olympus were becoming increasingly untenable, and many Romans were attracted to and interested in the monotheism of Judaism."

"Why then didn't they join Judaism?"

"Precisely for the reasons that led Paul to convince the other apostles to abolish circumcision as a requirement for joining the Christian movement. That is, to embrace Judaism, gentiles had to become Jews first and give up their identity as Romans or Greeks. Early Christianity abolished those ethnic divisions. One could become a Christian without giving up one's ethnicity. Furthermore, and in contrast to common beliefs, Stark shows that the Jews who lived in the big cities of the Roman Empire, away from Palestine, provided the foundation of the early Christian movement. Many of them, being Hellenistic Jews, were marginalized within the societies in which they found themselves and were therefore more amenable to conversion to the new religion. For them, Christianity must have seemed a modern version of Judaism with Hellenic elements, a synthesis of their Jewish background and the Hellenic world in which they found themselves.

"One of the most compelling reasons for the expansion of Christianity and its victory over paganism was, according to Stark, its superior capacity to cope with the massive calamities that befell the Roman world during the second and third centuries. Epidemics wiped out a large portion of the population. Christians looked after each other and after their neighbors, whether Christians or pagans. The notion of risking your life to help the infirm who were not your immediate family was alien to paganism. Even the great and celebrated physician Galen fled Rome and took refuge in his country villa. He felt no scruples in declaring openly that he saw no reason that he should risk his life to help strangers. On the other hand, the readiness of Christians to help strangers didn't go unnoticed. By giving out food and water to those plagued by the epidemics, they increased their odds of survival. Naturally, many of those who survived thanks to Christian charity were more likely to join Christian groups. It was also noticed that Christians had a higher survival rate than the pagan population, not only because they nurtured their sick but also because many of them, by taking care of the sick, had developed immunity from the diseases. The Christians' capacity to survive epidemics was interpreted by the pagans as the result of worshiping a superior god. In addition, Christians looked happier and more emotionally secure than their compatriots. Their theology, according to Stark, offered them hope. This impressed many pagans."

"It sounds as if the epidemics were sent by God."

"That's exactly how a Christian bishop saw it at the time. Stark points to two more factors that were decisive in the growth of Christianity: the rising status of women and the Christian opposition to abortion and infanticide, which were widely practiced in the Greco-Roman world. The ancients had no prohibition against exposing an infant to the elements and letting it die if, for whatever reason, they did not want it. Just think of what happened to Oedipus and the Spartan custom of throwing disabled or 'imperfect' infants over a cliff. Even the great philosophers didn't see anything wrong with abortion or infanticide. As a result, many female infants were killed at birth because, in a patriarchal world, parents preferred boys. By the time Christianity emerged, there was a severe depletion of females among the Roman population. Because Christianity, like Judaism, considered abortion and infanticide atrocious crimes, there was among the Christians an abundance of females of marriageable age. As a consequence, there was an increasing rate of marriages between Christian women and pagan husbands. The outcome of such marriages, Stark notes, is what sociologists call a form of 'secondary conversion.' Roman men were being converted to the new religion by their Christian wives."

"What was Constantine's role, then, in the rise of Christianity?" Antonis asked.

"Researchers like Rodney Stark would, I believe, say that Constantine simply made official what was already happening at the grassroots level. He saw which way the wind was blowing and followed suit."

"But what about his sky vision, his own mystical experience that led him to adopt Christianity?"

"Well, as I said before, that story doesn't contradict what the sociologists have uncovered. Constantine's vision coincided with the de facto development of Christianity within the Roman Empire. Constantine sealed the triumph of Christianity over all other rival religions.

"Once Christianity became the official religion of the Roman Empire, other social forces were activated that led to the historical development of Christianity and, by extension, of Europe as we know it. It also led to the Great Schism, the Crusades, the Inquisition, the takeover of the lands of Eastern Christianity by Islamic warriors, the Protestant Reformation, the survival of Byzantine monasticism on Mt. Athos and other parts of the Christian East, and so on.

"Rodney Stark," I concluded, "saw Christianity as a 'revitalization movement' within the Roman Empire. It revitalized, that is, the Greco-Roman world at a time of cultural and social disintegration, or of what sociologists would otherwise call severe conditions of 'anomie.' "

"Anomie?"

"It's a French word with Greek roots meaning a state of moral confusion and decline due, in the case of the ancient world, to the loss of faith in the pagan religions."

Like the ancient world, we were in decline, not because of any moral confusion but rather because our plane was beginning its descent to Larnaka airport. It was close to midnight when we reached Limassol.

TEN

MYSTERIES OF SINAI

When I woke up the next morning, Emily informed me that during my sojourn to Mt. Athos with Antonis and his friends, plans were made for a pilgrimage to the fourth-century monastery of St. Catherine in the Sinai. Unlike Mt. Athos, where only men are allowed, St. Catherine welcomes all pilgrims, regardless of the accident of their gender. That meant Emily and I could stay there together.

It was an opportunity I could not miss. At St. Catherine I could experience the very beginning of the Eastern Orthodox monastic tradition, where the fruits of the Holy Spirit have been systematically cultivated and uninterruptedly pursued for more than fifteen hundred years.

That very evening we chatted with Fr. Maximos. Emily mentioned in passing that we'd decided to venture into the Sinai desert. His face brightened, and he reassured us that it was bound to be an unforgettable pilgrimage.

"If you plan to climb Mt. Sinai, make sure," he urged us, "to do it very early in the morning."

"That's the plan," I said and nodded.

Since his arrival in Cyprus, Fr. Maximos had not only revitalized some of the island's monasteries but also launched a tradition of regular pilgrimages to holy shrines off the island. Destinations usually included Greece and the Aegean as well as Italy and some countries of the former Soviet Union. In recent years, pilgrimages into the heart of the Middle East were also organized. Fr. Maximos believed that sacred places are particularly charged with spiritual energy. He felt that while visits to such places were beneficial for relaxation and renewal, they were also, more important, opportunities to benefit one's spiritual life.

A central focus of our journey to St. Catherine, built in the foothills of Mt. Sinai, was to be at the site where, according to biblical tradition, Moses received the Ten Commandments. In fact, during my previous sabbatical, I had made plans with my friend Lavros to visit the desert sanctuary, but because of the outbreak of the Iraq war, we postponed our pilgrimage for a more auspicious time.

Lavros wasn't able to join us this time. He had visited St. Catherine two years earlier, after a promise he'd made to his wife, Maria, on her deathbed. As he explained to us, throughout her life Maria had felt an unusual affinity and deep reverence and affection for St. Catherine. What prompted him to make the difficult journey on his own was the fact that Maria's death occurred on St. Catherine's name day. In fact, a few days before her unexpected and untimely death, Maria, a deeply devout woman, had announced to Lavros that she saw St. Catherine in a vivid dream informing her that on the saint's name day she would come and lead Maria to Heaven. At the appointed time, Maria died peacefully, without fear or despair. Maria, like some of the elders that Fr. Maximos knew, experienced what the Orthodox elders call an *osiakos thanatos*, a blessed death.

Lavros advised us on how to prepare for the journey to the Egyptian desert. He furthermore offered us useful tips for the hike up Jebel Musa, Moses' Mountain.

Unlike most pilgrimages to St. Catherine, ours was not part of an organized tour. Olympia, an adventurous friend of Emily and a spiritual disciple of Fr. Maximos, invited us to journey with her and three of her friends to St. Catherine as well as to a few other Christian sites in Egypt. An enthusiastic and energetic woman in her late forties, Olympia had developed a deep fondness for and knowledge of Egypt as a result of yearly visits to Cairo and Alexandria. Coming from a wealthy Cypriot family, she was able to make these visits for over twenty-five years. This journey was not only a pilgrimage for her but also a voyage down memory lane. Olympia loved everything about Egypt: its extraordinary archaeological sites, its colorful bazaars, the warmth of the people, and the expansive hospitality of her friends. So great was her love for everything Egyptian that I once joked that she was an Egyptian mistakenly born into the body of a Greek Cypriot. Although Olympia had never visited St. Catherine's monastery, her confidence about the country and its ways was infectious and reassuring. Emily, who resonated the same energy and optimism as Olympia, helped me overcome my initial reservations about the trip because of the ongoing political tensions in the Middle East.

Only when the date of departure neared did I realize that the other three of Olympia's friends who had signed up for the journey were all women, of the same age and socioeconomic background as Olympia. Alas, their husbands, because of either their businesses and other preoccupations or their lack of zeal for pilgrimages, chose to stay at home. Consequently, I found myself the only man in our group of six. The makeup of our group made for amusing episodes, such as when a merchant in Cairo who was negotiating a sale with us in broken English and improvisational sign language inquired, in all sincerity, whether the five women were all my wives.

We left Cyprus at dusk on April 30 on an Egyptair flight to Cairo. We changed planes there for a one-hour domestic flight to Sharm El Sheikh, the newly created resort area on the Red Sea. Exhausted, we reached our hotel in the wee hours of the morning.

One way to go to St. Catherine would have been to travel by boat to Sharm El Sheikh and then endure a three-to-four-day camel ride through the forbidding desert peninsula. That is how pilgrims, writers, painters, and warriors made the journey over the centuries. Our trip would not be so romantic, as we would instead be traveling by taxi.

After only a few hours of sleep, we took a quick walk by the beach, which was full of sunbathing tourists, then boarded a boat with a glass bottom to enjoy Sharm El Sheikh's unique and extraordinary corals. We then hired a taxi for the three-hour journey north.

The young driver seemed to want to complete the monotonous desert journey as fast as humanly possible, making all six of us nervous. He had the peculiar habit of speeding up on curves. At one such critical maneuver, we felt as if we were about to flip over. Friendly as he was, our chauffeur was virtually immune to meaningful communication because of the lack of a mutually understandable language.

"You're sitting in front. Do something!" one of Olympia's exasperated friends begged of me. Repeatedly and discreetly, I sent signals to the driver to take it easy, signals he either didn't understand or simply ignored. I tried to stay calm myself and was careful not to get him agitated. The tragic accident that had taken place on that very road only a year ago, when a bus carrying pilgrims went over a cliff, did not make matters any more relaxed. To our great relief, our driver finally got the message and drove within the speed limit. Only then could I contemplate the desert and its historic significance.

It was an awesome feeling to travel across that strategically situated peninsula, steeped in biblical lore and ghosts of conquering armies. I imagined what it must have been like when so many diverse armies marched through that desert over the millennia: the ancient Egyptians, the Persians, Alexander's troops, the Romans and Byzantines, Mohammed's holy warriors, the crusaders, Napoleon's soldiers, the Ottoman Turks, and the Arab irregulars Lawrence of Arabia fought with, as well as the Israelis and Egyptians. All of them watered the desert with blood and tears and left their seal on the collective memory of humanity's follies. I imagined what it must have been like for the manna-gathering Hebrews during their forty-year wanderings as they tried to escape Pharaoh's sword and arrive at the promised land of Canaan.

The desolate landscape spread around us ominously. The road was now mostly straight and recently paved. We were surrounded by sheer rock and sand, with hardly any life to be seen, except an occasional lone camel driver. If I could imagine removing from vision our speeding minivan and the road, the scenery would probably have been no different than what existed during the time of Ramses the Great.

The most disquieting irritants were the military checkpoints at just about every crossroad: bored-looking, armed soldiers repeatedly examining our passports, inquiring about our destination and why we came to Egypt, checking to see whether we had paid the visa entry fee, and so on. Those were the times when a rush of adrenaline interrupted the monotony. Once the soldiers were satisfied that we were neither Israeli spies nor aspiring suicide bombers, they would let us through. Egypt looked like a country under siege. I told my fellow passengers that I personally would have felt less at ease if those checkpoints did not exist. Only a couple of years back a number of tourists at Sharm El Sheikh were massacred by Islamic jihadists. Egypt was threatened by extremists so much that not only the regime of Hosni Mubarak but the entire country's tourist industry and economic lifeblood were at risk of collapsing. None of us could have imagined at the time that the Mubarak regime's days were numbered.

We reached the last checkpoint, at the outer gate of the monastery, at about four in the afternoon. From there, it was a five-minute drive until we reached the monastery. In utter frustration we couldn't understand why the armed Bedouins who guarded the gate wouldn't let us through. Our driver was irritated and quarreled for a while with them in Arabic. We couldn't understand any of it and worried, unfairly, that in his frustration he was going to drop us off right there with our luggage and head back to Sharm El Sheikh. I suspected that because we were traveling as individuals rather than as a group with a designated tour guide, we had unwittingly created confusion and suspicions. After some negotiations using English mixed with Greek that the Bedouins had learned from the monks, and after many exasperating protests from my companions, we reached a friendly resolution. The guards simply and abruptly decided to let us through. In her relief, Emily gave them our leftover food. It seemed that when they realized we were mere Greeks from Cyprus, the ice melted. Since its creation in antiquity, the monastery was made up of mostly Greek monks, with whom the Bedouins had excellent relations. The steady influx of pilgrims from all over the world, and particularly from Greece and Cyprus, with money to spend provided the bedrock of the local Bedouin economy.

We all felt greatly relieved when we finally arrived at the ancient citadel, right in the center of that desert wilderness. The ancient historian Procopius could not have described more aptly the setting. The region, he wrote was "uninhabited . . . a barren land, unwatered and producing neither crops nor any useful thing."[1] Yet the monastery itself, thanks to drilled wells, was like a small oasis with an adjacent vegetable garden, several olive trees, cypresses, and almond trees. When the famous Greek writer Nikos Kazantzakis arrived at the monastery on a spring day in the twenties after an excruciating four-day caravan ride, he was so enchanted by the scent from the blossoming almond trees that he jotted in his dramatic and evocative style: "I wondered how was it possible for this monastic castle to survive these silent breaths over so many centuries and not crumble at some spring day like this."[2]

We were given a warm welcome at the monastery by Bedouin children. Lavros had warned us to arm ourselves with candy for the unavoidable assault by the little ones. After this delightful invasion, we were assigned to tidy and clean rooms. Unlike at other monasteries, married couples could stay together in the same room.

Before venturing inside the heavily fortified walls, we briefly rested in our rooms. I perused a book Emily had brought along that gave some of the basic facts about the monastery. St. Catherine, I read, is considered the oldest Christian monastery in the world, over fourteen hundred years old. Furthermore, it houses the richest collection of icons anywhere in the world. In terms of rare manuscripts, it comes second only to the Vatican. The Byzantine emperor Justinian (A.D. 527–565) decided to protect the monastic community by building around the Old Testament sites a mighty fortification. Before the high walls were erected, the monastery had suffered from repeated raids by neighboring tribes that ransacked the community and massacred many of the monks. In an effort to preserve Byzantium's influence in that strategic passage, Justinian built the walls of the monastery and brought along two hundred families to provide military protection to the monks and become their loyal workers and caretakers.

The descendants of those original Greek families converted to Islam and became assimilated into the surrounding Bedouin culture. They maintained, however, their special relationship with the monastery with an awareness of their Greek roots, participating in certain rituals, particularly those honoring St. Catherine and St. George. They are the Bedouin tribes that guard the monastery to this day, maintain the grounds, cook the meals, cultivate the vegetable gardens, groom the olive trees, attend to the pilgrims' needs, and serve as guides for the hike up Moses' Mountain. Thanks to Justinian's fortifications and to the original workers and military guards he sent there, the monastery has survived when most other Christian sites have withered away. I read: "Mohammed the founder of Islam, Arab caliphs, Turkish sultans, and Napoleon all took the Monastery under their protection, thereby preserving it from pillage: it has never in its long history been conquered, damaged or destroyed, and has through the ages kept its image as a sacred Biblical site."[3]

We learned more about the place when we walked into the monastery proper, passing through its massive walls, war towers, and embrasures. We traversed several narrow and dark corridors until we reached a small opening near the Church of the Transfiguration, another gift of Emperor Justinian. All six of us remained quiet, marveling at the magnificence of its architecture. Total silence prevailed, as if we were in a soundproof room.

I had never experienced anything like it. The monks must have been in their cells, praying or resting, as there was no sign of human activity.

The silence was broken when a vivacious Greek woman in her late twenties approached us, excited to discover that we were fellow Greeks. She introduced herself as Nikki and said she had come with her parents to climb the sacred mountain. She invited us to join them. Nikki claimed that she and her parents were experienced mountain hikers. We agreed to join them. Olympia wished to start the climb right away, after sunset, while the rest of us wanted to begin early the following morning.

"Please, please," an elderly monk implored us as he came down the steps into the yard, interrupting our conversation. "Lower your voices. You're disturbing the silence of the monastery!"

We apologized profusely to the good father, who introduced himself as Fr. Paul, originally from Athens. When we mentioned that we came from Cyprus with the blessings of Fr. Maximos, he warmed to us immediately. Fr. Maximos had, on several occasions, hosted visiting monks from St. Catherine at his bishopric in Cyprus. Fr. Paul generously volunteered to show us the art treasures housed at the monastery and tell us a few things about its life and history. When he heard of our plans to climb the mountain, he cautioned us to do so early in the morning with the help of an experienced guide. "Two weeks ago there was a terrible accident here," he told us. "A Russian pilgrim ventured to go there on his own at night without a guide and got lost. Trained alpinists with their ropes and special gear had to come from abroad to search for him. They found his body at the base of a ravine. So don't venture alone up there, please." It didn't take us long to convince Olympia to change her mind and begin the hike early the next morning with the help of a guide.

"You see this bush?" Fr. Paul said casually, pointing at a robust-looking plant in the middle of the yard. It was supported by a carefully crafted wall of dark brown rocks. "This is the Burning Bush where Moses heard the voice of God."

"Amazing," Olympia murmured. The monks have been keeping the bush alive for thousands of years. Rituals and services have been taking place next to it. Another pilgrim who visited the place on several occasions described to us how he felt uplifted during the chanting of a visiting choir right next to that mythic bush. We were told that that plant is the only one of its kind in the entire Sinai peninsula. Every attempt to transplant a branch of it to another location has reputedly been unsuccessful. The Burning Bush was one of the treasures that made the monastery famous throughout the centuries, attracting pilgrims from all three of the Abrahamic religions: Christianity, Judaism, and Islam. For thousands of years the faithful have learned of the legend of Moses and the bush through this famous verse in the Old Testament: "And he looked, and, behold, the bush burned with fire, and the bush was not consumed" (Exodus 3:2).

"This is Moses' Well," Fr. Paul said, pointing at an ancient looking well only a few meters from the Burning Bush. "According to tradition, it was here that Moses met Jethro's daughters, the oldest of whom, Zipporah, became his wife."

"This place fills your mind with Old Testament scenes," Emily said in awe.

"It's also been an inspiration for many famous painters and artists," I added.

I learned later from my artist friend Michael Lewis that in

1481 Botticelli painted a fresco on the left wall of the Sistine Chapel that includes images of Moses encountering Jethro's daughters and of God speaking to him from the Burning Bush. But Botticelli, as I told Emily, never saw the actual well and bush as we did that afternoon in May 2009.

Another great artist, who did visit the monastery and who painted an imposing image of it, was the Cretan master Dominikos Theotokopoulos, otherwise known as El Greco. His classic painting was the first image printed in a large book published by the monastery that exhibited its treasures.[4]

"Follow me," Fr. Paul said as he led us into a gallery of ancient icons and rare manuscripts. The room could have been part of any first-rate museum. Icons were protected behind glass with proper lighting and temperature control. There were beautifully gilded ancient Bibles, gospels, silver crosses, jewel-covered crowns, and other priceless religious relics that had been donated by rich patrons over the ages. It was breathtaking. We witnessed an assembly of artistic creations that took many years of negotiations before New York's Metropolitan Museum could bring them to New York for a first ever exhibition that had caused a stir in 2004. It was all in front of us, shown to our small group ever so casually.

"You can take pictures," Fr. Paul said, as if reading our thoughts, "if you don't use the flash."

One of the many exhibits that attracted my attention was a large, heavy-looking book in a prominent location. I looked more closely and inhaled sharply. It was Plato's *Ta Apanta*, the Complete Works. The place of publication was Venice; the date, A.D. 1513.

"It was published right after the discovery of the printing press by Gutenberg," Fr. Paul explained. I was in awe. In front of me was a masterpiece that had played a pivotal role in the emergence of the modern world, the Renaissance!

After the fall of Constantinople to the Ottoman Turks in 1453, most of the scholars of Byzantium escaped to Venice, carrying with them their books and knowledge of classical civilization that had been lost to the West during the Middle Ages yet preserved in the schools of Constantinople. I figured that I probably had in front of me the first ever publication of Plato's complete works! After all, Johannes Gutenberg, the inventor of the printing press, was born about 1390, and the first printed book was the Gutenberg Bible, circa 1455. The Neoplatonists had escaped from conquered Constantinople to Venice with their handwritten copies of Plato's works, and it would have taken some time after resettling before they could have published in the original Greek *Ta Apanta*. That meant we were looking at what was, most likely, the work that, along with the printed Bible, brought about a revolution in European culture. Before I could digest the impact of what I was gazing at, I heard the voice of our guide.

"The monastery has a rich collection of such books," Fr. Paul explained with a sweep of his hand. "But we don't have the space to exhibit them. Here is something that might also interest you." He pointed at a document with Arabic letters and the dark imprint of a human hand. "This may have helped the survival of the monastery over the centuries."

We learned that the document had none other than Mohammed's seal. It is said that the monks of St. Catherine sent a delegation to Medina in A.D. 625 to ask for Mohammed's patronage and protection. Their request was granted in the form of that document, which proclaimed that the Muslims would respect the autonomy of the monastery and that the monks could freely practice their religion and be exempt from taxation. The hand imprinted on the document is supposed to be Mohammed's, since the founder of Islam was illiterate and used his hand as signature and seal. According to tradition, during his travels as a merchant, Mohammed had visited the monastery and the monks had offered him hospitality. Because of that legend, when the peninsula was conquered by the Arabs, in A.D. 641, the monks carried on with their lives unmolested. Nevertheless, their numbers declined considerably. Many of the Christians of Sinai converted to Islam, such as the ancestors of the current Bedouins, and others fled. It is said that a little mosque built within the compound of the monastery was to placate less benevolent rulers during the eleventh century.[5]

The authenticity of Mohammed's document, the *Ahtiname*, has been questioned by some scholars. Nevertheless, Mohammed's request was respected by Muslim leaders throughout the ages. They considered the document genuine, and that's what mattered.[6] Fr. Paul showed us other important documents, including one signed by Napoleon that promised similar respect and protection to the monastery.

"Don't be shocked at what you will see next," he warned enigmatically. He led us into a room dimly lit for maximum effect. We found ourselves in front of a pyramid of human skulls, hundreds of them, neatly piled up. In another section of the dungeon was a pile of thousands of human bones, likewise neatly arranged. They were the remains of the monks who had lived at St. Catherine since its inception. Someday Fr. Paul's remains will be in that very room and his skull will be placed at the top of the pyramid, facing the visitors.

Surprisingly, none of us found the sight particularly gruesome. It was a reminder of the transience of our current existence, part of the fathers' training to overcome the fear of death. For me, it was more gruesome to see pictures of piled skulls of

Cambodians massacred by the Khmer Rouge during the seventies or the pyramids of butchered Tutsis during the genocide in Rwanda during the nineties. But the skulls of St. Catherine were not of people who had been tortured or beheaded. Most of the monks probably had peaceful lives, praying and fasting to secure their place in Paradise.

The skulls, mute and silent, were positioned as if they were looking at us, ready to strike up a conversation. "I wish I could have a dialogue with each of them," I whispered to Emily as I took a picture. "I'd like to learn about their stories. What made them decide to become monks and spend their lives in this desolate desert? Did they find what they were looking for?"

As these questions entered my mind, I thought of an identical question that Nikos Kazantzakis had asked of a monk named Moses during his sojourn to the monastery ninety years earlier.

"How did you become a monk, Fr. Moses?"

Fr. Moses laughed and with gusto and self-mockery replied:

"I wanted to become a monk since I was twelve years old. But the devil created obstacles for me. And what kind of obstacles you might ask? I had good jobs and doing well. I was making money. And what does it mean to make money? You forget God.

"I became a postman and a shoemaker; I worked in the mines of Lavrion [near Athens] and then at the railroads of Ikonio [Asia Minor]. I promised myself: the moment I lose my money I will become a monk. God loved me. I cut the rope, I left. You know how they cut the rope from a balloon? And the balloon climbs up to the sky? That is how I left from the world!

"I have been here twenty years now. What do I do? Whatever I did in the world. I work. I work from morning till night.

You might ask: Is it the same? I say not at all! Here I am happy. In the world I was not.

"And what do I do? I build roads. All the roads we just walked on I built them myself. This is my *diakonia* [divinely assigned task]. That's why I was born. If I go to Paradise I will march over the roads I built."[7]

"I wonder which one of those skulls looking at us is of Fr. Moses," I whispered to Emily. "I wish I could ask him whether he walked on those roads he had built and whether he found his paradise."

I thought of a recent book by the Athonite and much revered elder Ephraim Philotheou. Olympia had brought the passage to my attention while we were waiting for our flight out of Cyprus. It posited the elder's understanding of the infinite compassion of God and how God wants all His children to attain their salvation.

Had God not been so infinitely compassionate, no one could be saved. It is so because no one on earth has ever lived who was beyond blemish. No one can claim that he kept his heart spotless without stain and faults. God's compassion, however, is so stupendous, His medicine so awesome and powerful that it wipes out all blemish, turning everything sparkling clean. God makes monumental interventions and extraordinary surgeries in order to save man from certain psychic death.

We see souls that have left, that have left from this life without *metanoia* [repentance], and "*thia epemvasi kai thia pronoia*" [through the intervention of Divine Providence] and through the intercessions of saintly human beings, have returned back and received forgiveness. "*Meta thanaton ouk esti metanoia*" [After death there is no repentance] by the lost soul herself. In order for a

soul to undergo *metanoia*, she must return to life. Even such miracles the Providence of God has permitted in order to save a
person.[8]

I didn't know how to interpret these lines. I did mention to
Olympia, however, that it is a breath of fresh air to read such
words from the pen of an esteemed elder who implies that God
could not have constructed a hell into which He throws sinners
destined for eternal damnation. This Calvinist notion is totally
at odds with the Eastern Orthodox understanding of God's infinite compassion. God wants everybody to be saved. This is sufficient for me as a working hypothesis to conduct my life. I did
mention to Olympia that I believe in a subjective hell that each
one of us creates as a result of thoughts and actions that distance
us from God. But as far as God is concerned, only Paradise
is ultimately real. This is what I understand as the nature of
Orthodox eschatology, beautifully summarized in the words of
the Athonite elder. Having such thoughts as I stood in front of the
pyramid of skulls gave me an intuitive certainty that all those
monks, including Fr. Moses, had already attained their salvation
in Paradise.

My contemplation was interrupted by Fr. Paul, who wished
us good-bye and recommended the church service at noon the
next day, in which we would receive the "Ring of St. Catherine." "There will be a *paraklesis* [short prayer service], and then
you will be offered the silver ring," he said.

"A silver ring?" I whispered to Olympia, who raised her
shoulders, not knowing what it was all about. None of us knew,
but we looked forward to finding out.

"Remember! For your safety and joy, begin your ascent up the
mountain early in the morning and not in the late afternoon," Fr.
Paul repeated. "Most important, hire a guide."

During dinner we made arrangements for our hiking adventure. Only Emily, Olympia, and myself decided to go. Olympia's three other friends planned to stay behind and join the monks for the early morning service. We formed a group with Nikki, the enthusiastic young woman from Greece, and her parents. Together we hired Ahmet, a twenty-five-year-old Bedouin guide. He knew broken Greek and some English, and, given his easy-going disposition, we felt comfortable with him. I noticed other groups of pilgrims negotiating with other guides for the morning march up Jebel Musa.

"We start the hike no later than three in the morning," Ahmet instructed so that we would reach the top of the mountain before sunrise. We were told time and again that watching the sunrise from the top of Moses' Mountain was an unforgettable experience. The sun would come up from behind the distant desert mountains of Arabia shortly before 6:00. We set our alarm clocks for 2:30 A.M., hoping to get at least four hours of sleep before the challenging ascent.

Sleep did not come easy. The experiences of the day were too vivid in my mind for me to completely unwind. I was also concerned about a burst blister on Emily's right foot, which she reassured me would not interfere with the hike. But walking up a steep mountain is no easy matter, and a minor injury could become a major problem in no time. In any event, she had no trouble entering into a deep sleep while I ended up getting barely two hours of sleep.

By 2:45 we had assembled in the main yard, where other groups were gathering around their guides. Everybody carried a flashlight. It was a moonless night, and without flashlights we could not see beyond our noses.

"Oh dear!" Nikki exclaimed as she aimed her flashlight at Olympia's feet. "You can't hike up that mountain in those shoes!

You simply can't make it." Kostas, her father, nodded in agreement. Olympia was wearing ordinary street shoes. She insisted that she felt comfortable in them and that she could not foresee any problems. She said she'd used those shoes time and again walking the shopping district of Limassol. Besides, she hadn't brought any hiking shoes. Nikki checked Emily and myself with her flashlight, and we received her approval. We could make it to the top.

Ahmet stressed the importance of sticking together so that we wouldn't get lost in the dark or drift into other groups. He had his reputation to protect. If anything happened to people under his guidance, he could lose his license. Ahmet had just gotten married and needed the money he earned as a guide. As we exited the monastery, he had to show the license to the armed guards. Guiding pilgrims and tourists up and down the mountain was Ahmet's job. He mentioned that he had been doing that hike just about every day for several years. He would often do the hike several times in twenty-four hours, getting hardly any sleep.

With our flashlights in one hand and walking sticks in the other, we stepped outside the massive Justinian walls. Surprisingly, crowds of people with their guides were getting ready for the march up the biblical mountain. Not only pilgrims were there but also an army of sunbathing, scuba-diving tourists from the Red Sea resorts. They came by bus from Sharm El Sheikh to watch the sunrise from the top of the mountain. A visit to the monastery of St. Catherine and the hike up Moses' Mountain were part of their vacation package.

Following Ahmet's instructions, we stayed close together. The sky above was clear, starry, and moonless. In front of us, we could see a string of flashlights zigzagging up the mountain like moving stars. It was often difficult to separate the lights of the hikers from the stars above. We were in awe of the scene. On both sides of the path Bedouins awaited customers with their camels. It was hard to see them until we came face-to-face with a camel sitting silently and patiently on the side of the road.

Nikki and her parents walked in front of us, along with Ahmet. Emily and Olympia were behind me as I focused my flashlight on the ground to make sure we did not misstep. Ahmet would often stop and turn back, calling our names out to make sure that nobody was missing.

"Camel? Camel?" we would hear the Bedouins asking. "*Kamila? Kamila?*" they would ask when they overheard us speaking Greek. None of us wished to go up the mountain on the back of a camel. Olympia herself would hear nothing of it. Alas, after hiking about a mile, she realized the wisdom of what Nikki and her parents had told her regarding her shoes. Olympia reassured us that she could make it back to the monastery alone by following the hikers with their flashlights coming from the opposite direction.

It was only later that we learned Olympia's return was not so easy. She got disoriented in the mix of hikers, Bedouins, and camels and did not know which path to follow. It was then that she heard a young Bedouin boy call to her in Greek with the words "*Ela apedo*" (Come this way). He took her by the hand and guided her all the way to the monastery. When she offered him a tip, he refused. That was extraordinary; everywhere we traveled in Egypt tipping was expected, for even minor favors. Lavros had advised us always to have plenty of change on hand.

We accelerated our pace. Everybody wished to reach the top of the mountain in time to experience the famed sunrise. Every so often we came across rest areas where we could refresh ourselves for a few minutes. Illuminated with kerosene lamps and decorated with colorful carpets woven by the Bedouins, these stops were additional attractions. Hikers could buy bottled water and other refreshments and fraternize with others. There were hikers from all religious persuasions.

During our first rest, we struck up a conversation with a cheerful Saudi father and his four equally merry daughters and son. The young ladies could not have looked more unlike the stereotypical, fully covered Saudi woman. They wore tight blue jeans and had no scarves or veils over their heads. "We wear our blue jeans under our dresses when we are in Saudi Arabia. The moment we get home or as soon as we step into another country, we just take off our veils and gowns and remain with our blue jeans," the eldest daughter said.

It was still very dark, and we needed our flashlights until we reached the last leg of our path, where the 750 steps began and no camel could tread. As we started climbing, one step at a time, light was beginning to break through. It was a difficult ascent, which required on occasion the use of both legs and hands. Fortunately, Emily's foot did not create any problems, and we felt relieved that Olympia had decided to turn back. She definitely could not have made it to the top in the shoes she was wearing. There was heavy traffic, because all the groups converged and were trying to reach the top before sunrise. At the base of the stone ladder were young Bedouins asking whether we needed assistance. For a tip they would help untrained hikers move from one step to the next. "Help? Help?" they inquired in earnest. If they thought we were Greeks, "Voithia? Voithia?" I don't recall how many times I said "No thank you."

We kept climbing, nearing our destination. We no longer needed our flashlights. As we climbed up those endless steps, I

wondered how many of them had been hewed out of the granite rock by Fr. Moses. I mentioned to Emily, who was behind
me, that it may not have been accidental that St. John of Sinai,
the seventh-century abbot of the monastery, otherwise known
as St. John Climacus, titled his classic spiritual work *The Ladder of
Divine Ascent*.[9] The book is a series of homilies on how to work on
oneself one step at a time to climb up to and unite with God. He
must have gotten the idea not only from Jacob's vision in Genesis but also from climbing these steps some spring morning to
catch a glimpse of the sun rising over the desert mountains of
Arabia.

We rested at the last stop. We were only ten minutes from
our destination. Improperly dressed tourists and pilgrims could
rent handmade blankets from the enterprising Bedouins. Nikki
marveled how they managed to make money every step of the
way: first with camels, then with personal assistance at the start
of the steps, and finally with blankets.

It was cold up there. Fortunately, thanks to good advice, we
were dressed in layers so we could put on and remove garments
as the need arose. At 2,285 meters, the wind was strong and penetrating. Ahmet announced that we could go the last ten minutes
on our own. He would wait for us at the rest area below. He said
there was no point in his joining us since we could not possibly
get lost from there to the top. Our guide must have seen the
sunrise innumerable times.

At last we arrived. Already there were a couple of hundred
people sitting by the edge of the precipice, eagerly awaiting the
sunrise. Our immediate preoccupation was to protect ourselves
from the cold. We found a spot on a rock protected from the
wind near another slightly taller rock, and all five of us squeezed
in, making sure to stay far back from the precipice. It was 5:45.

At any moment we were going to witness the rising of the sun the way Moses saw it. Only ten yards away, at the very top, were an Eastern Orthodox chapel and a mosque. I found the symbolism compelling, but we would have to explore them after sunrise.

Finally, the first rays of the sun appeared over one of the mountaintops. There was thunderous applause from the hikers. I can't recall another moment when people showed such great excitement at the appearance of the sun. It was as if at that very moment God had revealed his Commandments to humanity and the applause reflected our appreciation for His fatherly love. I felt chills going down my spine, not from the cold but from the realization that we stood on holy ground, sanctified over the millennia by pilgrims' devotion and yearning for union with their Maker. Certain passages from Huston Smith's classic work *The World's Religions*, which I had read several times, came to mind. Writing about Judaism and the role it played in the Western understanding of God, Smith compared the difference between God as understood by the Hebrews and the surrounding cultures' understanding of their gods.

> The God of the Jews possessed none of these traits [immorality, vindictiveness, and capriciousness] which in greater or lesser degree characterized the gods of their neighbors. . . . The Greeks, the Romans, the Syrians, and most of the other Mediterranean peoples would have said two things about their gods' characters. First, they tend to be amoral; second, towards humankind they are preponderantly indifferent. The Jews reversed the thinking of their contemporaries on both these counts. Whereas the gods of Olympus tirelessly pursued beautiful women, the God of Sinai watched over widows and orphans. . . . [God as revealed through the Jewish prophets] is a God of righ-

teousness, whose loving-kindness is from everlasting to everlasting and whose tender mercies are in all his works.[10]

Smith states how Hebrew morality embedded in the Ten Commandments (Thou shalt not murder; Thou shalt not commit adultery; Thou shalt not steal; Thou shalt not bear false witness, et cetera) affected the history of the world: "Appropriated by Christianity and Islam, the Ten Commandments constitute the moral foundation of most of the Western world."[11]

I shared these thoughts with Emily, who was equally moved. But Kostas, Nikki's father, a retired schoolmaster, was not impressed. All along the hike he'd cracked one joke after another, helping us forget our fatigue. This time he was not joking; he felt let down. "I've seen better sunrises in Zakynthos," he said somberly, referring to his Ionian island. "So what's all the big fuss about?"

"I have also seen more spectacular sunrises, both in Cyprus and in Maine," I agreed. "The colors were more vivid and there was a greater variety of shades of red and yellow. But this isn't the point. What's important is that for more than two thousand years people have believed that Prophet Moses met God and had a conversation with Him right here. The God of Abraham, of Isaac, and of Jacob," I went on to say, "is a talking God. He has communicated and continues to communicate to humanity through His prophets. He's not an impersonal and indifferent deity that keeps the universe going but a fundamentally personal, omniscient, all-powerful, and all-loving God. This is the significance of what we are experiencing here, not the physical colors, which may vary with weather conditions and the particulates in the atmosphere."

"I understand, I understand," Kostas said, his attitude now markedly different.

After the sun made its full appearance and upon contemplating further the religious significance of the ground we were treading on, we spent some time exploring the narrow summit and peeking into the locked doors of the tiny Orthodox chapel and the equally tiny neighboring mosque. Others chose to do their morning meditations or prayers, facing east, sitting cross-legged on boulders with closed eyes. Half an hour later, we began our descent to meet Ahmet at the rest area.

We arrived at the outskirts of the monastery around eight thirty, when the sun was beginning to heat up the earth. Outside the monastery's walls, in an area of solid, smooth rock, about a hundred people were assembled for an outdoor mass. They knelt while a priest, who must have been either Catholic or Anglican, blessed them and began offering holy communion. On the other side, not far from the monastery's fortifications, passengers who had opted for public transportation for the return journey got off their camels and traipsed by. The mix of camels, hikers, and Bedouins was a sight I would not ever forget. It appeared like a scene from Exodus.

During our six-hour experience, the presence of the Bedouins with their camels had offered us a reassuring feeling. They were the equivalents of standby ambulances with seasoned hands to offer help in case of an emergency. The Bedouins of the area, while always eager to make money from the pilgrims and tourists, also saw themselves clearly as part of the monastery and considered the institution their own. According to Fr. Paul, the monastery could not exist without them.

It was clear that the survival of the monastery for over fourteen hundred years was due not only to the mighty fortifications of Emperor Justinian and Mohammed's *Ahtiname* but, most important, to the centuries-old, mutually interdependent lives of the Muslim Bedouins and the Christian monks. And it is not just the division of labor between these two groups that has held them together but also the clearly identifiable, underlying consensus of values that stem from their respect of each other's traditions and sense of strong identity with St. Catherine.

After breakfast we bade farewell to our hiking partners and exchanged addresses: their tour group was leaving for Cairo that very morning. We then went to our room for a shower and some rest. But although I'd hardly slept the previous night, I again could neither rest nor sleep. Somehow I felt energized by that pilgrimage adventure. We went instead around the monastery in search of the other members of our party. But they were nowhere to be found.

At noon we went to the Justinian-built Church of the Transfiguration in the middle of the monastery to attend the brief service and receive the mysterious silver ring of St. Catherine promised to us by Fr. Paul. It was the first time we saw a number of monks gathered in one place. There were plenty of tourists and pilgrims present. It was easy to distinguish the two categories of visitors. The pilgrims looked devout, appropriately dressed, and were kneeling and crossing themselves at various times during the service. By contrast the tourists looked like visitors to a quaint museum and were usually inappropriately dressed, in shorts and sandals.

After the service was over, the pilgrims were invited to receive a blessing from the presiding priest, who gave each one of us a silver ring with the Greek inscription *Agia Aikaterini*, St. Catherine. It was the second ring I was ever given; the first was during my wedding to Emily.

I learned the details about the ring only after returning to Cyprus. Our friend Erato, Stephanos's wife, who was thoroughly steeped in Orthodox literature, gave me a copy of the *Synaxaristis*, a compilation of the life stories of all the saints celebrated by the Eastern Orthodox Church. It recounts the tragic story of young Catherine who, because of her faith and martyrdom, became a celebrated saint of both the Eastern and Western churches.

St. Catherine was born in A.D. 294 in a wealthy, aristocratic family of Alexandria, a center of Hellenistic culture equal, if not superior, to Athens and Rome. Stunningly beautiful and having mastered philosophy, rhetoric, music, and poetry as well as the natural sciences and mathematics, she was considered one of the most educated women of antiquity. Very much like Penelope, wife of Ulysses, she had an army of suitors. But Catherine was not interested in marriage. To fend off family pressures to marry, she declared: "Find me a young man who is my equal in all the gifts and virtues that you claim I excel in and I will marry him. Search everywhere to find one who is like me in gentleness, wealth, wisdom, and beauty. If any one of those gifts is lacking, such a suitor is not worthy of me."[12] Her relatives knew that such a man would be impossible to find and suggested the son of the Roman emperor, along with the sons of other aristocrats who were richer than she but no match for her in wisdom and beauty. Catherine's reply was that she, who was steeped in classical philosophy and culture, could not possibly live with an illiterate husband. According to the story, her mother, who was a closet Christian, brought her in contact with a hermit who was hiding outside the city. The hermit triggered Catherine's curiosity when he told her cryptically that he knew of a prospective bridegroom who was infinitely superior to her in all knowledge and virtue and who would have made a perfect match for her. After that encounter she met Christ in two vivid dreams, which led to her conversion. According to the *Synaxaristis*, during her second dream Christ offered her a wedding ring.

"When the young woman woke up she discovered that she truly wore a ring on her right hand. Her heart became captive to the divine Eros of Christ the King."[13]

During the persecutions of Christians, Catherine confessed her faith publicly, and that confession led to her beheading on November 25, A.D. 305. After her execution, her body mysteriously disappeared. Tradition has it that angels transported it to the peak of the tallest mountain of Sinai, which is now known as Mt. St. Catherine. Three centuries later, guided by dreams, monks found her body. They brought it down to the monastery and placed it in a golden casket inside the church. It is said that to this day her sacred remains ooze a sweet fragrance that is considered a perennial miracle. Since the eleventh century, the monastery has been known as the Monastery of St. Catherine.

As I fiddled with the ring, another renowned woman martyr came to my mind, a fellow Alexandrian of St. Catherine's. Born in A.D. 370, about three generations after St. Catherine's death and after Constantine elevated Christianity to be the official religion of the Roman Empire, Hypatia became a leading philosopher and mathematician of her time. She was head of the Alexandrian Neoplatonist school and teacher of philosophy, mathematics, and astronomy. Like St. Catherine, she was considered one of the most beautiful, virtuous, and educated women of antiquity, refusing all suitors and preferring instead the life of the mind. However, unlike St. Catherine, who was killed by pagans, Hypatia was murdered in 415 by a fanatical Christian mob headed by a monk who considered her a pagan heretic. I found these parallel tragic Alexandrian lives poignant. Fanaticism, alas, is a demon that has plagued all historical religions.

~~~

In spite of her failed attempt to watch the sunrise from the top of Mt. Moses, Olympia beamed with joy when we met her during the early afternoon at the monastery's Bedouin-run coffee shop. She was having tea with her three friends. "I found what I was looking for," she informed us with supreme satisfaction. She then told us that at first she was very disappointed when she was forced to abort her hiking adventure. But it turned out for the better, "the way things were supposed to be," as she put it. Olympia attended the early morning service, after which the four Cypriot women were treated to coffee at the *archondariki*, the guesthouse of the monastery, where she met a monk who helped her contact a much revered hermit and spiritual elder. Fr. Moses, a favorite name at St. Catherine's, lived alone in the desert within walking distance from the monastery. It was an easy hike that Olympia and her friends could do in a little over an hour. "He gave us the kind of spiritual advice that was relevant for each one of us," she claimed. The other three women nodded. Olympia then shared with us the hermit's extraordinary abilities. "It was an unbelievable experience," she claimed. "He read my soul like an open book."

Fr. Moses was not only a spiritually gifted hermit but also a first-rate social organizer and activist. He had helped the women of four hundred Bedouin families become economically independent by setting up a cooperative to promote native handcrafts. He raised money from visiting pilgrims, imported looms and sewing machines, and trained the women to weave traditional fabrics and related products, which could be sold to tourists and visitors to the monastery. We heard that thanks to his efforts the status of Bedouin women in the area was beginning to rise. Olympia was so impressed that she volunteered to import their products to Cyprus. In fact, upon her return home, she organized a gathering of women at her spacious, Egyptian-looking home, cooked for forty or so guests by herself, gave a presentation on the work of Fr. Moses, and gathered a substantial amount of cash, vitamins, medicine, and hand creams for the Bedouin women.

Olympia had hardly finished describing her experiences with Fr. Moses when a tourist bus entered the monastery grounds. A horde of noisy and excited pilgrims got off the bus, storming the vine-covered coffee shop. All the empty tables filled within seconds. They were all Greek Cypriots from Paralimni, a coastal fishing village turned tourist attraction. Their tour guide, from the same village, was a rough-looking and rough-mannered man, like a football coach who barked orders and announcements. "Be here at three thirty to start the hike up the mountain," he commanded.

We were surprised. How were they going to do the hike in the heat of the day? We chatted with some of the pilgrims who were sitting next to our table about our experiences and suggested that a morning hike would be preferable to an afternoon trek. They had arrived after a tiring all-day bus ride from Cairo, and in less than an hour they were expected to start walking up the mountain. When some women raised the question with their tour guide, he shouted back that he was their guide and they should listen to nobody else. He boasted that he had come to St. Catherine many times before and knew what he was talking about. However, pressed further, he was forced to admit that he had never hiked up Moses' Mountain himself. Nevertheless, the hike at three thirty in the afternoon was on schedule. No further questions.

I wondered how many of these pilgrims, especially those of advanced age, would make it to the top. Few of this crowd seemed to have the physical characteristics of hikers, let alone proper footwear. What they did have in great abundance, which many of the hikers we encountered did not, was religious zeal and enthusiasm.

"I don't care when we start the hike. I know that I will get there no matter what," declared an obese grandmother who was sitting next to our table. "That's why I came here," she added, striking her cane on the pavement. "Nothing can stop me. I won't go back to Cyprus until I complete my pilgrimage and kiss the ground where Moses received the Ten Commandments."

I noticed that when the pious woman arrived at the coffee shop she could hardly move without breathing heavily. I leaned toward Emily and whispered, "For this poor grandma to reach the top intact would require no less a miracle than the one when the angels brought the remains of St. Catherine from Alexandria to Sinai." Both Emily and Olympia, who overheard me, burst into laughter, although Emily also playfully reprimanded me for spiritually counterproductive thoughts.

We did not find out what happened with that crowd of pilgrims from Paralimni. Therefore, I couldn't verify, at least at that moment, whether the overweight grandma had fulfilled her vow.

~~~

When we arrived at the Cairo airport on our return trip, the air was heavy and the wind was blowing with demoniacal intensity. Employees wore white masks while reassuring us that our plane was on schedule and that there was nothing to fear from the sandstorm that swept the area.

"This is tougher than climbing Jebel Musa," I mused as we sat, recovering from the onslaught of sand, waiting at the gate for our flight out of Egypt. At that point, we noticed that also on our flight was the group of Cypriots from Paralimni whom we had met at St. Catherine. We were surprised and pleased to hear that, with the help of the Bedouins and their camels, most had managed to climb to the top, including the heavy-breathing and overweight grandmother. She fulfilled her dream to kiss the rocky ground where Moses received the Ten Commandments thanks to a couple of muscular Bedouin lads who helped her climb up the last 750 steps.

"That's what it means to have faith," Emily reminded me as I nodded meekly in disbelief. "It moves mountains."

When the plane lifted off, I watched out my window as Cairo and its lifeblood, the Nile, faded away. The sky above and the Mediterranean below acquired their familiar blue and turquoise colors in no time. In a few minutes, we were beyond the reach of the sandstorm that had caused so much discomfort. Emily dozed off, and I used the time to jot down a few thoughts on the spiritually meaningful, albeit taxing pilgrimage that we'd just completed. I then perused a copy of an English-language compilation of Egyptian news. A disturbing piece of minor news stood out for me.[14] I read that two Muslim Brotherhood members of the Egyptian parliament were working on a draft law that would severely penalize Muslims who converted to any other faith. These MPs based their action on a controversial fatwa claiming that conversion is forbidden and that Muslim converts should be considered apostates. According to one of the proponents of this bill, "It is not 'right' for Muslims to convert to Christianity because it entails the denial of Prophet Mohammed's message, which is a step down, while Christians who convert to Islam continue to honor Jesus." The other sponsor said, "Muslims who convert because they are convinced that Christianity is the true faith deserve the maximum punishment." The two MPs' proposal was met with disdain by human rights activists, who claimed that it had no chance of passing and went contrary to the Egyptian constitution.

"The fact that two MPs could even propose such a law," I said to Emily, who had just emerged from her power nap, "is in itself disturbing Christians in a country like Egypt, which is noted for its relative openness and tolerance to other religions, particularly its Coptic Christian minority."

That piece of news was a reminder of the unpalatable fact of religious intolerance, which had begun to raise its ugly head in recent years. "What would happen," I asked Emily, "to the Monastery of St. Catherine, with its twenty-seven monks, if people with such notions came to power in Egypt and in other countries of the region?" Would such regimes continue to honor the *Ahtiname* of Mohammed, which had played such a key role in the survival of that most ancient of monasteries?

In fact, the future of Christianity in the region that gave birth to it two thousand years ago appears quite grim. Various international reports have documented the mass exodus of Christians from the Middle East as a result of political violence, lack of economic opportunity, and the rise of radical Islam. It is estimated that a century ago Christians composed 20 percent of the population of the entire region. Today, they are about 5 percent and rapidly diminishing.[15] Christianity's most famous and historic shrines, such as those we'd just visited, could, therefore, soon become no more than museum relics, with no relevance to those who live among them. The ultimate extinction of Christianity in the Middle East is a prediction shared by many knowledgeable observers.[16] Alas for Christians, Islam has replaced nationalism as the central force of personal identity in the Middle East. According to a *New York Times* report, since Islamic culture, particularly in its more fundamental expression, often defines itself in contrast to the West, Christianity has in some places become the enemy culture. The pessimistic assessment of some Christian journalists in the area is that without a turn toward secularism in the Arab world, there is no future for Christians there.[17]

Those were the issues I was discussing with Emily as the plane began its descent toward Larnaka airport. Our brief yet rich exposure to one of the key remnants of ancient Christianity brought home those realities.

ELEVEN

INNER RIVER

Two days after our return from St. Catherine I visited Fr. Maximos in his office. He was signing a pile of papers, including a number of marriage licenses. "I remember very vividly my first day at the office as the newly enthroned bishop," he said while carrying on with that routine task. "Not having any prior experience, I sat right here behind my desk wondering how I would cope with the many problems I was about to face. Then a very nice priest, an employee of the bishopric, knocked at my door and requested that I urgently sign a pile of papers, just as I am doing now. Due to the transitional period and the turmoil of electing a new bishop, they had been left unsigned. 'I'll be happy to sign them, Father,' I said and got my pen ready. I was curious to see what my first act as bishop would be. Lo and behold, all the papers he brought to me to sign were divorce papers! I was shocked and depressed." (Unlike Catholicism, Eastern Orthodoxy allows for divorce after all attempts at reconciliation fail.)

Fr. Maximos told me that he was further shocked when he found out that one third of all the marriages that take place each year in his diocese end up in divorce.

"At least," I said, "one third is better than fifty percent, as is the case in the United States."

Fr. Maximos said that he realized the seriousness of family and marital problems in the confessional. He listened to the problems of hundreds and thousands of people, young and old, men and women, and began a series of measures to support the family. Among other things, he planned to create a refuge for women who were victims of domestic violence. He had already organized Agia Skepi, a drug rehabilitation center, unique in the region. Furthermore, he inaugurated a series of talks to young people to help them prepare for married life.

In fact, while I was chatting with him in his office, a group of twenty or so young men from a nearby village walked in with their guide. They belonged to a young men's association for "self-improvement" and ranged in age from eighteen to thirty. The purpose of their meeting was to talk with the bishop about matters that concerned them. Marriage was on top of their agenda. Fr. Maximos gave them a brief talk on how the Church views marriage as a sacrament, a form of *askesis* for self-transcendence and union with God. Then he invited them to ask their questions. The young men were eager for advice and asked a torrent of questions, mostly related to courtship and marriage.

A lad in his mid-twenties with great bravado announced that on weekends he does not go home before five o'clock in the morning.

"Really! Why so?" Fr. Maximos asked. "Are you working that late?"

"No. I am looking for a bride." He said he frequented discos and nightclubs.

"And you think you will find a wife in those places and at that time?" Fr. Maximos asked with incredulity and then, half jokingly, continued. "Why don't you bring me the divorce papers now? I can sign them and spare you another trip here."

After our laughter quieted down, a twenty-eight-year-old

policeman complained that women don't know how to cook nowadays.

"Is that so important to you?" Fr. Maximos asked. "Why don't you cook yourself?"

"But that would be a violation of how things should be," the policeman answered soberly. I tried to keep a straight face. "Housework is natural to women but not to men. St. Paul said that women should obey their husbands."

Fr. Maximos shook his head. "No, no! The type of obedience that Paul refers to in that passage must be understood as obedience to the love of Christ, not obedience to their husbands. That goes also for husbands toward their wives. In reality, Paul urged husbands and wives to obey each other, that is, to feel total love and commitment to one another and a readiness to sacrifice even themselves for the sake of the other. If you start your marriage with an exclusively hedonistic expectation, that is, that marriage is a means of gratifying your wishes and desires, then you are setting yourself up for failure."

"Well, what's the purpose of marriage, Father?" the policeman asked with a quizzical look.

"The purpose of marriage is to transcend marriage itself," Fr. Maximos replied. Realizing they did not understand what he was talking about, he went on to say that the primary purpose of marriage is neither to procreate, as people commonly assume, nor to maximize physical pleasures. "It is good and a blessing to have children. And it is good for two people to enjoy each other's company. But the deeper reason for their marriage, as the Church understands it, is for the two people together to restore their relationship with God and work toward their deification. That is the foundation for a successful marriage. Everything else is a by-product of that supreme purpose.

"Don't assume your married life is going to be easy," he cautioned. "Family life is a training in how to think and take care first and foremost of others and then of yourself."

"It is a training to overcome selfishness," their guide, a soccer coach, interjected.

"Yes. You go beyond the boundaries of the ego. I have come to realize over the years through confessions that being a monk and being a married person have much in common. To be successful in either of these two roles you must overcome your narcissism. The Church blesses married life because in reality it is a means to reach God by uniting in love with another person. If you expect endless pleasure and happiness, you will be grossly disappointed. This is what happens to many couples. With the slightest of difficulties they seek a way out through divorce or an extramarital affair."

Fr. Maximos offered the young men pocket-size icons of the Holy Virgin and blessed them individually as he bade them farewell.

That evening we attended a lecture he gave to a different audience, many of them university students. The University of Cyprus had set up a branch in Limassol, adjacent to the bishopric. Many university students found in Fr. Maximos a wise elder to counsel them on their personal problems and existential questions. In his talk, Fr. Maximos again addressed marriage, elaborating further on some of the key factors that he believed led to divorces.

"Based on what I hear in confessions," Fr. Maximos said, "a key factor that leads to divorce is the inability to communicate. I have noticed that this problem starts with our schools. We learn from a very early age that what is important in life is to speak and behave well, to be courteous, to use language properly and intelligently. However, we have forgotten, or we have never learned, that to communicate with others presupposes not only speaking but, most important, listening. No one has taught us this art. This is sad, because in our culture there is a marvelous tradition of instructions on how to be a good listener. I have in mind, of course, the teachings of the holy elders. They have placed tremendous emphasis on listening and on attentiveness to what another human being is saying."

Fr. Maximos gave as an example the teachings of St. Nicodemos of the Holy Mountain, the author of the *Philokalia*,[1] who lived in the seventeenth and eighteenth centuries.

"St. Nicodemos, a hermit himself, gave instructions to Athonite monks on how to become good listeners, a prerequisite for them to become effective spiritual guides and confessors. What he taught, I believe, applies to ordinary human relationships, particularly as they relate to married life. He instructs his disciples in great detail on how to sit on their chairs during a confession, how to look at the other person, how to be conscious of their facial expressions while listening. He tells them to be very careful not to make any bodily or facial movements that would cause discomfort to the other person. He even instructs spiritual guides on how to breathe while listening, regardless of what they hear.

"Going over his instructions, one becomes awed by the refinement in our spiritual tradition on how to listen to and communicate with another human being."

Fr. Maximos went on to say how pleased he was to learn that in some European universities one can take seminars on the art of listening. "The first time I heard about this was from a young woman from Nicosia who got a scholarship to get training in proper listening. I said to her, 'My dear, did you have to go to London to learn how to listen?' I soon realized that in fact we do need training in this area of our lives. So I am glad Cyprus is a member of the European Union. Perhaps we can finally learn how to listen to each other!"

Fr. Maximos continued, "I see people who come as couples searching for mediation for their problems. Most of them are very sincere. They fervently wish to live in harmony with each other but cannot because they are listening-handicapped. They just don't know how to pay attention to what the other person is saying. Each side simply presents over and over their very compelling arguments and complaints. It is like having in front of you two finely tuned tape recorders playing simultaneously. There is no communication between the two, none whatsoever.

"I can tell you from personal experience that ninety percent of divorces take place not because of the involvement of third parties but primarily from this inability to listen to the other. Third parties usually enter the picture afterward, as a result of this problem. The spouses just shut themselves within themselves. The husband gets absorbed in his work, often handling two and three jobs to offer what he thinks is the good life to his family, and the same applies with the wife. They both come home exhausted. Not only do they have no time to sit and talk, but they also project on each other all the accumulated frustrations and fatigue from the day's work. If they have children, they try to convince themselves I am a good father or I am a great mother because of this or that. Their entire life is an endless sacrifice for their children. They don't realize that what their children truly need is harmony between them.

"I often go to high schools and have dialogues with teenagers. A standard question students ask me is 'Father, why is it wrong for us to have sex? Why is the Church so strict about premarital relations?' I tell them that indeed the Church is against premarital sex, not because it wishes to undermine relationships between men and women but because it wants these relationships to be built on solid foundations. If you do not learn from your teenage years to see another human being not merely as a man or as a woman but first and foremost as a person, then you are bound to create problems in your marriage. You will be unable to see the other as an individual and not merely as an object of pleasure. At least this is what seems to be happening here in Cyprus.

"For a successful marital bond to emerge, it is important that a man and woman first learn how the other feels and thinks and how they see the world. The aim is not to conquer, subjugate, and absorb the other person, to obliterate the other's personality, but rather for the two to become a new person. We have, I believe, a unique word in our language when we refer to a married couple. We call them *androgyno* [manwoman], a new personal reality, the loving union between a man and a woman. Such a situation emerges when each party brings into the union his or her respective gifts, leading to a new joined personality, which defines them both. This is the ideal that one should strive for in a marital bond."

After answering a series of questions, Fr. Maximos ended with a prayer as he usually did and then walked into the yard of the bishopric. A group of students surrounded him, asking for his blessing and continuing with the questions.

We too walked outside and chatted with several of our friends who had attended the talk, including Lavros; Antonis; his wife, Frosoulla; Stephanos; and Erato. They were all close associates of Fr. Maximos as well as close friends of ours. When Fr. Maximos spotted us, he waved to ask that we follow him to the cafeteria of the bishopric for some refreshments and further conversation. After a day of uncomfortably high temperatures, the cool of the evening was refreshing.

Fr. Maximos sat in the middle of a rectangular table as we sipped freshly squeezed orange juice. Responding to a question by a young professor from the University of Cyprus concerning Fr. Maximos's decision to remain single and become a monk, he began reminiscing about his early life. Now that he was no longer in a monastery, he had the freedom to speak of his past, which young novices are discouraged from doing.

"I decided to become a monk at the age of fifteen," Fr. Maximos said. "My mother was so upset that she threatened to end her life by swallowing poison. Thank God she was only bluffing. One day, I decided to just leave my home. I got on my bicycle, and in four hours I was at a monastery several miles outside of Limassol. I didn't know that it was a women's monastery. I announced to the abbess that I wanted to stay there as a monk. I remember her as a large woman who needed four chairs to accommodate herself! Upon hearing my words, she made the sign of the cross and said: 'Christos jai Panagia mou!' [Lord Jesus and Holy Mother of God!]. She waved to one of her assistants. 'Sister,' she said, 'please call a taxi, immediately, to take this kid to his mother.'

"Later on, I decided to travel to Nicosia in order to speak to Archbishop Makarios himself. (At that time the archbishop was also the first president of the Republic of Cyprus. The archbishopric, where the archbishop-president resided, was heavily guarded.) Strangely, the police paid no attention to me as I entered. I just walked in and found my way to Makarios's office, where he was alone having breakfast. He looked at me puzzled and asked, 'Who are you and what are you doing here?' I replied, 'I want to become a monk at the Kykkos monastery,' the monastery where Makarios himself began his monastic career. Makarios replied, 'Go a couple of offices down the hall to see

St. Konstantias. He may be able to help you.' I thought I was going to meet some kind of a saint! I didn't know it was just a title. St. Konstantias was in fact Bishop Chrysostomos of Paphos, who later succeeded Makarios as archbishop. After I explained my intentions, he shook his head and said, 'A bad idea!' He invited me to go to Paphos instead and finish high school. And that's what I did. In a way, I was adopted by the bishop. I was housed at the bishopric while going to school in Paphos. Before accepting his offer, I asked him whether I could wear a cassock at school. I had this obsession about giving up street clothes and putting on a cassock. 'You can, if you so wish,' he replied. With that understanding, I accepted his offer and went to Paphos, in spite of the reservations of my family. After I graduated from high school, the bishop sent me to Thessaloniki to study theology at the university there. The moment I got my degree I joined the monks of Mt. Athos."

"You were quite a rebel!" Emily joked.

"In fact, as a teenager I took part in a riot against the then bishop of Limassol, Anthimos. Do you remember when he and some other bishops tried to force Makarios to quit the presidency? Well, as a teenager I was fanatically pro-Makarios, and I participated in a demonstration that got out of hand. We stood outside the bishopric, right here, shouting slogans and hurling stones at the building. Imagine! The police arrived, and we ran away. I almost got arrested. Now when I stand at the steps of the bishopric, the memory of throwing stones as a teenager at those very steps often comes back to me."

Fr. Maximos was in a light mood, and he went on sharing more hilarious stories and details from his early life in Cyprus, before he went to Mt. Athos.

"I recall you telling me some time ago that your first impressions of Mt. Athos were not very favorable," I pointed out.

"Yes! At first, I was terrified by what I saw there and wanted to have nothing to do with that place. I remember during night services at the monastery of Dionysiou, everything was dark, with only one candle lit. Monks stood silently in prayer. I thought that I was in the land of the dead. There seemed to be no life in them. How could I survive in such a place? Those were the first thoughts that crossed my mind. Then out of the darkness, a monk who was praying in front of the icon of the Virgin approached me and whispered in my ear, 'These monks that you see in prayer are not dead. They are the ones who are truly alive. It is the people on the outside, who live in the world, who are the truly dead.' Then he walked away. As you can imagine, I was flabbergasted. I had never met that monk before. How did he know what was going on in my mind?"

Fr. Maximos soon realized that many of those very monks he thought were "dead" were filled with joy and inner peace because the Holy Spirit was fully activated within them. He then remembered the case of Elder Enoch, a Romanian Athonite monk whose actions were often hilarious. He described how he had once escorted the elder to Thessaloniki for medical treatment. They were in an apartment building when there was an earthquake that reached 7 on the Richter scale. There was massive destruction. "The apartment building," Fr. Maximos said, "was shaking like a leaf. Everybody ran out into the parks. I was ready to do the same when I thought of Elder Enoch. I opened his door, and I saw him sitting there praying with his *komboschini* [knotted rosary]. I said to him, 'What are you doing? There is an earthquake and we must run out.' Old Enoch looked at me and said in his broken Greek, '*Mbre, Enoch den fevgi* [Enoch will not leave]. If God wants Enoch to die, Enoch will die. If not, then Enoch lives. *Mbre den echis pisti!* [You don't have faith yourself!]' I could not convince him to leave with me, so I ran out. Everybody was gathered in the street, many of the buildings had collapsed, and all the balconies fell down. Only one structure was still standing in the neighborhood, and that was the building Enoch was in. After the earthquake, he came out on the balcony to watch everybody in the park."

For Fr. Maximos, old Enoch represented a model of the fool in Christ, one who has total faith and trust in God no matter what happens to him.

Before we dispersed, I reminded Fr. Maximos once again of his promise to complete the discussion on the fruits of the Holy Spirit that we had left unfinished in Boston many months ago. "We still have not talked about love as the apex of the hierarchy of the fruits of the Holy Spirit according to St. Paul," I pointed out.

He nodded, smiling. "So let's talk about love before you return to Maine."

Fr. Maximos thought for a few seconds, took out from his briefcase his large calendar book, and looked through his busy schedule. Gone were the years when, as abbot of the Panagia monastery, he had time for informal conversations on important questions about the spiritual life. During those years, he did not have to consult an appointment book.

"How about Monday morning at Mesa Potamos [Inner River]?"

"That would be just fine." I felt the venue Inner River was auspicious.

~~~

On Monday at six thirty in the morning, Lavros drove Emily and me to the monastery of Mesa Potamos in the Troodos mountains. The SUV that Lavros drove, a four-wheel-drive Pajero, was better fit to climb up the steep and unpaved, pinecone-covered road to the monastic hideout than our aging Honda.

Mesa Potamos, until recently an abandoned medieval ruin, was renovated thanks to the initiative of Fr. Maximos. He recruited seven young disciples from the Panagia monastery, where he'd served as abbot, to man the resurrected monastery. With several million euros from a wealthy Cypriot philanthropist, the monastery became yet another architectural gem and a new hub of monastic life in the heart of the Troodos mountains, surrounded by a pristine pine forest. A robust and sparkling stream runs next to it, hence the name Mesa Potamos.

The early morning liturgy was over when we arrived. We parked next to the outer gate. Fr. Maximos was standing in the inside yard, surrounded by several monks. He waved us over. After we chatted for a while, he asked Lavros and me to join him along with the other monks for breakfast in the dining hall. According to Athonite monastic protocol, men and women must eat separately, a custom not always compatible with modern ways. I remember when I drove with Fr. Maximos to the women's monastery of St. Heracledios, the two of us had to eat separately in the kitchen while the abbess with the other nuns and some women visitors dined at the adjoining hall. How ironic, I thought at the time, that Fr. Maximos, the confessor of those same nuns, who for years on end listened to their innermost thoughts and secrets, had to eat separately with me.

Fr. Maximos gave instructions to bring breakfast to Emily, who sat at the edge of the yard, in a corner covered with vines and shaded by a large oak tree. She assured us that she was perfectly happy having breakfast there on her own, reading her book and listening to the nightingales.

After our forty-minute breakfast, we found Emily chatting

with Stephanos and Erato. They too had come to hear Fr. Maximos's discussion on the last fruit of the Holy Spirit. Fr. Paisios, the young, jovial abbot of the monastery, also joined us. All seven of us sat on benches under the oak tree.

I opened the discussion by going over my notes and sharing with the others what Fr. Maximos had said many times on the subject of love. Love is the most perfect fruit of the Holy Spirit, and it emerges within one's life after one cultivates all the other fruits enumerated by St. Paul in his letter to the Galatians (5:22–23): love, joy, peace, patience, kindness, goodness, faithfulness, gentleness, and self-control. Authentic, divine love is a quality of the soul that manifests last, after the cultivation of all the other virtues, starting with self-mastery and self-control.

"There is much talk about love these days. All human beings yearn for it," Fr. Maximos commented. He paused for a moment and, in a humorous tone, continued. "Love and peace are fashionable topics of conversation nowadays."

"They're both in short supply," Lavros quipped.

"People have turned love and peace into slogans. But let it be so," Fr. Maximos added. "It's good to be preoccupied with such meanings, even as slogans. Let's say it is a step forward, even when we contemplate love in the abstract.

"However, love as it is taught by Christ and as the *Ecclesia* understands it through the experiences of the holy elders and apostles is not a simple sentiment. It does not have the same meaning as saying, 'I love so and so,' or 'I love my friends' or my students or my wife my children, or even 'I love the whole world.' These are human sentiments that are, of course, manifestations of an integral part of our deepest nature."

"We are made for love," Lavros noted.

"Yes, but not only are we made for love. We *are* love! It is so because God is love. John the theologian unambiguously states this in the Gospel: 'Beloved, let us love one another,' he says, 'for love is of God, and he who loves is born of God and knows God. He who does not love does not know God; for God is love' [1 John 4:7–8]. Therefore we are love because we are icons of God. A human being through Grace has what God has in His very essence.

"It is important to clarify something here," Fr. Maximos continued. "God is love, but love is not God."

"I don't see the difference," Lavros stated.

"There's a huge difference. For us God is the Person who is love. Love, however, is not a person. In worldly ways of understanding, love often becomes a form of idolatry. It becomes God. We say, for example, 'Love is everything. Love is above everything else.'"

"Well, isn't it?" I asked.

"Of course it is. But we forget that it is God who is love and not the other way around."

"This could be confusing," Emily interjected.

"Look. What a human being really searches for is God. It is in God and in his or her relationship with God that a person will find real joy and real peace and all those things described by St. Paul as the fruits of the Holy Spirit, including love. When we are graced by the fruits of the Spirit, we feel complete. We lack nothing. But it is important to remember that what we truly search for in our lives is God and not the fruits of the Spirit."

"It's easy for someone to assume that there is no difference," said Stephanos, who like Erato had been mostly quiet.

"Let me clarify. Our real objective is not joy, or peace, or self-control, or love, or any other fruit mentioned by Paul. Our objective is God. Everything else is a consequence of our relationship with God. Do you follow?

"To reach God I must exercise self-control and temperance,"

Fr. Maximos continued. "I must put in enormous effort to learn how to truly love. I must struggle for equanimity. When I unite with God, all these qualities that I formerly had to relentlessly work to acquire come effortlessly. They are now natural by-products of my relationship with God.

"For example, there will be times when you become angry or upset. What is important is to struggle so that you don't allow anger to control you or dominate you. You must struggle not to let wickedness, hatred, agitation, and the like strangle you and push you in a direction to do or say things that are unbecoming of you, things that you don't want, that are the opposite of love. Let's say this personal struggle is an instrument, a step that will lead us to God.

"So again, when we meet God, that which we could previously attain only after valiant effort emerges naturally, without any effort. In this God-realized state, we do not habitually allow anger or malice to enter our hearts. We don't get agitated, we don't get angry, we don't get upset. All such states wither away. They belong to our past."

"But as you mentioned earlier, at the highest state of our spiritual development we may get angry without falling into sin," I said.[2]

"Exactly. We can mobilize the powers of our soul naturally. That is, when we reach God, we have mastery over the gift of anger, which God planted in our heart for us to resist evil. As we said before, anger is very important in its natural state. It is a God-given power of the soul. But anger must never be mixed with egotistical passions. It must not be used against fellow human beings but rather against the temptation that threatens to cut us off from God. In short, anger must never undermine love. The only legitimate anger is the type that could help us establish ourselves in Truth and cement our relationship with

God. It is the kind of anger that should be directed only against our destructive passions."

"But couldn't someone assume that the inability to experience anger may in fact be a sign of apathy and indifference?" Emily asked.

"This is a total misunderstanding of what is meant here. I should marshal all the powers of my soul to free myself from lowly passions. And that includes not only anger but love as well."

"Love!"

"Definitely love. Let me explain. Love is the grandest power of the soul. That is why we must channel it properly, free from egotism."

"I assumed all along that love, by definition, is free from egotistical passions," I interjected.

"Not necessarily. Love can get severely distorted if energized while under the dominance of lowly passions."

"How so?"

"By idolizing human creations, such as various philosophical systems. People give themselves to such things with loving abandon. Love, you see, has as its central characteristic the giving of yourself to another. In this case you turn what you love into an idol."

"Even people that I love?" Emily asked.

"Even people that one loves, of course. Anything. It could be your wife or husband, your children, your political or religious ideology, your intelligence, your position in society, your scientific knowledge, your wisdom, your wealth, your youth. In short, a myriad of things could become idols for you."

"It is clear that people can fall into idolatry when they worship created things, such as their political beliefs or their cleverness and intelligence," I commented. "We all know people who are enamored of their own shrewdness, knowledge, and intellectual prowess. Their entire presentation of self is about feeling superior to those who aren't as clever as they are. We see such phenomena everywhere, particularly in academic circles. But what if love is directed toward other human beings? How could that become idolatrous?"

"All human beings, you see, have inside them the pure, unadulterated, and passion-free love that is characteristic of Divine Grace. When your love is directed toward others, it is this divine love that bursts forward. However, when it gets mixed up with lowly passions, then serious problems may emerge."

"In what way?"

"To repeat once again, love in itself has great power. I should also add that it is potentially very dangerous," Fr. Maximos said cryptically.

"Dangerous!"

"Yes. It can bring you to God's throne and destroy you at the same time, if you're not vigilant."

"That's why the holy elders teach that while love is the greatest of virtues, discernment is even greater," interjected Stephanos, who, like his wife, Erato, was steeped in Orthodox spirituality and had absorbed Fr. Maximos's teachings on the subject in a real and practical way.

"Exactly!" Fr. Maximos exclaimed. "Discernment should guide and have authority over love."

"I'm not sure I follow," I said.

"Lack of discernment can lead a person to adventures that at first may appear innocuous and praiseworthy," Fr. Maximos responded.

"Perhaps giving an example of what you have in mind will make things clearer for us," I suggested.

Fr. Maximos nodded. "I encounter this problem all the time

during confessions. Let's say that a family man, motivated by sheer compassion, is ready to offer his time and energy to help a woman friend in trouble. She may be experiencing a personal crisis, a family or professional problem, or whatever. The male friend, however, although motivated by good, loving intentions, lacks discernment. He isn't aware that he is not liberated from his personal desires and passions. Therefore, he is not conscious of the fact that there is a danger lurking there. He may lose control of the love that motivates him to help his friend. He is also not aware that the vulnerable woman is herself not passion-free. He may say to himself, 'Well, I don't feel anything personally.' Okay, you may not feel anything personally, but are you aware of how the other person feels? Are you aware of the strength and endurance of the soul of the other person? So without discernment, convinced that he is motivated by unadulterated, altruistic love, he volunteers to become a good listener to her problems and to help her bear her cross. Things, however, can get messy, and another kind of love between them begin to emerge, with tragic consequences for everybody. You understand what I am talking about, right?"

"It's a very common problem among psychotherapists and their clients," I said. "Psychiatrists even have special terms for when clients fall in love with their therapists and vice versa. They are *transference* and *countertransference*, a major risk of that otherwise professional relationship. Yes, things can get messy."

"Such problems emerge because the psychotherapist suffers from lack of discernment. He has not healed himself from his own lowly passions in order to offer the kind of selfless assistance that's required of him as a true psychotherapist," Fr. Maximos replied and went on.

"I have known many cases of the kind of love that started with good intentions and ended up in family tragedies. And the cause of all this suffering was the absence of discernment. Okay, you try to assist the other person. But are you sure you are capable of doing so? Or are you sure the person you are trying to rescue will not bring you down with him or her? Abba Isaac the Syrian gives a very telling example of this. He says that if you notice someone is about to drown in the river and out of love you extend your hand to pull him out, the likelihood is that he will pull you in, without intending it, of course. The result is that both of you will drown. It is more prudent to give him your cane instead and try to pull him out. If you succeed, great. If not, you can let him take the cane with him, but at least you will be saved.

"Abba Isaac wished not to put limits to love," Fr. Maximos hastened to add, "but rather to stress the importance of discernment when we are dealing with the power of love. Love is truly without limits. But if you think you can love without discernment, then you are bound to suffer great spiritual damage. Many times out of real love you must make the other person experience even sadness and disappointment. You may have to cause the other person to shed tears and deprive him of many things. For if you do not do that, you may destroy the other person. This is particularly true with parenting. I notice indiscreet love in the way many parents relate to their children. Parents oftentimes ruin their children from excessive love. Their deep love prevents them from practicing discernment that could offer real and healthy pedagogy to their children. A common problem is that they set no boundaries or limits."

"Setting limits is often difficult and painful," Emily said.

"Of course. Usually children don't like rules and regulations. They don't like boundaries. Parents often rationalize by saying, 'Well, they're just kids, they want to play, they want to run around.' Limits are painful for young people who cannot understand the logic for such restrictions. Setting limits is, of course, also painful for parents. It isn't easy to hear children cry because parents impose restrictions on them. So, out of love, the parents give in and lift those limits. They tell their children, 'Don't cry and I will buy you this or that' or 'We will do what you want.' Children, therefore, learn that whenever they want something, all they have to do is cry.

"So, yes, it is love that motivates parents to act that way. They are ready to die for their children, to become doormats for them. This is the nature of love."

"Self-sacrifice," Emily added.

"That's what it is. Love in itself has all these characteristics, including offering yourself totally to the other person. However, it is discernment that will put everything in its proper place and create healthy boundaries so that the flame of love does not burn both people and things. It is similar to machines that get destroyed when the electrical current is too powerful for them.

"If you offer more love than the others can hold, you can ruin them. They cannot contain it. They cannot function. They are paralyzed."

"That's when love becomes dangerous, the bread and butter of great literature," I mused.

"Well, of course it's dangerous, regardless of how beautiful and perfect it may be. It is truly the most perfect and priceless expression of our existence. After all, love is our true nature, our real self. God, motivated by love, created everything for us and offered Himself as a sacrifice to show His infinite love for us humans. Therefore, love is the deepest motivation of every human being."

"We're often ready to give our lives for those we love," Emily commented.

"Absolutely. This brings to my mind what a young woman told me the other day. 'When I became a mother,' she said, 'I realized for the first time that I could give my life for another human being, my child. I don't think,' she admitted, 'that I could die for my husband. I may love him and tell him that I love him unto death, but I am not sure if I can die for him. It is iffy.'"

Fr. Maximos paused as we laughed. "Motherhood, you see, has this inner quality. You notice it with animals, the way mothers are protective of their offspring. Have you ever seen a mother hen turn ferocious against intruders to protect her chicks? When we were kids, we were scared of them charging after us!"

"So discernment places even love within boundaries in order to contain it," I concluded.

"No. A better way of putting it is that discernment channels love in a healthy direction. If love tricks you and gets attached first to something other than God, then you have a problem, a spiritual problem. Yes, love is indeed fire that can burn you if you lack discernment. Actually, all the virtues are dangerous in the absence of discernment. Discernment is the steering wheel that guides all the virtues without exception.

"You see, it is important to know that love is the highest virtue, because people often destroy themselves or get traumatized in the name of love. But as the holy elders taught us, what makes all the virtues function perfectly is discernment. It is discernment that offers us right judgment about everything. When studying the lives of saints, you realize that they are characterized by such great discernment that they are not vulnerable to being swept away by human sentimentality, whether positive or negative."

"How can one develop discernment?" Emily asked.

"It is not easy. It develops with time and after arduous spiritual labors and many experiences. That is why it is important to ask for advice from an experienced spiritual guide whenever we face serious dilemmas. When we grow up spiritually, discernment comes easily. But at least at the beginning of our spiritual work, it's important that we seek out advice.

"A common problem of people who become enthusiastic about spiritual work," Fr. Maximos continued, "is that they do things which are beyond their capacity to endure. As a result they burn themselves, or they get ruined. Trying to imitate the life of an elder like Paisios, for example, could be disastrous for a neophyte. It is like giving a hard *paximadi* [baked and extremely dry bread, rusk] to a little baby who doesn't even have teeth. It will cause the baby's gums to bleed."

"The notion that love could be dangerous might appear strange to some people," I said.

"It is always so, even when you are advanced on the spiritual path."

"How so?"

"When a person becomes gradually liberated from the toxins of egotism, when he is freed from wickedness, hatred, or anger, and as he becomes more compassionate, tolerant, and loving, then he can fall in love with himself. This is a danger in the higher spheres of spiritual attainment."

"Strange."

"It happens because a human being in his essence is a very beautiful being. When we reach a point that we can become a witness to how we function with harmony, just like a classical symphony, then we run the risk of becoming enchanted with ourselves. That's where a lot of spiritually advanced people may suffer a great fall."

Our discussion was interrupted when a young novice, in charge of hospitality, arrived with tea and some baklava that pilgrims had brought to the monastery. We passed them around.

"Whenever I ask people what they suppose God's number one commandment is, their response always impresses me," Fr. Maximos said while munching on a piece of baklava. "Most of them answer: 'Love thy neighbor as thyself.'"

"In what way does that impress you?" Emily asked.

"Well, the first commandment is 'Love God thy Lord.' Love God with all your heart and with all of your power. Loving your neighbor is a natural by-product, a consequence of loving God. He gave us this commandment precisely to show us that in order to avoid the various love distortions that we talked about, we must focus our attention first and foremost on God Himself. Whatever a human being does, such as getting married, having children, or being in love, must be baptized within the love of God. If you transform all these relationships into absolutes, they could become idols. You would then end up worshiping them instead of God.

"When you tell people that 'Love thy neighbor' is not the first commandment of God, they look at you with an enigmatic grimace," Fr. Maximos went on. "But if we subtract this primary commandment of first loving God, it is like cutting the Gospel in two. The Gospel then becomes a social manifesto for the creation of an ideal society, a perfect society of good human relationships. But it is no longer a Gospel for the salvation of humanity."

"This is what happened to the Western understanding of the Christian Gospel. Focus on the world and try to make society more just," I said.

"This is fine and good. But the Gospel of salvation does not spring out of a vision for perfecting this world. Instead it is a blueprint for how to commune with God. If we don't understand this, we will not be able to understand the entire practice and life of the *Ecclesia*. We will not be able to understand the lives of saints and their struggles to become one with God." Fr. Maximos reflected for a few seconds.

"The Gospel tells us to be ready to sacrifice ourselves for our fellow human beings, all human beings. That means that God breaks down all boundaries between people. Okay, it is easier to understand how you can die for your child or even your friend, but to die for a stranger? And what about the request to die even for your enemy? Christ has done that. In a sense we are the enemies of God. He died not for His friends but for His enemies. It means that God does not allow us any fences between ourselves and anybody else. Authentic divine love has no boundaries. No restrictions. From the moment that love has boundaries, it is no longer love. That is why the elders taught that God loves everybody infinitely and without exception, including the devil himself."

"That could be considered a scandal by many Christians," I pointed out.

"It *is* a scandal! God loves Satan as much as He loves the Holy Virgin. God does not have limits and imperfections in His love for any part of His Creation. And that's how we, ourselves, must love, ideally speaking. After all, Satan is a fallen angel. In his original state, coming out of God's hands, he was good. It is Satan's works that we must repudiate and shun. That's why saints often pray even for the salvation of Satan himself."

"For most of us this is extremely difficult, if not impossible."

"Of course it is. It is certainly for me. But why is it so? Is it because such a state is difficult in itself? The answer, according to the Gospel, is no. Indiscriminate love is an inherent aspect of our nature as icons of God. We are created to love. It is our passions that distort love from being selfless and God-centered to becoming self-centered. From a passion-free love it is transformed into a passion-filled, pleasure-centered love."

"The kind of love that prevails between us, as ordinary human beings, is a form of exchange," I noted. "In essence we say, 'I love you and I expect equal love from you.'"

"During confessions I encounter such attitudes all the time. It is something like the 'I love him, why doesn't he love me?' syndrome. I hear this complaint all the time."

Fr. Maximos continued: "Real love is a perfect motion in the direction of the other person. If I do that and the other loves me in return, that's wonderful. But even if others do not love us, it is sufficient that we ourselves love them. I honestly think our fundamental existential need is not to be loved but to love."

"Of course," I added, "if people can love in that selfless way, the likelihood is that they will also be loved by others. I have never known a person who truly loves and is hated by others."

"But even if it does happen," Fr. Maximos went on, "our true being is to love everything and everybody like God does. We must make it a daily habit to remember that our supreme goal in life, the only goal in life in fact, as I never tire of repeating, must be our love for God."

"You mean of course to have a direct experience of God that fills our being with His love," I clarified, "not just belief but direct mystical experience."

"Naturally. But again, do keep in mind that such a state does not come automatically. We must work for it. If we achieve this goal, everything else will fall into its right place. A human being, then, will be able to cope with whatever problems come his or her way.

"Let us say I have a difficult marriage. My husband or wife is tormenting me. Or my mother-in-law creates problems for me. Or a thousand other things cause me grief, which leads to anger. More often than not, however, if I truly analyze myself and search for answers in the furthest recesses of my being, I will discover that the real cause of my problems is my lack of love for God. If I loved God truly and absolutely, then the difficulties with my marriage, the problems with my health, the troubles at work, my economic woes, my discomfort with aging, and even the problems of my country would work themselves out in a positive direction. My frustration means that somewhere my love for God does not make a perfect contact.

"For example, I face problems in my marriage. I feel suffocated. I tell myself, 'Get a divorce.' Or 'How wonderful it would be if she dropped dead!' Sometimes such thoughts do enter people's minds. They may not accept them. But they do enter their minds. Or 'My mother-in-law has plenty of money and doesn't give us a penny. How long must I wait for her? Let the Good Lord take her with Him, the sooner the better!'" Fr. Maximos paused until our laughter died down.

"In reality, the difficulties, as I said earlier, be they our marital problems, economic woes, or whatever, are not our main underlying problem. All problems stem from our estrangement from God. We must elevate everything that happens to us, positive or negative, and transform it into a ladder upon which we can climb to reach God.

"It is so difficult to climb that ladder," Stephanos said, sighing.

"To be sure, it is. But when we manage to get into the habit of doing so, we will eventually realize that our greatest benefactors are these very people who we thought were the causes of our grief.

"Elder Paisios used to say that when we die and the eyes of our souls open up, the first thing we will do is glorify God with all our might for our previous tribulations on Earth. Only then will we realize that it was those very difficulties that helped us grow spiritually."

"To tell somebody that our spiritual benefactors within eternity are not those who praise us but rather those who create problems for us, those who bad-mouth us, appears like a form of spiritual masochism," Lavros said with a chuckle.

"That's the worldly way of thinking. Those who create problems for us do so not because they want to benefit us. No. As far as they're concerned, they are responsible for the evil they cause. But if we transmute all that into a spiritual lesson, then all those difficulties that others cause us can become bridges upon which we can travel to the Kingdom of God."

Fr. Maximos leaned back, his posture suggesting that he was ready to conclude the discussion. "So the highest fruit of the Spirit is love, but the kind of love that does not become an idol in itself. Love for us is embodied in the love of God as a Person. We are not in love with love. This is the meaning of the Eucharist. The experience of the love of Christ is the greatest experience that a human being can have. It is infinite, and it has no boundaries or limits. Unlike worldly experiences, which always reach a saturation point, God's love has no end. We never reach the point when we say, 'We've had enough.' The path toward God's love is a never-ending, infinite, and eternal dynamic movement upward. It has no boundaries because God has no boundaries. We may be tired of things of this world, but we can never tire of the experience of God. The love of God is a state of perpetual enthusiasm. It is a state of continued enchantment and doxology in the infinite and absolute taste of God's eternal love.

"This love," Fr. Maximos continued, "springs from the struggle to commit oneself to the commandments of God. That's the aim of the *Ecclesia*. The homilies and teachings of the saints are a therapeutic pedagogy offered to us to heal our sick and passion-filled hearts so that they may function naturally as pure and unadulterated love. When that happens, a human being becomes indeed an image of God, compassionate and just, like our Father in Heaven, who is compassionate and just."

None of us doubted that Fr. Maximos was speaking with the authority of one who had experienced what he was teaching. It was this quality that led to his increasing recognition within the Eastern Orthodox world.

~~~

We lunched at the monastery. Emily and Erato ate together under the cool shade of the oak tree, whereas Stephanos, Lavros, and I joined Fr. Maximos and the other monks in the dining hall. To our delight Fr. Maximos asked us to give him a lift back to Limassol. The trip would give us additional time for conversation.

We remained at the monastery until the midafternoon, waiting for the high temperatures on the plains to subside. It was siesta time in all of Cyprus.

Fr. Maximos sat next to Lavros in the car as we began our descent from the mountains. On the way down, we stopped at the youth camp of the bishopric, which Fr. Maximos had created. The year before, there had been a fire. It was depressing to witness the once lush green area around the camp almost completely gone. "It was hell on earth," Fr. Maximos said. The fire encircled the camp and burned everything in its path. But as you can see, the chapel and the buildings remained intact."

Fr. Maximos went on to say that when the fire started, they first rushed to evacuate the children. He then returned with a silver case of sacred relics, believed to be pieces of the remains of St. Luke. Holding these relics firmly to his forehead, as priests do during liturgies, Fr. Maximos walked around the camp, chanting prayers and making petitions for Divine intervention. We found the image of him praying in such a manner within a burning forest particularly poignant. Fr. Maximos considered the saving of the camp a "miracle" and refused to take any credit himself.

"After I left, the firemen informed me, erroneously, that the camp was gone," he went on. "What saved the camp, however, was not the actions of the firemen but the help of God and the heroic work of five lads who stayed behind and fought the flames with hoses."

The major damage to the camp was the destruction of the forest around it and of the station for filtering and recycling water, which had cost close to a hundred thousand dollars.

"It will take two to three generations before the forest is restored," Lavros, a passionate environmentalist, said sadly. "I consider the government the foremost culprit for this catastrophe," he added angrily. "There is too much spending on so-called defense and not enough on helicopters and small planes to fight forest fires. Cyprus is vulnerable to forest fires. Pretty soon we will run out of forests, and we will be left with cement buildings and asphalt. They don't realize that if our environment is destroyed there will be nothing here to defend!"

In the mind of Lavros, who was elected a member of parliament many years back, military defense of the island is a useless expenditure anyway. The island of no more than seven hundred thousand Greek Cypriots is practically defenseless in the face of Turkey, a country of seventy-five million.

I couldn't agree with my friend more. Lavros was so frustrated with the environmental policies of the establishment and the serial blunders of the local governing elite vis-à-vis the "Cyprus problem" that, had he been younger, as he once told me in utter frustration, he would have left the island for good. But as an agricultural economist with a doctorate from an American university, he stayed on as an advisor to Fr. Maximos on environmental issues while spending the last portion of his life valiantly fighting the many enemies of the island's ecosystem.

In spite of the fire, the camp was full of young life. So excited were the youngsters at Fr. Maximos's unexpected visit that they sang and danced for us, a performance that included the hymn of the camp, which they had composed under the direction of a music teacher.

We reached Limassol in the late afternoon. Our hearts and minds were still reverberating with Fr. Maximos's words on love and discernment. Later in the evening, sitting on our balcony, Emily and I contemplated Fr. Maximos's magisterial vision of love. I fixed my gaze on the lit boats awaiting their turn to enter the harbor. One of the most powerful elegies that came to my mind was Viktor Frankl's ruminations on the subject of love. The Viennese psychiatrist and Auschwitz survivor described in his classic work *Man's Search for Meaning* a mystical experience he had on a bitterly cold morning while being marched by sadistic Nazi guards to dig ditches in the snow-covered land. A vivid image of his wife, a Holocaust victim, entered his mind, triggering his epiphany on the nature of love.

> A thought transfixed me: for the first time in my life I saw the truth as it is set into song by so many poets, proclaimed as the final wisdom by so many thinkers. The truth—that love is the ultimate and the highest goal to which man can aspire. Then I grasped the meaning of the greatest secret that human poetry and human thought and belief have to impart: *the salvation of man is through love and in love.* I understood how a man who has nothing left in this world still may know bliss, be it only for a brief moment, in the contemplation of his beloved.[3]

I shared my thoughts on Frankl with Emily. Then I felt the urge to read once again St. Paul's paean to love, arguably the most riveting homily on this ultimate gift of the Holy Spirit in all of world literature. I fetched a copy of the New Testament and read as Emily listened to my recitation in the original Greek:

> If I speak in the tongues of men and of angels, but have not love, I am a noisy gong or a clanging cymbal. And if I have prophetic powers, and understand all mysteries and all knowledge, and if I have all faith, so as to remove mountains, but have not love, I am nothing. If I give away all I have, and if I deliver my body to be burned, but have not love, I gain nothing.
>
> "Love is patient and kind; love is not jealous or boastful; it is not arrogant or rude. Love does not insist on its own way; it is not irritable or resentful; it does not rejoice at wrong, but rejoices in the right. Love bears all things, believes all things, hopes all things, endures all things.
>
> "Love never ends." (1 Corinthians 13:1–8)

TWELVE

A HERMIT'S JOY

A year later, in mid-May 2010, shortly after we'd finished our academic year, Emily and I were back in Cyprus for further discussions with Fr. Maximos. I assumed that my work was virtually completed and, therefore, that I was in no need of further material for the manuscript.

Emily, however, insisted that I meet a Cypriot businessman whom she had never met but who, according to her close friend Thekla, had an extraordinary tale that I should hear. Having heard many miraculous and paranormal stories, I was reluctant to invest more time in new acquaintances. But, as usual, Emily's intuition was right on the mark. I was finally persuaded to meet Yiannis, the stranger with the unusual experience.

Yiannis was at first suspicious of Emily's intentions when he received her phone call. "How did you get my number?" was his immediate reaction. Apparently his story was a secret, shared only by a small coterie of trusted friends. Thekla had heard about it indirectly, through friends in her parish; it's always a challenge to keep secrets in Cyprus. But when Emily explained the reason for her call, the stranger softened somewhat. "I've read your husband's books," he said. "I'd be willing to share my story with him."

Yiannis, accompanied by his friend Sotiris, a retired government employee, arrived at our apartment on a Monday morning, two days after Emily's phone call. He seemed apprehensive at first, but when we began talking he lost his stiffness. The fact that his companion was a spiritual disciple of Fr. Maximos helped us to strike a friendly note from the start. After a few minutes of introductions, Yiannis began to narrate his adventure in detail.

He was a fifty-year-old entrepreneur, married, with two teenage girls. On a business trip to a former Soviet republic, he was arrested and sent to jail on trumped-up charges of human trafficking. We were told that his jailers were, in fact, part of an alleged mafia-type ring. Their operation was intended to extract ransom for his release. They demanded thirty thousand euros. According to Yiannis, the local mafia was in collusion with corrupt politicians who had connections with the country's justice system. "I was going out of my mind," he lamented. "I had no idea what would happen to me, and the conditions of my incarceration were deplorable. I was cold and poorly fed."

Not knowing the local language and without anybody he could trust to defend him, Yiannis found himself in a Kafkaesque nightmare. His family back in Cyprus was in desperate agony. His horrified wife managed to hire a lawyer, who made contact with him. Through the lawyer, his devout mother smuggled to him the Bible and a book about the lives of the saints. "I was not religious," Yiannis explained. "I never read the Bible before, or any other religious book for that matter. But in my utter despair and isolation, I began reading those two books whenever the guards weren't watching. I wasn't allowed to read any books."

One night, as Yiannis was lying in bed, shivering and feeling miserable, an elderly monk miraculously appeared in his cell and introduced himself as Elder Paisios of the Holy Mountain. Yiannis hastened to reassure us that he had never heard of

Paisios before and had no clue as to who the elder was. The book on the lives of the saints his mother had sent him did not include anything about the life of that specific elder.

"Elder Paisios in that vision said to me, 'Son, don't be afraid. Have faith and I will help you leave this place. But you must promise me that upon your return to Cyprus you will seek out Elder Seraphim and have him as your spiritual guide and confessor.'

"I had never heard of Elder Seraphim either," Yiannis said. He noted that he had several more visions of Elder Paisios in his cell, offering him courage during his six-month ordeal. Yiannis was emphatic that he was not in a state of delirium and thus seeing things that did not exist. Furthermore, his visions were therapeutic. He lost his fear and developed hopefulness that his suffering would soon end.

Had conventional psychologists or psychiatrists been present to hear Yiannis's story, I'm certain they would have defined his visions as hallucinations, the products of a brain under extreme duress. They could not have thought otherwise, since mainstream science, operating within the reductionist worldview of modernity, offers no other explanations. I was confident, however, that Yiannis's experience could not be explained through such conventional terms. Having personally met mystics, healers, and hermits who were perfectly sane and normal but who had had such experiences, I was open to the possibility that Yiannis's experience was authentic.

He went on to stress that he had no doubt his visions were real. With the help of his lawyer, he was temporarily released to await his kangaroo court appearance, as he put it. His lawyer advised him, however, to take advantage of the offered opportunity and escape because, as he warned Yiannis, "You can't find justice here, and you won't be able to leave the country alive."

Yiannis managed to sneak out of the country. He was still worried that the mafia ring might pursue him in Cyprus. It was for that reason that he'd reacted with suspicion when he received Emily's phone call.

Upon his return to Cyprus, Yiannis discovered that Elder Seraphim was indeed a real person, an old hermit affiliated with one of the ancient mountain monasteries of the island. Fulfilling the request of Elder Paisios, he contacted Elder Seraphim for confession and spiritual guidance. Elder Seraphim, in turn, accepted Yiannis as one of his disciples. From being an agnostic, Yiannis became deeply devout.

"In retrospect," he told us, "my ordeal was the best thing that ever happened in my life. Through it I discovered God."

A week later, Emily and I, along with Yiannis and his friend Sotiris, traveled to a wooded, out-of-the-way area in the foothills of Stavrovouni (the mountain of the cross) to meet Fr. Seraphim. We arrived at his hermitage at seven in the evening. As it was the middle of June, there was still plenty of sunlight when we reached his monastic retreat.

Elder Seraphim was a real surprise. For a ninety-one-year-old monk, he was extraordinarily robust and full of radiant energy. In fact, he looked at least thirty years younger than his real age. Lean, and of average size, he struck me as one of those rare and larger than life nonagenarian athletes who could run marathons. We soon realized that the elder exemplified all the fruits of the Spirit that Fr. Maximos had discussed with us and St. Paul wrote about. In fact, Fr. Seraphim reminded me of Elder Paisios, whom I had met in 1991, two years before his repose. Very much like Paisios, he radiated abundant and disarming love and an electrifying joy. His humorous disposition, also reminiscent of Elder Paisios, made for a warm conversation and an immediate, heart-to-heart connection. On a personal note, it pleased me when he mentioned that he had read the Greek translations of *The Mountain of Silence* and *Gifts of the Desert* several times and expressed his great admiration for Fr. Maximos.

After we lit our candles in his small chapel, where he carried on his nightly vigils and prayers, Elder Seraphim showed us his lush and well-kept vegetable garden, which he tended by himself. He and Emily shared information about various plants and their secrets. Then all five of us sat on benches under a vine while Elder Seraphim talked to us about his life. In the meantime, Yiannis, demonstrating familiarity with the hermitage, prepared refreshments.

Until the age of seventy, Elder Seraphim was an atheist and one of the early members of the island's Communist Party. "I joined AKEL [the Communist Party of Cyprus] at fifteen," he told us, "because very early in my life I felt a burning passion for justice. I looked around me, and all I could see was the exploitation of the poor by the rich. The only people who struggled for fairness and justice were the labor unionists, who, at that time, were all Communists. So, I joined them. It seemed to me that Communism had the answers to our miseries. Religion was not for me. It was the opiate of the people."

Elder Seraphim got married and had three children, two sons and a daughter. "Unlike me," he told us, "my wife was deeply religious and attended church every Sunday. I would walk her to the church and then go to a nearby coffee shop to play cards or backgammon until the service was over. Then I would walk with her home. Imagine, I never, ever stepped into a church from the age of fifteen until the age of seventy. I was an atheist for fifty-five years!" Elder Seraphim laughed heartily. Then he went on to tell us that the Communists of the island he had known were not bad people. They meant well and were genuinely interested in the common good. They were the ones who, during British rule, actively worked for legislation that set the eight-hour workday and other legislation protecting the rights of workers.

At a certain point in his life, because of financial difficulties, Fr. Seraphim migrated with his family to London, where he became a successful entrepreneur in fish and chips restaurants. All the while he was committed to the Communist ideology. "I also loved to gamble," he added with a laugh. "It was one of my many vices. I believed in nothing other than matter, you see."

After several years in England, Fr. Seraphim returned to Cyprus and invested his savings in a Limassol hotel. His children started their own families, while he resumed his political activities.

A personal crisis that he did not tell us about radically changed his worldview. "In a desperate moment," he went on, "I fell on my knees and cried out, 'If there is a God, show me a sign of your existence and help me out of my troubles!'"

That was a turning point in the life of Fr. Seraphim, whose name before his tonsure as a monk was Andreas. He had a mystical experience, a classic road to Damascus epiphany, when, in his words, "all of a sudden the heavens opened up and I saw the dazzling glory of God." He shook his head and said that, alas, there were no appropriate words to explain what happened to him. One thing was certain: at the age of seventy Fr. Seraphim's consciousness was radically altered. From being an atheist he was transformed into a deeply devout believer, so much so that, with his wife's consent, he decided to become a monk and spend the rest of his life in continuous prayer and contemplation. His wife, in fact, decided to become a nun and together with her husband devote her remaining years to pursuing union with God. Unfortunately, she died three months after their decision to follow the monastic lifestyle.

Fr. Seraphim visited a couple of monasteries, asking to become a novice, but was rejected on grounds that he was too old to start a monastic career. In one of the monasteries, a monk told him that "monasteries are not nursing homes. Besides we don't accept married people here." Fr. Seraphim (or Andreas at the time) visited Mt. Athos and consulted with a revered holy hermit. The hermit urged him to return to Cyprus, assuring him that they would accept him at the monastery that had last rejected him. Upon his return to the island, he went back to that monastery and declared, "I came here to stay and have no intention of leaving." The elder of the monastery, a reputed holy man who was endowed with clairvoyant vision (and who also played a role in Fr. Maximos's early spiritual life), had a long conversation with him. He realized that Fr. Seraphim's experience was a true manifestation of the Holy Spirit. Consequently, he gave permission for Fr. Seraphim to remain at the monastery. Fr. Seraphim then passed on his material wealth to his children and joined the monastic community.

"For two years," Fr. Seraphim told us, "I tried to be an exemplary novice, showing total obedience to the monastic way of life and to the elder. At the same time, since I had many practical skills from my experiences in the world, I made myself quite useful. I was not a burden to them, as they feared at first, and they came to appreciate my stay there."

But Fr. Seraphim found life in the monastery too easy, and he longed for greater spiritual challenges. He was a man in a hurry. His passion was to unite with his Maker as soon as possible, before he exited this life. His mystical epiphany made him impatient with anything less. The elder of the monastery, who himself was four years younger than Fr. Seraphim, recognizing his special gifts and spiritual condition, tonsured him a *megalos-chemos*, the highest formal status in a monk's career, the equivalent of earning a doctoral degree. Furthermore, he offered him his blessing to become a hermit and devote the rest of his life to a more rigorous regimen of prayer.

Fr. Seraphim was allowed to use a hermitage owned by the monastery farther down the pine-covered mountain. There he lived the life of ceaseless prayer for nearly twenty years. He ate only once a day, fasted most days of the year, and worked a few hours every day in his garden for his physical sustenance. In addition, every day between nine and eleven in the morning, he welcomed pilgrims seeking spiritual guidance. Most of his time, however, was spent in prayer, with little sleep. Every night was an all-night vigil for Fr. Seraphim. He prayed for the good of others and the world, and for his own salvation.

"I have never been happier in my entire life," he assured us, with emotion in his voice. Fr. Seraphim was a living example of the joyous individual. Based on the time we spent with him, we had little doubt that what he told us was his genuine state of being. "The love and compassion of God for every human being is indescribable, believe me!" he repeatedly informed us. It was the same message I had heard Elder Paisios repeat when I met him with Antonis and Fr. Maximos in 1991. It was also the message that we had heard from another venerated hermit on our recent trip to Mt. Athos. In fact, that Athonite hermit could hardly control his tears as he spoke to us about the intensity of Christ's love for all human beings. Like Fr. Seraphim, he spoke with the certainty of one who had a direct experience of God's love for His creatures.

Fr. Seraphim urged us to visit him again in his hermitage and with delight agreed to Emily's request that on our next visit we bring along our friend Vladimiros. Since both of them were former members of the Communist Party, he and Vladimiros would have much to talk about. Emily's ulterior motive, however, was for Fr. Seraphim to help Vladimiros overcome his depression and fear of old age and death.

When the following week we drove our friends from Limassol to Fr. Seraphim's hermitage, the elder received both Vladimiros and his wife, Elena, warmly, calling them "my dearest comrades" and sharing with them many of the stories related to his personal transformation from Communism to the single-minded pursuit of God. A large part of the conversation, however, between Fr. Seraphim and Vladimiros, revolved around people and events from their many years in the Communist Party. That in itself invigorated Vladimiros and made him feel comfortable with Fr. Seraphim. Whether the encounter had any impact on Vladimiros's worldview, however, was not clear to us at the time.

On our return trip to Limassol, I shared with Emily and our friends some of my thoughts about how to make sense of the former Communist's radical transformation.

During the twentieth century, I said, many reputable explorers and scientists, from William James to Richard Bucke and from Rudolf Otto to Joachim Wach, concluded that the mystical experiences many people have had throughout the ages reflect realities that cannot be explained—or explained away—by reducing them to chemical reactions in the brain or to simple psychological or cultural factors.[1] The phenomenological studies of those pioneers, I pointed out, led to the conclusion that those who have mystical experiences, such as Fr. Seraphim, undergo massive transformations in their consciousness and worldview.

According to the Eastern Orthodox understanding of mystical ecstasy, I added, Fr. Seraphim apparently experienced the

Uncreated Light, the light of God. It is that experience which propels the person to abandon everything else in his or her life in order to pursue that glimpse of Heaven with wholehearted and extraordinary zeal. Nothing else matters. Joachim Wach, a leading philosopher and sociologist of religion, pointed out that the mystical experience is the most intense experience a human being is capable of having, the *mysterium tremendum et fascinans*, in Rudolf Otto's words—something totally beyond our ordinary range of experiences, which is awe-inspiring, overpowering, and completely separate from ourselves, and to which we are attracted with both curiosity and trust.[2] People who have had such experiences consider them contact with ultimate Reality. Regardless of one's previous beliefs, religious loyalties win over all other loyalties. From a Communist atheist, Fr. Seraphim became overnight a spiritual zealot, in the same way that St. Paul, after falling off his horse on the road to Damascus, turned from a zealot persecuting Christians into the foremost apostle responsible for spreading Christianity to the Roman Empire. The person who experiences ultimate Reality, Joachim Wach noted, develops within himself or herself an urgency to act. All other pursuits and activities are considered trivial by comparison. This is apparently what happened to Fr. Seraphim. He had a mystical experience, identical to that of St. Paul.

I wasn't sure whether my explanations of Fr. Seraphim's state of mind made any sense to our friends, but they both mentioned that they planned to revisit their former comrade.

I wished to discuss Elder Seraphim with Fr. Maximos before leaving for Maine on the Fourth of July 2010. More specifically, even though on several occasions Fr. Maximos had spoken of the importance of prayer for one's spiritual life, I still wanted to explore it further. I wished to hear more on the role of ceaseless prayer in Elder Seraphim's life, or in anybody's life for that matter. Not only did Elder Seraphim seem not to get tired of or bored by that form of intense and continuous prayer, but in fact, as he repeatedly assured us, prayer offered him extraordinary energy and joy. This ninety-one-year-old hermit, who appeared to be like a character straight out of a Dostoevsky novel, was one of the happiest people we had ever met. He was a man intoxicated by God. He was already in Paradise. Fr. Seraphim reminded me of the homilies of St. Maximos the Confessor, who claimed that the God-realized individual is possessed by an *Eros Maniakos*, a maniacal form of love that is infinitely more powerful than any worldly erotic passion. The metaphors he used to express such states of God intoxication often scandalized puritanical Christians.

Three days before we left Cyprus, Lavros organized a get-together to discuss our visit to the hermitage of Fr. Seraphim and to bid us farewell. He invited our close friends from Limassol, who for many years had been part of my exploration of the mystical tradition of Eastern Christianity. There were Stephanos and Erato; Antonis and Frosoulla; Lavros and his friend Jasmine, a neophyte disciple of Fr. Maximos; Olympia, our friend who'd organized the pilgrimage to St. Catherine; Emily; and myself. To our pleasant surprise, Fr. Maximos accepted our invitation to a potluck gathering in Lavros's small but magnificent permaculture garden, which he'd created over the years around his humble and traditional house.

"To understand hermits like Elders Paisios and Seraphim," Fr. Maximos stated after we had dinner, "we need to understand the nature of ceaseless prayer and its importance in our spiritual life. The holy elders called such practice by a variety of names, such as the Jesus Prayer, Noetic Prayer, Prayer of the Heart, or simply the Prayer, and by that they meant the well-known prayer 'Lord Jesus Christ, Son of God, have mercy on me.' The saints considered that form of prayer the royal road to salvation and the means by which the mysteries of God are revealed to the human heart."

Fr. Maximos reminded us of the key principles of Christian eschatology as a preamble to helping us understand the radical transformation that a hermit such as Fr. Seraphim undergoes. "According to the tradition of the *Ecclesia*," he went on, "the healing of fallen humanity presupposes a return to our natural state, the way we were originally created by God. Adam and Eve in Paradise were in constant contemplation of God. That was the sole activity of their hearts and minds. They lived in a state of uninterrupted memory and awareness of their Creator. This meant that humanity in its prefallen state had a continuous communion with God's Grace.

"As a consequence of this ceaseless contemplation of God," Fr. Maximos added, "human beings were the beneficiaries of God's divine love and of every other gift that this state implies. That is how the original humans lived in the Garden of Eden. This is our divine endowment, which lies dormant in the depths of our being. We are invited to restore in our hearts and minds our natural state, that is, to be in continuous contemplation of God.

"The Fall interrupted this connection with our Creator. Our *nous*, or the core and center of our consciousness, was scattered on things of this world and away from the continuous Divine contemplation. The image of God within us was torn apart.

"But God, as the great Healer, offered us the medicine that we need to enable us to return to our original healthy condition. He offered us His one overarching commandment: "Thou shalt love the Lord thy God with all thy heart and with all thy soul, and with all thy mind." That is, your entire existence and focus should be redirected toward the love of God, the Great Beloved.

"This is the only commandment of God. There are no others. The remaining commandments that God gave us are consequences of the first one. 'Thou shalt love thy neighbor as thyself' and 'thou shalt not steal,' 'thou shall not kill,' and so on are by-products of the first commandment, while at the same time they are the means by which the primary commandment can be actualized.

"But in order for us human beings to love God with all of our heart and with all of our mind, we need to return to the way we functioned before the Fall. That means God must become once again our permanent and uninterrupted focus and preoccupation. Our minds, and the center of our consciousness, must get reattached to the love and contemplation of God. This must become the primary activity of our minds, as it was in the beginning, before the Fall.

"We may be able to understand this condition as it takes place in ordinary, worldly life. What happens in our lives when we are deeply in love with another human being? The beloved is constantly in our minds, whatever we do, wherever we are. Our minds are in continuous communion with that person. In fact, we are totally absorbed by the beloved even when we are asleep. That person is constantly with us, in our dreams, in our conscious state, in our hearts, and in our minds. We are continuously in conversation with our beloved even if we are not physically together. Furthermore, we behave toward that person in a way that is consistent with the depth of our love."

"What kind of behavior do you have in mind?" Jasmine interjected.

"We are ready to give up even our lives for the beloved person," Fr. Maximos continued. "So if this state of mind emerges in us in our worldly relationships, imagine how much more intense it is when it happens in our relationship with God, when we literally fall in love with God."

"This is the state of the *Eros Maniakos* that is characteristic of hermits like Fr. Seraphim," I pointed out.

"That is what the holy elders say," Fr. Maximos added. "Fr. Seraphim was blessed to reach that state of having fallen in love with God all of a sudden. Ordinarily, for our minds to return to their original function to ceaselessly remember God, the primary instrument in our fallen state is ceaseless prayer."

"This is what St. Paul urges us to do," Stephanos said.

"Yes. We've talked about this many times before."

"Does this mean that only hermits can reach this state of continuous contemplation of God?" Olympia asked.

"Not at all. Your question reminds me of a conversation that St. Gregory Palamas had with an ascetic, addressing this very point in a dialogue that was recorded by others who were present. The ascetic insisted that ceaseless prayer is an activity to be engaged in by monks and hermits but not by ordinary people. St. Gregory, on the other hand, claimed that the Prayer of the Heart is for all people because all human beings are invited to reestablish their spiritual health and become true children of God. He argued vigorously that there is no particular gospel for ordinary people and another for monks, nor is there a specific holiness for monks and another for ordinary people.

"Well, the ascetic was not persuaded, even though he was a virtuous and devout person. It is said that St. Gregory prayed fervently to God to enlighten the mind of his fellow ascetic. According to the story, God informed the heart of the dissenting brother through an angel who conveyed to him that the practice of ceaseless prayer is indeed appropriate not only for monks but also for all human beings. All human beings are, after all, called to become lovers and children of God."

"In practice, however, one wonders how ordinary persons like us who live in the world could achieve such a feat," Lavros said. "We hardly have time to think of our existence, let alone to pray ceaselessly. How do you propose we do that?"

"The holy elders of the *Ecclesia*, based on their personal experiences, discovered that the most practical way of having the mind focused on God is to get into the habit of continuously repeating God's name through the prayer 'Lord Jesus Christ, Son of God, have mercy on me.'

"It is a theological prayer par excellence. By invoking the Holy Name and by saying 'have mercy on me,' we ask to be offered whatever our deepest need is, be it spiritual strength, solace, or illumination. This continuous repetition of the Jesus Prayer gradually energizes our hearts and minds and replaces all other thoughts or *logismoi*.

"You see, our minds are so constructed that they never cease to work. The Fathers claimed that the mind is like a flour mill that never stops turning round and round. If in that mill we throw good, healthy seed, it will give us good, healthy flour, with which we can bake nutritious bread."

"Unfortunately," Stephanos interjected, "we all know from personal experience that our minds are capable of producing not only the most silly and pointless thoughts but also the most diabolical and criminal ones."

"Right. They ceaselessly produce all types of *logismoi*, all kinds of thought forms. They never stop. Our aim, therefore, should be to inject in these constantly working minds the Jesus Prayer, which, according to the Fathers, we must try to recite at all times and in all places. It is important, in other words, at the beginning of our practice to remember to engage our minds as much as possible with the Prayer."

"How much time should one spend in prayer?" Jasmine asked.

"At the beginning of our practice, the quality is not as important as the quantity of our prayer. In fact, initially we should not be concerned with quality. What is important is the volume of our engagement."

"This is true of everything we do at first," I pointed out, "whether playing the piano or learning how to write. The more we do it the better it gets. It also works in a negative way. We could, for example, do something wrong repeatedly, such as have self-deprecating thoughts, and that makes us very good at being bad to ourselves. We become conditioned."

"Precisely. In reference to the Jesus Prayer, it is also important to remember that because this particular prayer is so short, we can recite it at all times and in all places. We don't need books, and we don't need to be well read. You can be anywhere in the world, and within your heart and within your mind, you repeat the Prayer over and over. No external conditions can neutralize it. It's easy to practice."

"A psychologist would say this is a form of delusion, a practice of self-conditioning and autosuggestion," Emily said.

"Okay. As we recite the Prayer repeatedly, we do become addicted and conditioned to it. One can certainly make that argument. We get attached to the words of the Prayer, which displace all other thought forms and distractions. Believe me, the Jesus Prayer has enormous spiritual power because it is imbued with divine energy. As such, it sanctifies our existence. It sanctifies our hearts and minds and our entire being. Gradually our souls get glued to the Prayer and become obedient to its meaning."

"Fr. Maxime, it is important to remind people that at the

beginning of our effort the greatest enemy is distraction," Stephanos pointed out. "It is hard to remain focused on the Prayer." Stephanos and Erato had been practicing the Prayer for many years, having become spiritual guides themselves.

"That's right. The mind is like what Abba Isaac calls an 'impudent bird of prey,' which flies everywhere, particularly to places where there are corpses and filth. It seems impossible to control it."

"Because of that tendency, many beginners in the practice become disheartened and finally give up," Stephanos noted.

"Yes. This is a real problem," Fr. Maximos agreed. "I hear people tell me, 'I pray and pray and my mind is all over the place. I cannot keep it still. The moment I begin to recite the Prayer, time flies and I feel lost. At the end I can't even remember that I had been praying.'

"I keep reassuring people that, at the beginning, this situation is unavoidable. We must not feel disappointed or disheartened. What is happening is not unique to ourselves. It's important to be persistent and never to give up. What is of value is to be in a state of continued effort. We must keep reciting the Prayer and, when we become aware that our minds are wandering, gently anchor them back to the Prayer. The mind will unavoidably wander again. Again we bring it back to consciousness. That is how our minds will gradually be strengthened and remain focused on the Prayer.

"It is no easy work, but it is a sheer delight. A person like Elder Seraphim, whom Emily and Kyriacos have just met, who has devoted the rest of his life to that activity, is like an eagle who opened his wings and flew toward the horizon. He has seen the mysteries of God and tasted the sweetness of the love of Christ."

"What's more important, to pray silently or to recite the Prayer out loud?" Emily asked.

"The elders advise that in the initial stage of the Prayer it is helpful if we recite it out loud," Fr. Maximos replied.

"This is difficult," Antonis interjected. "We live and work with other people. Reciting prayers aloud would be awkward. Imagine being in a business meeting and starting to pray aloud." There was an outburst of laughter.

Fr. Maximos nodded. "I appreciate the difficulty. In such situations we can recite the Prayer silently, without anyone noticing. Our minds may still be constantly preoccupied with God. After all, that's what's important. But when conditions permit, it is better to recite it aloud."

"Why?" Jasmine asked.

"Because that makes it easier to focus the mind on the Prayer at these early stages," Fr. Maximos replied and continued. "I should add that when we pray we should focus exactly on the words of the Prayer so that our minds may overcome the tendency to wander. We must not even imagine images and episodes from the life of Christ. Such distractions and fantasies may in fact be counterproductive and even harmful for the spiritual life. Instead, with great humility, we must focus on the meaning of the words themselves and recite the Prayer as many times as possible.

"I assure you, the person who practices this form of prayer and guards his conscience by adhering to the commandments of God can become a marathon runner of the spiritual life. Nothing can stop him."

"Is prayer alone sufficient for the spiritual life?" Jasmine asked.

"It is central, of course. But one must keep in mind that our prayer will be for naught if we do not at the same time practice charity and compassion. Our prayer will be useless if at the same time we constantly blame and criticize others. We cannot pray and at the same time surrender ourselves to passions that undermine the spiritual foundations of our lives."

"So parallel to prayer we must work to overcome our egotism through various activities and spiritual exercises," Jasmine added.

"Of course! We've talked about this many times. We must work on the stage of *Catharsis* in order to free our souls from egotistical passions. This is necessary before we can taste the fruits of the Spirit that will lead us to *Fotisis*, or enlightenment, and then to *Theosis*, our final unification with God."

Fr. Maximos went on to point out that, for the Eastern Orthodox, the sacraments of the *Ecclesia*, such as confession and communion, are always available to assist the spiritually struggling human being.

"A person may wonder, what if I can't live up to such high spiritual expectations?" Lavros interjected. "Alas, we succumb to temptations all the time."

"That's a given," Fr. Maximos replied. "But what reconnects us with the energy of the Prayer is *metanoia*. A human being learns how to repent and, by doing so, asks for God's mercy and forgiveness. Then the Grace of God returns in his or her heart through the practice of the Prayer."

"But once again," Lavros said, "many people I know wonder how they can do this effectively while living in the world. We are neither hermits nor nuns."

"If we really wish it, we can find plenty of opportunities to practice the Prayer while living ordinary lives. We engage daily in all kinds of activities that do not require special concentration, such as traveling to work, cooking, cleaning the house, or taking a walk. Why not fill up these time slots with the invocation of the Holy Name? It is my humble opinion that a person who does that on a regular basis needs no other form of prayer.

This habit may be sufficient to get the heart to work in the way of ceaseless prayer."

"But is it really enough?" Olympia asked.

"Well, two conditions can help enormously for the Prayer to get activated in the heart of the praying person. First, it is advisable to implement a short spiritual program. A person can devote a few minutes in a quiet place every morning and every evening to exclusively focus on the Prayer. At the beginning one does not need many hours for this practice. Devoting a few minutes each day to cultivate the Prayer should be sufficient. Second, in order to help the Prayer penetrate the heart and stay there during the day, it is important to do what the Fathers call *protonoia*. That means that upon awakening and within seconds after opening our eyes, we make the sign of the cross and begin invoking the Holy Name. It is like filling up the gas tank of our car to last us for a day's journey."

Fr. Maximos went on to say that it is important to start with the Prayer right at the point of awakening in order to prevent other thought forms, or *logismoi*, to enter the mind. This way the mind gets attached to the invocation of the Holy Name right from the start of our waking day.

"When we do the Jesus Prayer," Fr. Maximos continued, "it is also important to remember not to leave time between one prayer and the next. One invocation should immediately follow the next so that no negative thought forms can find a way to enter our minds between the two prayers. That way, the cycle of prayer remains uninterrupted.

"Needless to say, in this work God is always present to give us a hand. Furthermore, as members of the *Ecclesia*, we can benefit from its sacraments: its rich prayers, its chants, and all its other spiritual practices work in a synergistic way to help us in our continuous effort to master this supreme science of the spiritual life. With such systematic effort on our part, we may then be blessed with *Fotisis*, the illumination of our soul through the experience of the Uncreated Light, as it has happened throughout the ages in the lives of saints and holy elders like Paisios and Seraphim."

"I suppose with such an illumination our existence will no longer be a problem," Lavros commented.

"Exactly! The Prayer can unlock for us the mystery of our life in this world," Fr. Maximos responded. "It is like a key that will lead us back to Paradise, the place where we should be. All human beings have the capacity to return there. That is God's wish for all of us.

"By energizing the mind through the repetition of the Prayer, Grace gradually comes and propels the person from the first stage of verbal prayer to what the Fathers call the Prayer of the Heart. The Prayer, that is, becomes self-activating and an effortless and natural activity of our minds and souls, just like breathing."

"I suppose," I added, "it's like learning how to swim or ride a bicycle or drive a car. At first, it's very difficult, but once you master these tasks, they become automatic and effortless."

"I think you can make such an analogy," Fr. Maximos said. "The person prays harmoniously with all his or her powers. Neither the mind nor the heart gets distracted. This activity is no longer tiresome for the praying person. Prayer now becomes natural to the soul, feeding it with very sweet honey. The prayer never stops, whether the person is asleep or awake."

"Should one practice the Prayer in church while the service goes on?" Antonis asked.

"Absolutely. That is a space particularly conducive for the Prayer."

"In reference to our daily lives, what are the immediate,

tangible results of practicing the Prayer?" Emily asked. "I don't mean the great achievements of the saints and ascetics, but rather what impact does prayer have on us, ordinary people?"

"First and foremost, the person who practices the Prayer tastes the love of Christ. This is what we all truly need and what our supreme objective should be. This is what we lack. When the Prayer is activated within our hearts, it awakens in us the sense of Divine zealousness that prompts us toward valiant spiritual engagements. Together with the sacraments, the Prayer can ignite within our hearts the flame of Christ's love."

"Is this perhaps the meaning of what is written in the Gospel when Christ said that He has come into the world to spread fire?" Olympia asked.

"Of course! What else could it be? It is the fire of God's love for humanity. Where else could that fire be ignited but within people's hearts? When that happens, everything in us that is useless and harmful is burnt out. We become purified, distilled. That's when we discover who we truly are, while becoming aware of the beauty of our souls and existence. We come to know how God made us so that we may become harmonious, balanced, and beautiful. It is that stage in our spiritual development when we become truly friends with ourselves, with our brothers and sisters, with our environment, and with God."

"So prayer eliminates loneliness, the problem facing so many people today in crowded cities," I said.

"Absolutely. People who know how to pray are never alone, even if nobody knows them, even if nobody speaks to them, even if no one pays attention to them. It is so because God is actively present in their souls. Being alone is not a problem for praying human beings. In fact, they 'delight in isolation,' as the Fathers say. They are happy and feel particularly blissful and delighted when they are alone, as is the case with hermits such as Fr. Seraphim."

"It seems like a paradox," Lavros observed. "They are alone but not lonely."

"It may seem like a paradox, but in their isolation, hermits like Seraphim feel with greater intensity the presence of God. And they are joyous within that isolation from the rest of the world because of God's Presence. When other people visit such hermits, they welcome them and commune with them lovingly. And when people are absent from their lives, it is not a problem for them because the energy of the Prayer maintains the presence of God within their hearts. Had they not been in communion with God, people living like hermits would go insane. That is also the reason only a few monks are ever given permission to live like hermits.

"In addition to overcoming loneliness," Fr. Maximos continued, "praying persons are also victorious over the other major problem of our times, angst. It's impossible to have angst if you pray systematically. Through prayer, people can transcend all anxieties about worldly things. When God is present, emotions like angst and depression are absent. This is why we chant in church that we should entrust our entire lives into the hands of God. Such persons are a hundred percent certain, and can see it, feel it, know it, that God truly cares for them. Under such conditions, it is impossible to experience depression even if they try. They have surrendered everything to God. For this reason, praying people feel an intense form of peacefulness, an inner quietude."

"That's precisely what we felt when in the presence of Fr. Seraphim," Emily added.

"I'm not surprised," Fr. Maximos said. "That is what one

feels in the presence of authentic holy elders. At least this is what I've experienced in my years on Mt. Athos.

"Another problem of our times is fear. How could praying persons feel fearful? It's impossible. Through prayer all fears are transcended. Nothing worldly can terrify praying human beings or cause them to feel lonely, anxious, or fearful. The world exists because there are people like Fr. Seraphim who constantly pray."

Fr. Maximos then pointed out that there are many people who live in the world and pray like hermits. These are people who are not known publicly. "I assure you, based on my limited experience as a spiritual confessor and guide during all these years, I have met people, ordinary laypeople, in their daily activities and work, young and old, men and women, rich and poor, healthy and sick, who are capable of fiery prayer. Such people have reached extraordinary levels of holiness that hardly anyone recognizes."

"They are invisible and anonymous saints," Antonis murmured.

"Yes. These are the people who, through their prayers, keep the world together. If they stopped praying, the world would disintegrate, and I'm not saying this metaphorically," Fr. Maximos added.

"We have an amazing wealth of traditional prayers that each of us can employ in our daily spiritual work. The Jesus Prayer is the crowning of this tradition. It fills us with the greatest of joys and opens up our hearts to the most supreme love imaginable, the presence of Christ in the depths of our being."

With that last remark, Fr. Maximos looked at his watch and signaled that it was time for him to return to the bishopric. It was ten in the evening, and there were several people waiting for confession. He would not retreat to his sleeping quarters until way past midnight, a daily routine of self-renunciation that none of us could fathom. Both Emily and I bade Fr. Maximos farewell because we were leaving in two days for Maine. We promised to return the following summer, hoping for further opportunities for spiritual encounters and conversations like this one.

~~~

It was interesting that, upon our return to Maine, the first e-mail I opened was on the Jesus Prayer. It was from the librarian of a Jewish American liberal arts college. After reading *The Mountain of Silence*, he expressed his appreciation for the wisdom and teachings of Fr. Maximos. I was pleased to read that the content of the book had made an impact on his life. "But I have a problem," he wrote. "I am Jewish, and I find it very awkward to pray 'Lord Jesus Christ, Son of God, have mercy on me, a sinner.' What do you think I should do?"

Without hesitation I wrote back suggesting that he use a version of the Prayer introduced by St. Gregory Palamas, who said "Lord, enlighten my darkness, Lord enlighten my darkness." The Jewish librarian wrote back several weeks later to let me know that he was systematically practicing that version of the Prayer and that he felt "extraordinarily blessed."

"What do you think the meaning of this story is?" my friend Mike Lewis asked after I brought to his attention this e-mail correspondence.

"It means," I responded, as we resumed our regular walks through the University of Maine woods, "that God does not discriminate. He generously spreads His blessings, love, and wisdom to all human beings, regardless of ethnic background or religious affiliation. I am certain that Fr. Maximos would agree. In fact, I will make a note to ask his views on this matter next time I meet with him."

Mike raised a further question. "So, what do you think the spiritual tradition you have been studying all these years could offer to the modern world?"

I thought for a second and then replied: "It offers an integrated system of spiritual practices within Christianity that can lead to a direct experience of God, what the elders of Eastern Orthodox Christianity call *Theosis*."

Those last words reverberated in my mind as I walked back to my office in Fernald Hall. I sat for a while outside the building on a bench facing west as the sun was beginning its descent behind the thick forested area on the other side of the Stillwater River, a familiar, most soothing scene in several of Mike's paintings. Since I had just finished reading the monumental work of Diarmaid MacCulloch on the history of Christianity,[3] Tertullian's classic question "What does Athens have to do with Jerusalem?" came to my mind. That question has percolated in my mind, consciously or unconsciously, ever since I encountered the reality of Mt. Athos twenty years ago. That is, what is the proper relationship between my secular learning as a rational sociologist and my quest for a transcendent faith grounded in my Orthodox Christian upbringing? In short, what is the proper relationship between reason (Athens) and faith (Jerusalem)?

In my mind's eye I have never been able to forgive the Byzantine emperor Justinian for the crime he inflicted on Western civilization by shutting down the philosophical schools of Athens. He based his fateful decision on the disastrous premise that Jerusalem alone was sufficient for human existence. Yet the doctrines of Christianity were shaped precisely within the creative encounter between Greek philosophical thought and Christian experience. Without that we would never have had such founding theological giants as St. Basil of Caesarea (331–379), his close friend St. Gregory of Nazianzus "the Theologian" (330–390), and Basil's brother St. Gregory of Nyssa (334–394). All three of them were brilliant classmates in the philosophical schools of Athens during that most creative of theological centuries. In fact, St. Gregory of Nyssa was known not only as a great theologian but also as a great philosopher. So what if the philosophical schools of Athens created by Plato and Aristotle had remained open and richly endowed by Byzantine emperors for the succeeding centuries? How many other Christian hierarchs would have been produced by an ongoing encounter between Athens and Jerusalem?

Based on my experiences and explorations of the Christian East, I came to the conclusion that the reintegration of reason and faith, scientific knowledge and spiritual knowledge, is crucial if humanity is to survive in the foreseeable future. In this effort to bridge the gap between Athens and Jerusalem, and to foster the spiritual and intellectual regeneration of the world, I believe Mt. Athos and the Eastern Orthodox mystical tradition can play a role.

Those were the thoughts and unanswerable questions that swirled in my mind as I watched the sun disappearing behind the trees in a cornucopia of blazing color.

ACKNOWLEDGMENTS

〰〰〰〰〰〰〰

I am very grateful to Father Maximos, who, as in my previous work, is the central character of the book. Without his readiness and generosity to share his knowledge about the Eastern Orthodox spiritual tradition, this book would not have been written. Of course, the responsibility for whatever shortcomings or errors are found in my current volume is exclusively mine.

I would also like to express my appreciation to my colleagues and the administrative assistant in the Sociology Department of the University of Maine for their friendship and sustained support over the years related to my research agenda. My thanks also to the University of Maine for a sabbatical leave in the spring semester of 2009 that allowed me to work full-time on the manuscript.

Special thanks to my literary agent of over twenty-five years, Ashala Gabriel, for her superb professional expertise and genuine commitment and belief in the value of my work. Likewise, I extend my deep thanks and appreciation to my editor, Gary Jansen, for his determined interest and faith in the importance of this material and for being such a great editor in every respect.

I am particularly thankful to my colleague from the Art Department Michael Lewis for his personal interest in my work, his friendship, and his critical reading of the manuscript. I am also grateful to him for being one of the active characters in the book. Likewise, I am thankful to all my friends in Cyprus who, over the years, have played a key role in my exploration of Eastern Christianity. As in previous volumes, some of them have become key figures in my present work.

My sister Maroulla and her husband, Vassos, have played, as always, a central role in making our stay on the island an intensely meaningful and emotionally fulfilling experience. No words can ever express our deep gratitude.

I feel blessed to have the type of family that I have. Many special thanks to our multitalented writer son, Constantine, for his astute editorial interventions, which strengthened and tightened the text considerably. I cherish the faith that our talented daughter has for the work I do and rejoice in her endeavors as an artist and filmmaker. Lastly, I would not have been who I am without Emily, who has been an integral part of my life for over thirty years, so much so that life is inconceivable without her nurturing presence and support. She has been a central figure in all of my books, sharing many of the spiritual adventures found in them. Without her, this work would certainly not have come into existence. Furthermore, her sharp and critical comments made all of my books better reading material than they would have otherwise been.

CHAPTER 1: REMINISCENCES

1. Robert Cowley, ed., *The Collected What If?* (New York: G. P. Putnam's Sons, 2001).

2. Kyriacos C. Markides, "Eastern Orthodox Mysticism and Transpersonal Theory," *Journal of Transpersonal Psychology* 40, no. 2 (2008): 178–198.

3. Cited in Seyyed Hossein Nasr, *Religion and the Order of Nature* (New York: Oxford University Press, 1996), p. 153; Wolfgang Smith, "The Plague of Scientistic Belief," in Mehrdad M. Zarandi, ed., *Science and the Myth of Progress* (Bloomington, IN: World Wisdom, 2003), pp. 228–229.

4. Pitirim A. Sorokin, *Social and Cultural Dynamics*, 4 vols. (New York: American Book Co., 1937–1941; rev. and abridged, 1 vol., Boston: Porter Sargent, 1957).

5. Jeffrey Mishlove, "Intuition: The Source of True Knowing," *Noetic Sciences Review*, Spring 1994, pp. 31–36.

6. Kyriacos C. Markides, *Riding with the Lion: In Search of Mystical Christianity* (New York: Viking Press, 1995).

7. ———, *The Mountain of Silence: A Search for Orthodox Spirituality* (New York: Doubleday, 2001); *Gifts of the Desert: The Forgotten Path of Christian Spirituality* (New York: Doubleday, 2005).

8. Sophrony (Sakharov), *Saint Silouan the Athonite*, trans. Rosemary Edmonds (New York: St. Vladimir's Seminary Press, 1999); Markides, *Mountain of Silence*, pp. 78–93; Gerontos Porphyriou Kavsokalyvetou, *Vios kai Logoi* [*Life and Words*] (Chania, Crete: Holy Monastery of Chrysopege, 2003).

CHAPTER 2: ATHOS IN AMERICA

1. Markides, *Gifts of the Desert*, pp. 17–38.

2. See Markides, *Mountain of Silence*, pp. 212–224.

3. Thomas Berry, *The Great Work: Our Way into the Future* (New York: Three Rivers Press, 2000).

4. Sophrony (Sakharov), *Saint Silouan the Athonite*.

5. See Matthew Gallatin's *Thirsting for God in a Land of Shallow Wells* (Ben Lomond, CA: Conciliar Press, 2002) for an extensive discussion of this matter.

6. Bart Ehrman, *Jesus, Interrupted: Revealing the Hidden Contradictions in the Bible (and Why We Don't Know about Them)* (New York: HarperOne, 2009).

7. Charles Templeton, *Farewell to God: My Reasons for Rejecting the Christian Faith* (Toronto: McClelland & Stewart, 1999).

8. John Romanides, *Patristic Theology* (Uncut Mountain Press, 2008). This extract was brought to my attention in an e-mail from Bishop Christodoulos of Holy Ascension Monastery, July 25, 2009.

9. Markides, *Gifts of the Desert*, pp. 98–126.

10. For an extended discussion of the *logismoi*, see Markides, *Mountain of Silence*, pp. 115–146.

CHAPTER 3: SYMPOSIUM

1. Joseph Gusfield, *Symbolic Crusade: Status Politics and the American Temperance Movement* (Chicago: University of Illinois Press, 1986).

2. Markides, *Gifts of the Desert*, pp. 58–77.

3. Philip Sherrard, *Christianity: Lineaments of a Sacred Tradition* (Brookline, MA: Holy Cross Orthodox Press, 1998).

CHAPTER 4: FRUITS OF THE SPIRIT

1. See Keith A. Roberts and David Yamane, *Religion in Sociological Perspective* (Belmont, CA: Wadsworth, 2004), pp. 239–249.

2. See Markides, *Mountain of Silence*, pp. 153–164.

3. Raymond Moody, *Life After Life* (New York: Bantam Books, 1976).

CHAPTER 6: FOGGY LANDSCAPES

1. Viktor E. Frankl, *Man's Search for Meaning* (New York: Pocket Books, 1984), pp. 143–144.

2. Jennie Yabroff, "Take the Bananas and Run," *Newsweek*, August 18, 2008, pp. 57–58.

3. Ernest Becker, *The Denial of Death* (New York: Free Press, 1998).

4. Peter Berger, *Pyramids of Sacrifice: Political Ethics and Social Change* (New York: Basic Books, 1974).

5. Richard Dawkins, *The God Delusion* (Boston: Mariner Books, 2008); Christopher Hitchens, *God Is Not Great: How Religion Poisons Everything* (New York: Twelve, 2007).

6. Munson attributed it to the sociologist Peter Berger.

7. Quoted in Richard Tarnas, *Cosmos and Psyche: Intimations of a New World View* (New York: Plume, 2007), p. 435.

8. Patrick Glynn, *God: The Evidence* (Rocklin, CA: Forum, 1997), p. 32.

9. Masaru Emoto, *Messages from Water* (Tokyo: Hado Publishing, 1999).

10. Tarnas, *Cosmos and Psyche*.

11. Moody, *Life After Life*.

12. Larry Dossey, *Healing Beyond the Body: Medicine and the Infinite Reach of the Mind* (Boston: Shambhala, 2003); Amit Goswami, *The Visionary Window: A Quantum Physicist's Guide to Enlightenment* (Wheaton, IL: Quest Books, 2000).

13. Michael Harner, *The Way of the Shaman* (New York: Bantam Books, 1982).

14. See http://spiritfaces.com. See also Mark Macy's *Miracles in the Storm: Talking to the Other Side with the New Technology of Spiritual Contact* (New York: New American Library, 2001); *Spirit Faces: Truth About the Afterlife* (San Francisco: Weiser Books, 2006).

15. See Amazon.com.

16. See http://spiritfaces.com.

17. Jung's original letter was printed in an op-ed *New York Times* insert, "Crazy Times," November 19, 1993.

CHAPTER 7: BEYOND DEATH

1. Huston Smith, *The World's Religions* (New York: HarperCollins, 1991), pp. 87–88.

2. Dannion Brinkley, *Saved by the Light: The True Story of a Man Who Died Twice and the Profound Revelations He Received* (New York: Harper Torch, 1995); Dannion Brinkley, *At Peace in the Light: A Man Who Died Twice* (New York: HarperOne, 2008).

3. Elisabeth Kübler-Ross, *On Death and Dying* (New York: Macmillan, 1969); quoted in John J. Macionis, *Society: The Basics*, 9th ed. (Upper Saddle River, NJ: Prentice Hall, 2007), p. 870.

4. See Dinesh D'Souza, *Life After Death: The Evidence* (Washington, DC: Regnery, 2009); Gary E. Schwartz, *The Afterlife Experiments: Breakthrough Scientific Evidence of Life After Death* (New York: Atria Books, 2002).

5. Kallistos Ware, ed., *Philokalia: The Complete Text, Compiled by St. Nikodimos of the Holy Mountain and St. Makarios of Corinth*, vol. 4, trans. Kallistos Ware, Philip Sherrard, and G. E. H. Palmer (London: Faber & Faber, 1999).

6. Sherrard, *Christianity*, p. 183.

7. Ibid., p. 187.

8. Ibid., pp. 189–190.

9. Ibid., p. 195.

10. Ibid., pp. 18–199.

CHAPTER 8: PILGRIMAGE

1. Bill Mollison, *Introduction to Permaculture* (Tyalgum, Australia: Tagari Publications, 1997).

2. Porphyrios, *Wounded by Love* (Limni, Evia, Greece: Romiosyni Books, 2005).

3. Markides, *Riding with the Lion*.

4. Paisios, *Spiritual Counsels: With Pain and Love for Contemporary Man*, vol. 1, trans. from the Greek (Souroti, Greece: Holy Monastery of John the Theologian, 2006); *Spiritual Counsels: Spiritual Awakening*, vol. 2, trans. from the Greek (Souroti, Greece: Holy Monastery of John the Theologian, 2008).

5. Andrija Puharich, *Beyond Telepathy* (London: Souvenir, 1974), pp. 33–34; quoted in Richard Smoley, *The Dice Game of Shiva: How Consciousness Creates the Universe* (Novato, CA: New World Library, 2009), pp. 35–37.

6. See Thomas Kuhn, *The Structure of Scientific Revolutions*, 2nd ed. (Chicago: University of Chicago Press, 1970).

CHAPTER 9: MONASTIC HOSPITALITY

1. *The Service of the Akathist Hymn to the Most Holy Theotokos*, new English trans. Seraphim Dedes (Pittsburgh: Greek Orthodox Diocese of Pittsburgh, 2000), p. 38.

2. Judith Herrin, *Byzantium: The Surprising Life of a Medieval Empire* (New York: Penguin Books, 2008), p. 323.

3. Rodney Stark, *The Rise of Christianity* (Princeton: Princeton University Press, 1996). The discussion in this section is based on the brilliant work of this contemporary sociologist.

CHAPTER 10: MYSTERIES OF SINAI

1. Quoted in Judith Herrin, *Byzantium: The Surprizing Life of a Medieval Empire*. (New York and London: Penguin Books, 2007), p. 42.

2. Nikos Kazantzakis, *Taxideuontas: Italia, Egyptos, Sina, Ierousalem, Kypros, O Morias*, 2nd ed. (Athens: Eleni Kazantsake Publishers, 1965), p. 104.

3. Evangelos Papaioannou, *The Monastery of St. Catherine* (St. Catherine Monastery Press, no date), p. 1.

4. Constantine Manafes, ed., *Sina: Oi Thesavroi tes Mones* [Sina: Treasures of the Monastery] (Athens: Ekdodike Athenon Publishers, 1990).

5. Papaioannou, *The Monastery of St. Catherine*, p. 10.

6. Manafes, *Sina*, p. 14.

7. Nikos, *Taxideuontas*, p. 121.

8. Gerontos Ephraim Philotheou, *E Techni tis Soterias* [*The Art of Salvation*] (Holy Monastery of Philotheou: Mt. Athos, Greece, 2006), p. 37.

9. John Climacus, *The Ladder of Divine Ascent* (Brookline, MA: Holy Cross Orthodox Press, 1996).

10. Smith, *World's Religions*, p. 275.

11. Ibid., p. 286.

12. Mathew Larngris, ed., *Megas Synaxaristis tes Orthodoxou Ecclesias*, 11th ed. (Athens: Iera Mone Metamorphoseos, 1991), p. 621.

13. Ibid., p. 623.

14. *Daily News* (distributed with the *International Herald Tribune*), May 4, 2009.

15. *New York Times*, May 13, 2009.

16. William Dalrymple, *From the Holy Mountain: A Journey Among the Christians of the Middle East* (New York: Holt Paperbacks, 1999).

17. *New York Times*, May 13, 2009.

CHAPTER 11: INNER RIVER

1. Kallistos Ware, ed., *Philokalia: The Complete Text, Compiled by St. Nikodimos of the Holy Mountain and St. Makarios of Corinth*, vol. 4, trans. Kallistos Ware, Philip Sherrard, and G. E. H. Palmer (London: Faber & Faber, 1999).

2. Markides, *Gifts of the Desert*, pp. 58–77.

3. Frankl, *Man's Search for Meaning*, p. 57.

CHAPTER 12: A HERMIT'S JOY

1. William James, *The Varieties of Religious Experience* (New York: Longmans, Green, 1902); Richard Maurice Bucke, *Cosmic Consciousness* (1901; repr., New York: Penguin Putnam, 1991); Rudolf Otto, *The Idea of the Holy: An Inquiry into the Non-rational Factor in the Idea of the Divine and Its Relation to the Rational* (1950; repr., New York: Oxford University Press, 1970); Joachim Wach, *Types of Religious Experience* (1951; repr., Chicago: University of Chicago Press, 1970); Joachim Wach, *Sociology of Religion* (1944; repr., Chicago: University of Chicago Press, 1962).

2. Michael Winkelman and John R. Baker, *Supernatural as Natural: A Biocultural Approach to Religion* (Upper Saddle River, NJ: Prentice Hall, 2010), p. 63.

3. Diarmaid MacCulloch, *Christianity: The First Three Thousand Years* (London: Allen Lane, 2009).